JUST LEISURE:

Policy, Ethics and Professionalism

Edited by

Mike McNamee, Chris Jennings and Martin Reeves

LSA

Publication No. 71

First published in 2000 by
Leisure Studies Association

A catalogue record for this book
is available from the British Library.

ISBN: 0 906337 81 X

Layout design and typesetting by Myrene L. McFee
Binding by Kensett Ltd., Hove

Contents

Just Leisure?
Policy, Ethics and Professionalism

Ethics and ethics and Just Leisure

The idea that leisure might centrally be related to matters of ethical significance is not a new one. This volume attempts to situate the broadest range of ethical concerns in leisure in a single volume in a manner that is driven both by philosophical and social scientific disciplines. In this regard it does not privilege any one conception of ethics. But a word of clarification may be helpful here. Ethics is often conceived of as a branch of philosophy. So Ethics (with a big "E") might be thought of as the philosophical study of morality. Ethicists in this vein are solely concerned with conceptual matters about the nature of "good", "bad", "just", "unjust". But the word "ethics" (with a small "e") is also understood coherently to refer to the description, evaluation and analysis of persons, practices and policies from any of the range of social scientific disciplines with their various methods and methodologies.

The book comprises three sections: Policy, Ethics and Professionalism. To a certain extent the sections represent an arbitrary classification. Many of the essays cut across these (and other) ethical and conceptual boundaries. Within these sections there is a balance between philosophical and social scientific essays. Importantly, the authors of this volume do not speak to the diversity of scholarship in ethics and leisure simpliciter, but do so from a range of national and international perspectives. While a majority of authors are UK-based, there are strong continental European, Scandinavian, and North American voices at play here. Each attempts to draw attention either to an old issue in a new light, or to a new issue in a significant leisure context.

Policy

In the first section of the book, a series of papers, using case studies from the UK and Scandinavia, examine the impacts of contemporary leisure policy initiatives and practices across the public, private and voluntary sectors.

Anna MacVicar, **Margaret Graham**, **Susan Ogden** and **Bernadette Scott** employ a multiple case study design to ascertain the extent to which current legislation has enhanced fairness and flexibility in working practices (particularly, but not exclusively, for women) within five Scottish leisure organisations. In addition to analysing the disparate policies of the respective organisations, MacVicar *et al.* further identify the gap that exists between the UK and many other European countries in respect of the integration of women into higher managerial categories. While recognising that Scottish leisure, in particular the public sector, is feminised to the extent that similar numbers of women have entered the leisure professions as men, there remains a concern about sex-segregation of traditional "feminised domestic" labour of cleaning and reception duties. Moreover, MacVicar *et al.* argue that the move from Public Sector Leisure to Charitable Trust Status may present threats to the family-friendly initiatives that have been developed in the publicly-funded leisure sector.

The impact, in terms of increased pressure on the structure, organisation and management of voluntary sports clubs in receipt of awards from the publicly funded Lottery Sports Fund, is the focus of the paper by **Richard Garrett**. Situating his study in the context of changing patterns of voluntary organisations, he critically questions the long-term value of the newly added bureaucratic burdens. In noting the increased pressures of the new administrative demands of Lottery Sports Funding upon volunteer labour in terms of skill, effort and time, he argues that these significant labour-effects will stay with the recipient organisations long after the lottery bid has been won and its outcomes are achieved.

The replacement of "Compulsory Competitive Tendering" with "Best Value" in Local Authority leisure provision, and its relationship to quality management systems (and practices), is addressed by **Christine Williams**. Williams examines the complex relationship between 'voluntary' qualitative assessment tools and mechanisms in the delivery of leisure services and the now mandatory Best Value approach. Williams concludes by highlighting the need to examine the 'culture' of the organisation before addressing the demands imposed by Best Value and the inspecting Audit Commission.

The policy ramifications for leisure and sports providers of ensuring safety for its participants in light of increasing legislation are highlighted by **John Hunter-Jones**, who makes use of a number of cases from the UK which have involved negligence, health and safety breaches and other related legal issues. Hunter-Jones demonstrates that interpreting current legislation and the inherent implications for the sector of the leisure industry (especially hazardous sports) is far from an exact science, given the difficulties in classifying such activities coherently and rendering legal considerations appropriately to the relevant contexts. He argues that the demonstration of "due diligence" and "risk identification and management", however, are prerequisites to the management of safe environments for customers.

Concluding this section on leisure policy, **Ari Karimäki** examines the shifting nature of public planning and the integration of social impact considerations in a case study from central Finland. The essay examines the impact on leisure participation created by the move to construct leisure-swimming pools in Finland from a stakeholders' perspective in the move beyond centralised economic planning with its focus on standardised facilities and services. His research enables the identification of winners and losers within a model of "Comprehensive Impact Assessment". He concludes that, in the new economic environment and its attendant planning policies, there is a pressing need for more locally-sensitive planning processes.

Ethics

The second section of the book deals with examinations of ethical issues in and of leisure, from both philosophical and social scientific perspectives, by scholars from the UK, North America and Scandinavia.

Heather Sheridan tackles the highly problematic issue of the conceptual and philosophical tensions inherent in "deviant" and "dark leisure". In order to shed light on the differences, she calls on the work of a number of philosophers, and notably the sociologist Chris Rojek (and his provocative thesis on serial killing as the dark side of leisure). Sheridan argues from a broadly Aristotelian position that the concept of leisure is itself loaded with positive moral force. The idea of "dark" or "deviant leisure" therefore becomes oxymoronic. While acknowledging this logical tension, she suggests that the ranges of behaviours that fall under this heading be re-described as "dark" or "deviant *pleasure*" and recommends, like Rojek, that the practices that constitute and support such a profitable, often illegal, industry are worthy objects of study for leisure professionals.

Alun Hardman considers the concept of 'change' as fundamental to the understanding of the development of sport and leisure activities. Hardman situates the problems of evaluating change in a variety of sports, but concentrates his analysis more specifically on problems related to technological developments in golf and whether they are to the good of the game or detrimental to it. Hardman presents a model, "The Pyramid of Constraints", in order to normatively classify and evaluate (potential) change in sports according to aesthetic, moral and structural criteria.

The importance of promoting both social and environmental justice through leisure is proposed by **Karla Henderson**. She introduces the notions of 'ethical fitness' in the light of three eco-philosophies: ecofeminism, eco-tourism and social ecology and illustrates their differing agendas. Henderson bemoans the lack of an eco-philosophical basis for outdoor recreation policies that are dominated by narrow political constraints and driven by the economic motive of controlling nature.

An ethical perspective from Scandinavia is provided by **Per Nilsson, Matz Franzén, and Thomas Peterson** in the form of a study examining 'The Ethos of the Game' using a case study of junior footballers in Sweden. Utilising a Bourdieuan perspective, Franzén *et al.* illustrate how, through the use of key concepts such as "habitus" and "social field", we can understand the ethos of different sports and more specifically of Swedish boys' and girls' football. Utilising a framework of factors (such as will power, ball skill, fair play) they conclude that boys and girls differ significantly in their perceptions of what constitutes "good" football. Interestingly, neither group valued fair play particularly highly. Moreover, neither sex valued team play significantly, though both valued toughness as a psychological capacity.

In a closely related essay, **Carwyn Jones**, addresses the methodological and philosophical difficulties of social scientific research into the ethics of sports. Given the nature of the subject matter, he argues, it is impossible to have a theory-neutral idea of what constitutes ethical goodness. In contrast to the dominant picture of ethical conduct as right action, Jones argues that we should shift ethical evaluations away from their narrow focus on moral judgement and instead recognise their place among a broader range of considerations to do with the evaluation of good and bad character. In this light he extols the role of sport as a valuable nursery of ethical conduct, in contrast to the extant psychological literature.

In this Olympic year, it is perhaps fitting that the final paper in this 'ethics' section is provided by **Graham McFee,** who poses the problem: 'Sport- a Moral Laboratory?'. McFee draws on a number of Olympic sports, including boxing and basketball, to 'test' their implicit capacity to provide an arena in which a sense of morality can be developed and explored. In contrast to the universalised conception of moral rules that so many philosophers have been persuaded by, McFee advances the heuristic value of moral particularism (as opposed to absolutism), especially in educational contexts. In the making of moral judgements and in moral action itself, we learn first in specific contexts and not by the comprehension of formal rules. He concludes, rather tentatively, that sport has the potential to function as an effective moral laboratory.

Professionalism

The advent of increased pressures on modern sport and leisure provision and consumption, whether it be through the requirement to provide a cost effective and continuously improving service, which meets (and surpasses customer's needs); the exponential growth in sports sponsorship, or pressure imposed through current legislation, has ultimately resulted in calls for increased 'professionalism'. The papers within the third and final section examine the impact of professionalism in diverse areas of sport and leisure.

Graham Berridge introduces Chernushenko's principles for "sustainable sport" and situates them in the context of event organisation. In particular he applies the principles as a "test" against which to evaluate the extent to which over fifty UK competition mountain biking events adopted "green practices". Utilising questionnaire and on-line survey methods to collect data, Berridge concludes that more strategic direction and leadership is required by the sports' Governing Bodies to assist race organisers. The sport satisfies many of the 'green' principles in terms of the behaviour of the riders and the administration of events, but still has a long way to go in the management of land erosion and terrain damage of the venues used for competition.

The role of coaches in 'forcing' their gymnasts into early retirement is the focus of the paper by **Konstantinos Koukouris**. His investigation into a cohort of elite predominantly female gymnasts in Greece uncovers the depth of unethical and unprofessional conduct in the coaching fraternity there. Using in-depth interviews. He analyses the extent to which the coaches' conduct may be identified as the key variable in the performers' decisions to disengage prematurely from the sport. Gymnasts reported that coaches' conduct frequently went beyond the commonly observed verbal and emotional abuse into actual physical beatings. Exacerbated by increased pressures for high performance, athletic engagement became viewed as hard labour under a regime of psychological warfare. Koukouris links the gymnasts' view of specific coaching practices (from beating to dietary control) to their premature disengagement from the sport.

Margaret Graham provides a Scottish context for discussion of the issue of professionalism, this time in relation to the role of volunteers in the museum service. In a multi-method approach, she presents data from questionnaires, focus groups and from participant observation, in order to underscore the processes of professionalisation. Graham examines issues of accountability and partnership as key to understanding the curious phenomenon of professionalised volunteering. She further demonstrates the growing reliance on the 'unpaid worker' in this sector and the parallel developments in the services approach to the management of this vital and cost-effective human resource.

Finally, in an appropriately sceptical tone for a philosopher, **Claudio Tamburrini** develops a position whereby cheating in sport ought not to be thought of as necessarily wrong. The contribution takes its title from the (in)famous 'illegal' handball goal by Maradona in the 1986 World Cup match between Argentina and England, and Tamburrini uses football as the primary context, differentiating between 'professional' transgressions of sports rules, foul play and blatant cheating. Increased professionalisation and commercialisation has led some critics to view rule-breaking in a high-handed and simplistic fashion. Tamburrini offers criteria by which to evaluate the (un)acceptability of rule-breaking, and in so doing agues that in certain instances these will enhance the value of sports. Against this model, and conforming to a consequentialist ethical position, Tamburrini invites the reader to take a more open attitude toward the 'professional' breaking of the rules as an acceptable part of contemporary sporting culture.

Taken as a whole, the collection invites philosophers and social scientists, policy makers and practitioners to rethink leisure in its manifold conceptualisations from a variety of ethical perspectives. No singular ethical perspective or theory is advanced here. Rather, the diversity of opinion and argument presented in this volume seeks to problematise our notions of the ethical and to treat with scepticism the idea leisure will necessarily be "just" or ethical without prior reflections on the nature of leisure and indeed the nature of ethics itself.

Mike McNamee, Chris Jennings and Martin Reeves

About the Contributors

Graham Berridge is a Senior Lecturer, Pathway Leader in Leisure and Event Management in the School of Tourism, Hospitality and Leisure at Thames Valley University. Teaching areas include leisure management (general), event management, planning and development of facilities, psychology of sport. Past work experience in sports and leisure development, event organisation and co-ordination. Previously BCF representative to the UCI Mountain Bike Commission. Currently member of LSA Executive Committee. Research focus is on designing leisure experiences, mountain biking and access to the countryside, television and sport.

Matz Franzén is Associate professor in sociology at the Institute for Housing Research Uppsala university. His leisure-related research interests are in the socialisation of youth into leisure activities and patterns of participation.

Richard Garrett is a doctoral student in the Leisure Management Unit at the University of Sheffield. His research examines whether the Lottery Sports Fund contributes to a change in the nature of voluntary sector in sport. He is also helping to compile the WLRA Volunteering Commission bibliographic database on Volunteering and Leisure.

Margaret Graham is Research Associate and Professor John Lennon Chair at Glasgow Caledonian University. She is a project officer for the Department of Hospitality, Tourism and Leisure Management. Her PhD focused on volunteering in the urban museum service. Recent research projects have included her contribution towards a UK wide study concerning the impacts of admission charging in the museum sector and a project considering to what extent the Scottish leisure industry as flexible workplace accommodates gendered lifestyles.

Alun Hardman is Lecturer in the School of Sport, Cheltenham and Gloucester College of Higher Education. He received his PhD from Pennsylvania State University. His research interests are in the philosophies of sport and leisure and the ethics of sport in particular.

Chris Jennings is a Senior Lecturer at The University of Wales Institute, Cardiff; Director of Leading Teams and a former local authority Assistant Chief Officer. He is current working in the area of quality monitoring and talent identification and tracking.

Karla Henderson is Professor and Chair in the Department of Recreation and Leisure Studies at the University of North Carolina in Chapel Hill. Her research in the past 15 years has focused on gender and diversity issues. She is co-author of both "Gains and Gaps: Feminist Perspectives on Women's Leisure." She is author of numerous articles on professional issues for women, feminist outdoor leadership, social justice and research methods.

John Hunter-Jones is a lecturer in Leisure Management in the School of Education at the University of Manchester. His teaching areas are law, economics and tourism. He gained a BA (Hons) in Law from the University of Cambridge and an Msc in Tourism from the University of Strathclyde. He has experience in commercial and public tourism, legal work and law enforcement. His research interests include securing safety in the leisure sector and the teaching of law to business/management students.

Carwyn Jones is Lecturer in Philosophy of Sport and the University of Teeside. He was awarded his PhD from the Open University in the area of ethics and sport. His research interests focus on the nature of moral action, fair play and character development in sport. He teaches philosophy, ethics and sociology of sport

Ari Karimäki is a full-time researcher and doctoral student in the Department of Social Sciences of Sport at the University of Jyväskylä, Finland. He is working on a project which aims to assess the social impacts of sport facilities. His particular interest concerns the how global and national economical and political changes which affect local planning can be revised so that the rational planning based on the expertise of the welfare state and local governmental planners is changed into a more comprehensive planning model.

Konstantinos Koukouris is Assistant Professor, Department of Physical Education and Exercise Science, Aristotle's University of Thessaloniki, Greece. Konstantinos completed his doctoral thesis in the field of sport sociology at the University of Manchester. He teaches courses in leisure and sport sociology and has conducted qualitative research on aspects related to disengagement of sports. He has been published in the International Review for the Sociology of Sport, "Disengagement of Advanced and Elite Greek Male Athletes from Organized Competitive Sport" (1991) and the Sociology of Sport Journal, "Constructed Case Studies: Athletes' Perspectives of Disengaging from Organized Competitive Sport."

Anna MacVicar is a lecturer in Human Resource Management at Glasgow Caledonian University. Her main interests include workplace flexibility in public sector leisure and the impact of Investors in People within the hospitality, tourism and leisure sectors.

Graham McFee is Professor of Philosophy at the University of Brighton. His major research interests include the philosophy of Wittgenstein, the problem of freewill, and aesthetics (especially the aesthetics of dance). Related interests include educational theory, especially arts education, physical education and dance education. His principal publications include *Free Will (Routledge, 2000); Understanding Dance* (Routledge, 1992); *The Concept of Dance Education* (Routledge, 1994); and 'The Surface Grammar of Dreaming' (*Proceedings of the Aristotelian Society,* 1994). He Vice President of the British Society of Aesthetics.

Mike McNamee is Reader in applied philosophy in the Leisure and Sport Research Unit at Cheltenham and Gloucester College of Higher Education. His main research interests lie in philosophy of education, leisure and sport, and in applied ethics. He is co-editor of *Ethics and Sport* (1998, Routledge) and of a series of the same name (also Routledge). He is currently president of the International Association for the Philosophy of Sport.

Per Nilsson is Associate Professor in Educational Research at Stockholm Institute of Education and Reader in Sport and Education at Stockholm University College of Physical Education. He was also a visiting Professor at Cheltenham and Gloucester College of Higher Education in the autumn of 1997. His doctoral thesis was on "Football and morality, a study of four Swedish elite football clubs" (1993). He is the author of several books including *Serious Leisure Time* (1994), *The Discourse of the Body* (1998) and *Leisure in Different Worlds* (1998). His main research interests centre around sport and socialisation, leisure and youth, and body and identity.

Susan Ogden is a lecturer in Management within the Department of Hospitality, Tourism and Leisure Management at Glasgow Caledonian University. Her research focuses on the impact of successive Government policies on public leisure and hospitality services with particular reference to the management of employees, organisational culture and service quality.

Tomas Peterson is Professor in Sociology in the Department of sociology at the University of Lund.

Martin Reeves completed his PhD at Loughborough University, examining the interrelationship between sport and tourism, followed by over 2 years as a lecturer lecturing at Cheltenham and Gloucester College of Higher Education. He has now moved into the public sector as Policy Manager for Reigate and Banstead Borough Council. His role there includes responsibility for managing Best Value reviews across Leisure Services, as well as all aspects of strategy formulation including the Local Cultural strategy. He is an active member of ILAM, now serving on the South East Regional Executive.

Bernadette Scott is a lecturer in Hospitality Management at Glasgow Caledonian University. Her research interests include workplace violence and gender related issues pertaining to working in the hospitality industry.

Claudio Tamburrini is a Senior Researcher at the Department of Philosophy, Gothenburg University. He has published "Crime and Punishment?" (his PhD dissertation) and articles on penal philosophy and philosophy of sports. He has recently co-edited *Values in Sport* (2000) with Torbjörn Tännsjö and has played professional soccer in Argentina.

Heather Sheridan is a doctoral student at Cheltenham and Gloucester College of Higher Education. Her PhD is in the areas of applied ethics and is a moral philosophical exploration of the concept of "fair play" in elite male tennis. Her Masters thesis in Leisure and Tourism Management, also at Cheltenham & Gloucester College, aimed to assess whether conceptual sense could be made of "dark leisure".

Christine Williams is a Senior Lecturer in Leisure and Service Quality Management at The Lancashire Business School, University of Central Lancashire and a Fellow of the Institute of Leisure and Amenity Management. In 1997 she completed a research project investigating quality systems and service delivery in the UK leisure industry, for which she was awarded a Master of Philosophy degree. Her area of research has now widened from the leisure industry to the public sector in general. Christine has published articles on service quality management and has presented papers at WLRA and ANZALS conferences. Prior to her career in education, Christine worked for over fifteen years as a practitioner in the public sector of the leisure industry where she designed and managed outdoor leisure facilities.

Part I

POLICY

Changing their Game:
The Effect of Lottery Sports Funding on Voluntary Sports Clubs

Richard Garrett

Sheffield university Management School,
University of Sheffield (UK)

Introduction

This paper presents initial findings of survey data collected from voluntary sports clubs (VSCs) regarding their organisational structure. All the clubs questioned were awarded Lottery sports funding in 1996. The paper first introduces the voluntary sports sector. An outline of institutional theory is given, applied to the Lottery Sports Fund (LSF) and then used to interpret the survey results. The objectives of the paper are therefore: first, to identify any institutional pressures exerted on VSCs in 1996 by the LSF; and, secondly, to identify whether the structure of VSCs that received Lottery sports funding in 1996 has changed from their pre-award structure.

Context

Sports volunteering is the most common form of organised voluntary activity in the UK (Davis Smith, 1998) and amounts to 1.5 million volunteers at an estimated value of £1.5 billion per annum in the UK (Gratton et al., 1997). No studies have calculated the number and value of volunteers in local sports clubs independent of national and international sports volunteers, although Gratton et al. (1997) estimated that local sports clubs accounted for 80% of the total number and value of sports volunteers in the UK. The value of VSCs goes beyond economic measures. Lying at the foot of the sports pyramid, VSCs form the grass roots of sports provision in the UK. Not only are the clubs crucial for sporting opportunities and participation within the local community, they are necessary for success at national and international level as they are the starting point for the elite performers of the future.

UK VSCs are typically self-supporting (Boothby and Tungatt, 1978) but may obtain resources from a variety of internal and external sources. However, VSCs are more dependent on internal member-generated income and resources (i.e. membership fees and volunteering) for their day-to-day existence than external sources. Funding from external sources tends to be capital funding and sponsorship to realise projects that might not be achievable through members' efforts alone such as a new club house or playing facilities. The importance of volunteering as a resource to VSCs ought not to be underestimated (Burgess, 1996; Gratton *et al.*, 1997; Taks *et al.*, 1998). Members turn their skills, manual or intellectual acquired through the labour market or leisure, to running the club.

However, the source of funding to local voluntary organisations is changing with an increasing amount coming from the state (Russell *et al.*, 1996) which is coming to recognise the value of the voluntary sector as a cost-effective means of delivering services and implementing policies (Home Office, 1990; National Council for Voluntary Organisations, 1992). State funding tends to be rationalised as it is often programme specific, ignores the administration costs of seeking and implementing the funding, and is related to the funding body's objectives (Joseph Rowntree Foundation, 1995; Leach and Wilson, 1998; Nichols and Sparrowhawk, 1999).

The acquisition of external funding by voluntary organisations has been associated with a change in the organisation's internal structure (Slack and Hinings, 1994) and also bureaucratisation (Rosenbaum, 1981; Thibault *et al.*, 1991). Bureaucratisation is characterised by, and among others, the specialisation, formalisation and professionalisation of structures (Frisby, 1982; Slack, 1985; Thibault *et al.*, 1991). If a voluntary sport club becomes increasingly bureaucratised with receipt of external funding, then it is reasonable to expect that the club's structures will change, demonstrating increased specialisation, formalisation or professionalisation. Bureaucrat-isation and a change in structure alters the context and nature of volunteering (Lewis, 1994), possibly influencing the balance between motivations for and barriers to volunteering as an individual. This raises concomitant issues for volunteer recruitment, management and retention.

Papadimitriou (1998) examined the structure of grass-roots voluntary sport organisations, but few have investigated change in structure over a period of time or centred around a significant event. Studies exist (Slack and Hinings, 1994; Thibault *et al.*, 1991; Slack, 1985; Frisby, 1982) of national voluntary sports organisations on this subject, which inform the examination of local voluntary sports organisations but, given the description of the latter above, it is unwise to assume that the findings of national studies are transferable to the local.

Kikulis *et al.* (1989) produced a structural typology of amateur sport organisations using measures of centralisation (of decision making), specialisation, formalisation, and professionalisation. In a study of local sport organisations in Greece, Papadimitriou (1998) noted that clubs had a simple structure (highly centralised decision-making, low formalisation and specialisation of tasks), which is the least bureaucratic of Kikulis *et al.*.'s typology. It was also apparent that Greek VSCs are more developed and structured than UK VSCs. Papadimitriou (1998) reports the necessity of technical staff, the employment by one third of her sample of one or more part-time coaches, that clubs establish links with doctors and physiotherapists, and finally that clubs are more likely to provide more than one sport. In the UK, VSCs mostly provide for one sport through the use of amateur coaches and officials, and are unlikely to have medical and technical support staff. However, we do not know whether these characteristics of UK sports clubs are changing. If change is taking place, it is important to locate the cause of this change and to understand its impact. Institutional theory offers this possibility.

Institutional theory

One of the central tenets of institutional theory is that "the engine of rationalization and bureaucratization has moved from the marketplace to the state and the professions" (DiMaggio and Powell, 1983: p. 147). Thus, we can expect that with the acquisition of external funding from the state, local VSCs will become bureaucratised. To progress with a delineation of institutional theory it is necessary to first define an institution as an objectified and legitimated structure, existing in a focal organisation's field, prescribing and proscribing ways of organising either implicitly or explicitly. These pre- and proscriptions are to be viewed as *normative* and *mimetic* pressures that are often reinforced through coercion and resource pressures. Normative pressures exist in an organisational field as conventional and rationalised knowledge. DiMaggio (1983: p. 158) explains:

> Commonly accepted structures or administrative approaches may be diffused throughout a field if key staff are trained in a few universities; if careers are launched in a few key organizations and develop in smaller ones; or if organizations learn by sending their staff to common training sessions or workshops or by calling on one of the few leading management consultants.

Mimicking occurs voluntarily when an organisation is uncertain of the actions that are expected of it by its organisational field. Consequently, "organizations are likely to identify organizations in their field that seem successful and adopt attributes of those organizations that can be reasoned to have caused their success" (DiMaggio, 1983: p. 158). Essentially, 'best practice' examples provided by the state or available from the organisational field are likely to be copied or used as a template. Coercive pressures emanate from powerful organisations in a field and encourage less powerful organisations to adopt suggested goals and structures (DiMaggio, 1983). These can be "both formal and informal pressures exerted on organizations by other organizations upon which they are dependent and by cultural expectations in the society within which organizations function" (DiMaggio and Powell, 1983: p. 158). Informal pressures may constitute the threat of withdrawing accreditation or funding from an organisation; whereas the legal framework enforced through the courts and the police represents formal pressures.

The LSF is viewed as a policy tool of Sport England, which is considered an agent of the state that employs a body of professional sports administrators. The LSF is therefore viewed as being a resource pressure used to reinforce the institutional pressures of Sport England. What Institutional theory proposes is that organisations within a particular organisational field are subjected to mutually reinforcing (Slack and Hinings, 1994), coercive, normative, and mimetic institutional pressures (DiMaggio and Powell, 1983), that pre- and proscribe ways of organising (Hinings and Greenwood, 1988). Thus, institutional pressures in a particular organisational field encourage greater similarity in the structures of organisations belonging to that field. Therefore, the structures of organisations in that field become isomorphic with each other and the institutional pressures. According to Scott (1995: p. xiv) then, institutional theory emphasises the:

> importance of the wider context or environment as it constrains, shapes, and penetrates the organization... To the earlier emphasis on the importance of the technical social environment — resources and technical know-how — institutional theory has called attention to the importance of the social and cultural environment, in particular, to the social knowledge and cultural rule systems.

According to this position, the institutional pressures of Sport England, reinforced through the LSF, encourage VSCs to adopt the practices and structures preferred by Sport England, and perhaps already adopted by some VSCs.

However, this assumes that VSCs will acquiesce to the LSF's policy values and norms. This is not always the case, as Oliver (1991: p. 145) points out:

> The institutional perspective has been increasingly criticised for its lack of attention to the role of organisational self-interests and active

agency in organisational responses to institutional pressures and expectations.

An organisation's response to institutional pressures will not be invariably passive. By accepting that a range of responses can be hypothesised from acquiescence, compromise, avoidance, and defiance to manipulation, this determinism can be overcome and a role for agency recognised in institutional theory (Oliver, 1991). Meyer and Rowan (1977) acknowledged the role of agency through the 'decoupling' process where an organisation apparently accepts institutional pre- and proscriptions of how to organise. They propose that, although organisational structures and practices may be established in line with these pressures, they are only adopted ceremonially, remaining decoupled from the organisation's operational structure and with little influence on the daily life of the organisation. Hence the organisation is *seen* as conforming to the prescribed way of behaving, therefore increasing its legitimacy and assuring its survival. Decoupling these structures from its daily activity though, means that the organisation avoids the full implications of change.

The Lottery Sports Fund: institutional pressures

Attention now turns to the first research objective of establishing the institutional pressures of the LSF. At present the LSF is probably the most significant source of new and additional funding that sport has ever received. The LSF has also resulted in Sport England being able to further its objectives through closer ties with VSCs and having a greater degree of influence in the way the sector develops and operates. This is just one example of the changing relationship between the state and the voluntary sector. Indeed, the LSF could be viewed as a microcosm of state-sector relations as a whole.

The LSF pressurises voluntary sector sports clubs in several ways, which can be grouped under three headings. Firstly, the application procedure where the clubs are subjected to the logic and rationality of the business world. For example, an LSF Monitoring Officer (English Sports Council, 1998) stated:

> We need the club to convince us that the extra demands will not force the club to go under, because sometimes they are quite short termist and we're obviously wanting to secure a kind of lasting sport legacy. So I think what we want is good planning, good financial management, we certainly don't expect the kind of standards you'd expect from a large government agency or organisation, but we would expect a club to be able to have some kind of provision for maintenance, to have some kind of financial projections.

Business plans need to be created by the club to convince the LSF that the project is viable. This requires that the club demonstrates a proven need for the facility and that the local community stands to benefit from the proposed project. The club is also asked to predict the increase in membership that the project will produce among Sport England's targeted participation groups (i.e. juniors, women, special needs, ethnic minorities). Clubs' fund raising skills are also tested, as they must raise at least 10% of the cost of their project and find a minimum 25% of the cost through matching funding from other sources. The intensive consumption of resources (e.g. time, effort and money) in the pursuit of funding is notable. The effort, skills and resources required to make applications for and manage the funding are great, and may be beyond the capacity of some small voluntary organisations. Such costs "are compounded by a lack of appropriate technology" (Russell *et al.*, 1996: p. 407) such as presentation and management skills (Gratton *et al.*, 1997; National Council for Voluntary Organisations, 1992).

If the bid is successful then the second source of demands is the operation of the facility. The new facility has to be managed and maintained. In some cases this demand may be greater if the operating the facility means an absolute increase in provision. In other cases, however, where a facility may have undergone renovation, it may be that less attention is required because it is easier to maintain. After the project is realised, the club has to put its plans into action to create links with the community, perhaps through schools liaison and also to foster minority use. Developing a junior section may create additional demands on the club. For example, it may be necessary to appoint a specialist coach, or to train a volunteer in junior coaching skills. Both these options may involve police checks. An increase in the demands placed on the club is possible due to the extra coaching time, additional fixtures and transport needs of the juniors, all of which must be manned and provided by volunteers.

The VSC must also ensure that the revenue costs of the club are continually being met. An organisation can only expand so far without broadening its base or strengthening its core operations. Future growth may require that short-term costs be borne which are not covered by the capital grant. This may or may not be possible for voluntary organisations without further aid. Even after a substantial award from the LSF that seemingly guarantees its future, a club may still have to develop new working practices and become increasingly professional to ensure a continued flow of income. The Secretary of a lawn tennis club that had successfully applied for Lottery funding outlined the effects of their award:

> We used to have relatively small amounts of money passing through the club but ... as we have developed the facilities we've had to manage our money much more carefully. Whereas before it was perhaps

a task which almost any competent person within the club could do, nowadays we try and have an accountant member as the treasurer.

This indicates an increasing need for volunteers with professional skills. However, with an apparent lack of volunteers, skilled or not, it must be asked whether VSCs can rely on their members to ensure its survival through voluntary activity. The Chairman of another successful lawn tennis club commented:

> I think voluntary help is going to be the biggest problem that this club and other clubs are going to have in the years to come. When you look around there are not as many volunteers coming into the game, into the administrative side of the game as there were in the past. And when people of my generation leave the clubs you fear that there won't be enough.

Sport England argue that the LSF application procedure requires enough forethought and planning for these contingencies to be anticipated and overcome (English Sports Council, 1998). Any project lacking evidence of sustainability would not receive funding. This places more emphasis on the planning and application stage of any project. Ongoing support is available through the Running Sport programme provided by Sport England, and aims to help VSCs in their operation. The Running Sport programme has seen a 55% increase in the number of seminars it runs for VSCs over the past two financial years (Sport England, 1999a). Whether this increase is due to supply finally meeting latent demand created by the LSF is problematic.

A third way in which pressures are placed on clubs by the LSF to conform to expected or prescribed models of behaviour is through the monitoring process. Detailed membership and usage records may be needed for the purposes of monitoring by Sport England (English Sports Council, 1998). Progress towards the fulfilment of the conditions of the award can then be checked. The 1997 White Paper on the National Lottery encourages a more strategic distribution of Lottery funds which "will produce results that *can be measured*" (Department of Culture, Media, and Sport, 1997: p. 20, emphasis added). Several problems exist with this short point as many projects do not and cannot produce quantifiable results, and in the present reactive application–distribution system, strategic distribution is difficult. Quantifiable results may be available in the form of participation or usage figures. Measurement of results inevitably necessitates monitoring systems which the club must establish and maintain. Should a club fail to meet the conditions of an award, Sport England has the legal right to recover the award from the club. An LSF Case Officer (Sport England, 1999b) states:

...the award letter is actually a legally binding document. Within the period that's specified in the award letter, and that's dependent on the size of the grant, there's a clawback liability period. Within that period we are at liberty to either get the grant repaid or take ownership of the facility.

The nature of the LSF community facilities capital grants scheme is such that the funding is discrete and not continuous as would be the case for revenue funding. Once the grant has been paid by the LSF to the club, the club is no longer dependent on the LSF. This short-term dependence may mean that the LSF's influence on the club is less than it would be if the club was to receive long-term revenue funding. Consequently, the bureaucratising influence of the LSF may be less than other sources. However, the new facility may leave the club with increased revenue costs, increased demands on volunteers, and an expectation to behave in a rational, accountable and professional manner. That is not to say that such clubs did not behave in a responsible way in the past, rather that the pressures to operate in a managerialist fashion have increased. Meeting these pressures may require a higher level of skill, time, and effort from volunteers. Some of these demands may be within the capacity of those volunteers who have sufficient skill and ability. For others, the demands may be too much.

In these greater demands on clubs and volunteers can be seen the isomorphic pressures that DiMaggio and Powell (1983) identify as existing in an organisation's institutional environment. The application for Lottery sports funding encourages applicants to operate in what Sport England sees as the logical and efficient manner for an organisational population receiving public money. This is the rational and appropriate way for organisations in this situation to behave — it is the norm. Mimetic isomorphism operates between clubs. If other clubs have adopted these norms and forms of operating, and have achieved success in their Lottery bids, then it is increasingly likely that similar clubs will adopt the same practices. Models of best practice heralded by Sport England are likely to be mimicked by other applicants.

However, early applicants to the LSF in 1995/1996 may have been left wanting for models of best practice due to the likelihood that only a limited number of projects had been awarded and completed. Coercive isomorphic pressures exist in the procedures and regulations of the application itself and also any conditions attached to an award. Gross failure of the club to fulfil the award provisos, as discovered through the monitoring process, means that Sport England are legally entitled to revoke the award, although this would of course be a last resort (English Sports Council, 1998).

Therefore a relatively independent set of organisations are subjected voluntarily to the external constraints and stipulations of the LSF, introducing prescriptions and proscriptions of means and ends. Isomorphism with these institutional pressures of the LSF may change the voluntary sports club structure and operation, thus altering the context of sports volunteering at the local level. Such changes in context may affect volunteers' participation in the provision of sporting opportunities. Given the importance of the VSCs' role in the sports pyramid, their characteristics, and the neglect of VSCs in the research, it seems pertinent to investigate the structural impacts of receiving Lottery sports funding on VSCs.

Methodology

A telephone survey investigating changes in VSCs' structural characteristics was employed to address the second research issue identified at the start of this paper. The sampling frame used for the survey was the *Lottery Link Newsletter* (English Sports Council, 1996) produced by Sport England. This lists all awards made from the LSF to recipients such as local authorities and national governing bodies as well as VSCs in the period summer / autumn 1996. Thus, the sample extracted contained all VSCs receiving awards in that period, constituting a 100% sample of the population (n=309). **Table 1** (page following) shows the constituents of the population and the survey's response pattern.

Selection of the sampling frame was important for two reasons. It was conjectured that the full impact of the award might not materialise immediately after receiving it. For this reason a significant amount of time needed to be left between the announcement of the award and the point of enquiry during which the project would have been implemented and the impact become apparent. However, too great a period of time between these two points would hinder the respondents recall of pre-award structures in the club. Therefore, the sampling frame had to be chosen carefully in the light of recall problems and also the emergence of the award's impact.

In accordance with Frisby (1982), Slack and Hinings (1987; 1994), Kikulis *et al.* (1989) and Thibault *et al.* (1991), structures of specialisation and formalisation were tested, but centralisation of decision making (locus of decision making) was substituted with professionalisation. The flat structure of VSCs means that decision making is already centralised within the committee structure and provides little opportunity for decentralisation. Furthermore, Theodoraki and Henry (1994) note that measures of centralisation are unreliable and not suited to quantitative investigation. Therefore it is more relevant to investigate the change in the number of paid

Table 1   Response pattern for the first 100 surveys

Number of responses			
Sport:	Number in Population	Number of clubs Contacted	Percentage of Population
Bowls	47	30	64
Cricket	66	16	24
Football	33	10	30
Lawn Tennis	67	23	34
Others	96	21	22
Total	**309**	**100**	**32**
Non-responses			
Reason for Non Response:			Number
No number obtained for club			92
Number obtained but contact could not be made			17
Contact made but club was not a suitable respondent			12
Refusals			0
Total			**121**

professional staff within the club. Also, as measures of organisational structure, professionalisation, formalisation, specialisation are three indicators of the level of bureaucracy in an organisation (Blau, 1974; Frisby, 1982; Hatch, 1997; Slack 1997). The questions investigating the indicators of bureaucracy were based on constructs examined by Slack and Hinings (1987; 1994) and Thibault (1991) and were designed to enable pre-bid and post award comparison of structures.

Specialisation concerned the extent to which a VSC was horizontally or vertically differentiated (Slack, 1997). Horizontal complexity is increased through the differentiation of activities on one organisational level into task specific units, for instance creating individual positions for new tasks or splitting existing tasks, and also the use of skilled specialists to perform specific tasks. An increase in the number of hierarchical levels in the organisation is characteristic of vertical differentiation, for example the creation of additional sub-committees in a club's committee structure. Specialisation questions investigated whether training was given to committee and non-committee volunteers, the number of committee positions and the existence of specialist coaches.

Formalisation concerned "the extent to which mechanisms such as rules and regulations, job descriptions, and policies and procedures govern the operation of a sports organisation" (Slack, 1997: p. 49). Formalisation questions concerned the existence of job descriptions for committee and non-committee volunteers also whether the constitution was altered or established as part of the bid.

Professionalisation was defined as the change in the total number of professionals in the club's structure. This definition covers both self-employed professionals such as some coaches, and professionals employed directly by the club such as club managers.

Results

The degree of change in each club's structure was quantified by calculating a total bureaucratisation score (Total B score). Positive scores indicated an increase in bureaucracy, negative scores a reduction and a score of zero meant no change in the level of bureaucracy. Fifty two clubs demonstrated positive Total B scores, six clubs had negative Total B scores, and forty two showed no change. **Figure 1** shows the distribution of Total B scores.

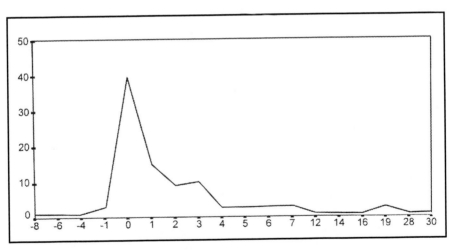

Figure 1   **Bureaucratisation scores**

It is evident then that, of the one hundred responses gained from the sample so far, the majority of clubs have become more bureaucratised, with Total B scores ranging from 1 to 30. However, the modal Total B score across all responses was that of *no change* [Total B = 0 (n=42)]. This shows that a large number of clubs did not experience change in the structures measured. Also, de-bureaucratisation was experienced by six clubs, with scores ranging from −1 to −8. Questions now arise of whether increases in bureaucracy are due to the institutional pressures exerted by the LSF, and also whether unchanged or decreasing levels of bureaucracy are indicative of resistance to these pressures. The implications of structural change or inertia on volunteering will need to be elicited through qualitative means, which is beyond the objectives of the present paper but is the focus of ongoing research.

Conclusions and further research

Institutional theory argues that bureaucratic structures emerge out of conformity to institutional pressures existing in the organisation's field. These pressures emphasise a professional and rational approach to a club's operation as valued by the administrators and agents of the state, and also out of the need for legitimacy, reflecting the central role of the state and the professions in structuring the organisation's field (DiMaggio, 1983).

The purpose of the survey was to facilitate a bureaucracy classification of VSCs awarded Lottery funding in the summer/autumn of 1996, which would enable further investigation through qualitative case studies. The classification was based on results from 100 surveys and holds the assumption that receipt of a LSF award subjects all the clubs to the same institutional pressures exerted by Sport England through the LSF. Indicators used to measure bureaucracy and organisational structure were designed so as to allow pre-bid and post-award comparison of VSCs' structures.

The survey's responses were divided into three categories: increased bureaucracy, reduced bureaucracy, and those which showed no change. The modal score was zero (no change). However, the greatest number of responses fell into the category of increased bureaucracy. Very few clubs reported a reduction in their level of bureaucracy. The majority of clubs therefore witnessed an increase in their level of bureaucracy associated with receipt of their Lottery grant, whereas slightly fewer clubs showed no change in their structure. Establishing causality between a change in a VSC's organisational structure and receipt of a LSF grant is impossible based on these results. Only further qualitative investigation with these clubs will elicit the relationship between LSF funding and a club's structure. A greater number of survey responses are also required if less tentative inferences are to be permitted. This would suggest that not only should the entire sample population eventually be surveyed but that a larger population than originally planned should be surveyed because of the high number of non-responses evident from Table 1.

Increased bureaucracy may mean a more formalised structured and obligated role for volunteers, which requires greater time, effort, and skill, selecting out those who feel unable to meet these demands. Alternatively, some may be attracted by the idea of a more clearly defined and demanding role. Meyer and Rowan (1977) and Oliver (1991) argue that increased bureaucracy in VSCs is not so straightforward. Instead, clubs may choose either to only ceremonially accept the prescribed structures and practices or to challenge and reject them. These ideas may help to explain the findings of the survey which show that some voluntary sports club's structures did not change whilst others actually showed de-bureaucratisation. In this case, the context of volunteering may go unchanged or change for the better, allowing volunteers to maintain their involvement and attracting additional volunteers. Again, the converse is possible, where a less specialised and formalised volunteering environment discourages those who desire a structured and accountable position. A further explanation could be that those clubs demonstrating no change in their structures had already adopted the institutionally prescribed structures long before applying to the LSF, whereas those clubs whose structures became more bureaucratic had not.

Clearly, further research of a qualitative nature is necessary to explain these survey findings. Whether the changes in VSCs' structure identified here are due to the institutional pressures of Sport England applied through the LSF, or the result of wider societal pressures, sports policy needs to take account of the implications for the volunteers upon which British sport is based.

References

Blau, P. (1974) *On the nature of organizations*. New York: John Wiley.

Boothby, J. and Tungatt, M. F. (1978) 'Amateur sport clubs: Their salient features and major advantages', *International Review for the Sociology of Sport* Vol. 13, No. 1: pp. 25–35.

Burgess, S. (1996) *Barclaycard volunteer investment programme*. Leeds: The National Coaching Foundation and the English Sports Council.

Davis Smith, J. (1998) *The 1997 national survey of volunteering*. London: The National Centre for Volunteering.

Department of Culture Media and Sport (1997) *The peoples' lottery: White paper on the national lottery*. London: HMSO.

DiMaggio, P. (1983) 'State expansion and organizational fields', in R. H. Hall and R. E. Quinn (eds) *Organization theory and public policy*. Beverly Hills CA: Sage, pp. 147–161.

DiMaggio, P. J. and Powell, W. W. (1983) 'The iron cage revisited: Institutional isomorphism and collective rationality in organizational fields'. *American Sociological Review* Vol. 48, No. 2: pp. 147–160.

English Sports Council (1996) *Guide to the Lottery Sports Fund.* Sports Council. London: English Sports Council.

—— (1998) Interview with Lottery Sports Fund Senior Monitoring Officer.

Frisby, W. (1982) 'Weber's theory of bureaucracy and the study of voluntary sport organizations', in A. O. Dunleavy, A. W. Miracle and C. R. Rees (eds) *Studies in the sociology of sport: Second annual conference of the North American society for the sociology of sport.* Fort Worth, Texas, pp. 53–71.

Gratton, C., Nichols, G., Shibli, S. and Taylor, P. (1997) *Valuing Volunteers in UK Sport.* London: English Sports Council.

Hatch, M. J. (1997) *Organization theory: Modern symbolic and postmodern perspectives.* Oxford: Oxford University Press.

Hinings, B. and Greenwood, R. (1988) 'The normative prescriptions of organizations', in L. G. Zucker (ed) *Institutional patterns and organizations.* Cambridge MA: Ballinger, pp. 53–70.

Home Office (1990) *Efficiency scrutiny of government funding of the voluntary sector: Profiting from partnership.* London: HMSO.

Joseph Rowntree Foundation (1995) *Mixed fortunes: The funding of the voluntary sector.* York: Joseph Rowntree Foundation.

Kikulis, L. M., Slack, T., Hinings, B. and Zimmerman, A. (1989) 'A structural taxonomy of amateur sport organizations', *Journal of Sport Management* Vol. 3, No. 2: pp. 129–50.

Leach, S. and Wilson, D. (1998) 'Voluntary groups and local authorities: Rethinking the relationship', *Local Government Studies* Vol. 24, No. 2: pp. 1–18.

Lewis, J. (1994) 'Voluntary organisations in "new partnership" with local authorities: The anatomy of a contract', *Social Policy and Administration* Vol. 28, No. 3: pp. 206–220.

Meyer, J.W. and Rowan, B. (1977) 'Institutionalized organizations: Formal structure as myth and ceremony', *American Journal of Sociology* Vol. 83, No. 2: pp. 340–363.

National Council for Voluntary Organisations (1992) *The efficiency scrutiny implementation: Report and recommendations on funding of the voluntary sector* (Draft). London: NCVO.

Nichols, G. and Sparrowhawk, J. (1999) 'Local authorities' role in distributing the lottery to sport', *Local Government Studies* Vol. 25, No. 3: pp. 1–15.

Oliver, C. (1991) 'Strategic responses to institutional processes', *Academy of Management Review* Vol. 16, No. 1: pp. 145–179.

Papadimitriou, D. (1998) 'Measures of organizational structure, context and performance in voluntary sport organizations', in G. Pires, F. Fernandes and N. Parry (eds) *Service quality in sport: Conference proceedings.* Madeira: European Association for Sport Management, pp. 7.14–7.24.

Rosebaum, N. (1981) 'Government funding and the voluntary sector: Impacts and options', *Journal of Voluntary Action Research* Vol. 10, No. 1: pp. 82–87.

Russell, L., Scott, D. and Wilding, P. (1996) 'The funding of local voluntary organisations', *Policy and Politics* Vol. 24, No. 4: pp. 395–412.

Scott, R. (1995) *Institutions and organizations.* London: Sage.

Slack, T. (1985) 'The bureaucratization of a voluntary sport organization', *International Review for the Sociology of Sport* Vol. 20, No. 3: pp. 145–166.

———— (1997) *Understanding sport organizations: The application of organization theory.* Leeds: Human Kinetics.

Slack, T. and Hinings, B. (1987) 'Planning and organizational change: A conceptual framework for the analysis of amateur sport organizations', *Canadian Journal of Sport Sciences* Vol. 12, No. 4: pp. 185–193.

———— (1994) 'Institutional pressures and isomorphic change: An empirical test', *Organization Studies* Vol. 15, No. 6: pp. 803–827.

Sport England (1999a) Interview with Education and Training Programme Manager.

———— (1999b) Interview with Lottery Sports Fund Senior Case Officer.

Taks, M., Duysters, A., Laporte, W., Verhoeven, M., Bollaert, L., De Knop, P. and Van Bunder, D. (1998) 'Motivating and de-motivating factors for volunteers in sports organisations: An empirical survey', in G. Pires, F. Fernandes and N. Parry (eds) *Service quality in sport: Conference proceedings.* Madeira: European Association for Sport Management, pp. 7.41–7.51.

Theodoraki, E. and Henry, I. (1994) 'Organisational structures and contexts in British national governing bodies of sport', *International Review for the Sociology of Sport* Vol. 29, No. 3: pp. 243–268.

Thibault, L., Slack, T. and Hinings, B. (1991) 'Professionalism, structures and systems: The impact of professional staff on voluntary sport organizations', *International Review for Sociology of Sport* Vol. 26, No. 2: pp. 83–97.

Issues of Legal Responsibility in Organised Sport and Outdoor Recreation

John Hunter-Jones

Centre for Physical Education and Leisure,
University of Manchester (UK)

The paper focuses on those organised sporting and recreational activities where there is a high degree of risk of injury to participants and consequently a need to identify those responsible, in law, for safety. Many of these activities carry inherent risks, for example the risk of injury through tackling in rugby, which participants are deemed to have accepted in their taking part. However, organisers have been subject to increasing scrutiny of their legal responsibility through civil actions, Health and Safety law and licensing conditions. Such scrutiny may well reflect society's concern to see that organisers of sport and recreation are not immune from the process of law, and that their actions are subject to the same regulation as other activities. The paper considers the relationship between organisers and participants and how far English law has sought to determine responsibility for the risk of injury.

Quantitative research into injuries sustained in Sport and Recreation

In spite of the number of agencies compiling statistical information on injuries, it is difficult to give a clear indication on the number of injuries arising out of organised sport and recreation. The reason for this is that the Agencies involved are concerned with injuries within particular contexts; the Health and Safety Executive and the Office of National Statistics (Labour Force Survey) are concerned with workplace related injuries; the Consumer Safety Unit, at the DTI, is concerned with injuries caused by equipment; and the Office of Population Census and Surveys (OPCS) is concerned with fatal accidents and poisoning. There are also difficulties in defining what injuries are worth reporting and the methods of recovering such information.

The OPCS, in its DH4 series of Statistics (1998), identified the number of accidental deaths in places for sport and recreation (excluding transport and drowning) from 1992 to 1996 as follows:

	1992	1993	1994	1995	1996
Male	67	70	67	68	58
Female	17	18	22	17	23

In 1993, the OPCS Monitor analysed the number of deaths occurring during leisure and sporting activities in 1992. One difficulty that was highlighted is that some accidents, for instance drowning, may happen because the victim suffered from another ailment at the time. Relevant to this paper is the following:

Deaths in 1992

	Climbing	Horse riding	Ball games	Athletic Sports	Drowning
Male	6	5	4	6	58
Female	1	7	0	3	06

When these statistics are reviewed by age (0–4; 5–14; 15–24; 25–34; 35–44; 45–64; 65+), the 15–24 group recorded the most deaths (41–30% of the total).

Between 1991/92–1995/96 the HSE recorded just 20 fatal injuries to members of the public and 5 to employees within sporting and recreational service industries (HSE, 1997). Falling from a horse accounted for 6 fatalities, and there were 2 from drowning in a swimming pool. Elsewhere, in the HSE publication *Managing Health and Safety in Swimming Pools* (HSE, 1999: p. v) it is recorded that "about 10–12 people drown in pools every year ... however ... open water ... claimed about 420 deaths in 1998".

The Leisure Accident Surveillance System (LASS) (HASS, 1998) is a survey of leisure injuries recorded by a sample of British Hospital Accident and Emergency Departments, conducted by the DTI's Consumer Safety Unit. LASS reports that 12% of all accidents treated in their Hospitals during 1996 were sport related, adding (p. 16) that 11% of all GP patient injuries are also sport related. The total number of sporting accidents in Britain was estimated at 990,000 (HASS, 1998: p. 31). Ball sports accounted for 64.3% of such injuries; stick sports 10.9%; combat sports 2.9%; animal sports 3% and water sports 3.4%. However, these figures do not distinguish organised activities.

In stark contrast, the HSE figures for 1995/96 show only 2,592 (hospital-treated) injuries to members of the public recorded by the Sports and Recreation Industry (HSE, 1997: p. 7). According to OPCS data on sporting fatalities, about 8% appear to occur within workplaces, whereas only 2–3% of sports injuries reported to hospitals appear to occur in workplaces. The Labour Force Survey (HSE, 1997) shows that only 33% of reportable injuries to employees are reported. This may well explain the low numbers of workplace injuries that are reported to the authorities, in spite of it being a legal requirement under the Reporting of Injuries, Diseases and Dangerous Occurrences Regulations 1995. The statistics suggest that sport does pose a notable risk of serious injury to those involved in ball and stick games, water sports, riding and combat sports. It would appear that the great majority of injuries occur outside the workplace, and so are beyond much of the Health and Safety and licensing regulations.

The need for risk vs the need for regulation

In considering safety regulation, Dawson (1988: p. 154) states that "a reduction [in accidents] may entail costs or require control over individual behaviour at work, and so there exists the possibility of a trade off between safety and other issues". The play-off between the reduction of accidents and a reduction in an activity is a central concern raised in this work.

Barker (1998: p. 10) comments: "If risk is over-regulated [in sport], the challenge and appeal of a particular activity are diminished". The Consumer Protection Unit (CPU) at the Department of Trade and Industry (DTI) in 1989 produced a research report which sought to establish the link between risk-taking and satisfaction in sport. It stated:

> ... if it is the case that people are deliberately seeking risk in the leisure aspect of their lives, difficulty may arise in attempting to remove or at least reduce that risk. Individuals will then either not partake in the activity any more or will possibly take more risks when they do. (CPU, 1989: p. 13)

Sport, clearly, poses the problem that a reduction in regulated risk opportunities may cause sensation-seekers to participate in less regulated, hence more dangerous, activities/environments.

Further, this is not a problem concerning just adults. Psychologists have identified a need, particularly in young males, for sensation-seeking through risk-taking (Zuckerman, 1994) and some see risk-taking as a positive contributor to quality of life: "A life without risk-taking is a life without mastery, achievement or social status" (Nell, 1998: p. 19). Children's exposure to risks is seen by others as an important part of their development "Children need risk in order to develop" (Jones, 1998: p. 15).

Criminal law and safety in sport and recreation

Although criminal prosecutions are quite rare against organisers of sport and recreation, it is an area that reveals much about society's willingness to apportion blame to those who may be at fault. Most criminal law protecting the individual from physical harm requires proof of deliberate or reckless intention to do harm, such prosecutions are typically made against individuals rather than organisations. However, organisers can be (and are) prosecuted in Criminal law where they have failed in their duty to provide specified minimum safety standards to participants. Three areas of Criminal law are relevant: *Corporate Manslaughter*; *Health and Safety* and *Licensing*.

a)   Corporate Manslaughter

Corporate Manslaughter can be proven by showing that death was caused by an unlawful act of the organisation — e.g. failing to observe Health and Safety regulations. At present it is a difficult crime to prove against an organisation because the prosecution must first succeed in prosecuting at least one manager whose negligence led to the death. One such case, though, R v Kite and OLL Ltd (1994) is a good example of how the criminal law has been applied. It is commonly referred to as the Lyme Bay prosecution.

In 1993, four school children drowned whilst they were on an organised canoeing trip at a commercial outdoor activity centre in Dorset. The Managing Director of the centre, Peter Kite, had been warned by staff that practices at the centre were dangerous. He ignored such advice and the accident followed. In 1994 both Kite and the Centre were successfully prosecuted, and Kite received a prison sentence of 2 years. The centre, at the time of the accident, was not subject to licensing, but was expected to comply with Health and Safety legislation. In many ways the case demonstrates the difficulty of prosecuting large organisations where it is more difficult "to align the managing director with the company itself" (Gardiner *et al.*, 1999: p. 131). This area of criminal law is, at present, unlikely to be successfully used to apportion blame in most accidental deaths.

b)   Health and Safety Legislation

The Health and Safety at Work (HSAW) Act 1974 is very wide in its application and can be regarded as that part of the criminal law most likely to identify responsibility for accidents occurring in organised sport and recreation. It does not seek to say what activity can or cannot be performed, but concentrates on the manner of its doing (Canterbury City Council v Howletts and Port Lympne Estates Ltd, TLR 13 Dec. 1996). This distinction is relevant to those sports where the risk of danger is intrinsic to the sport itself — for example, ice climbing which exposes participants to severe and unpredictable winter weather; and white-water rafting, the distinguishing feature of which is the dangerous state of the water. The Act protects not only those persons at work but also members of the public and volunteers affected by work activity (s.3). The Act sought to create a new safety environment where both the employer and worker could regulate the workplace to make it safer, with support provided by both the Health and Safety Executive, the Commission and local authorities. In the final analysis action can be taken against those parties failing in their duties. The act also provides for the creation of regulations (e.g. Management of Health and Safety Regulations 1992).

Much Health and Safety legislation has been, in recent years, driven by Directives from the European Union. In considering criminal liability there is a need to identify the extent of the duty to comply, so that the main Health and Safety offences (s.2–s.6) are subject to compliance being "reasonably practicable" (see Edwards v National Coal Board 1949), which clearly allows a balance between the extent of the risk and the cost of dealing with it.

Another aspect of Health and Safety law is whether a civil action can be based on a breach of the criminal law (breach of statutory duty). Elsewhere that opportunity generally exists, but s.47 of the HSWA prevents actions based on s.2–8 and also permits its prevention in the Regulations. The approach of Health and Safety law is illustrated by the Management of Heath and Safety Regulations 1992, Regulation 3, which states:

> Every employer shall make a suitable and sufficient assessment of:
> a) the risks to the H&S of his employees to which they are exposed whilst they are at work; and
> b) the risks to the H&S of persons not in his employment arising out of or in connection with the conduct by him or his under-taking.
>
> Where risks are identified it is the duty of the employer to eliminate or control them.

The failure to carry out a risk assessment can have far-reaching results. In November 1997 the London Borough of Hounslow was fined £25,000 under s.3 (1) for failing, through one of its schools, to check the qualifications of swimming pool attendants (not Hounslow's employees) at a Scout Camp, in advance of a day visit at which a pupil drowned (Gaskin v Hounslow 1997 unreported). Clearly, where organisers of hazardous sporting activity contract out to other bodies, such as happened at Lyme Bay, Health and Safety law places an additional burden of responsibility on the organisers. If the effect is that fewer bodies are willing to go through this process, because of additional time and cost, then this may indirectly deny many the opportunity to participate in controlled hazardous activities. The principle of risk assessment, although in keeping with the ideal of HSWA 1974 in the prevention of accidents, can also be seen as in conflict with the idea of "creating the conditions for more effective self regulation by employers and work people jointly" (Robens para. 452).

Robens felt that the "greatest obstacles to better standards of safety and health at work are indifference and apathy" (para. 46) borne out of a complex safety environment. It might appear that the State has taken too great a lead and that keeping up with the Regulations is the priority of most businesses. Dawson (1988), however, in considering self regulation, identifies the need for the system to create an environment where there is "motivation and capacity to act amongst all parties in the workplace so that nationally agreed laws and standards would be maintained and even improved upon" (p. 154). He identifies small firms, especially those with part time workers and low union representation, as having particular difficulty because of organisational constraints, an observation of much relevance to the leisure sector (p. 176). Willingness, Dawson argues "is likely to be affected by the costs to the employer of accidents versus the costs of safety provision, the likelihood of prosecution under the Act for safety shortcomings and the strength of the requirement to demonstrate to employees, customers or the public at large that the workplace is safe" (p. 249).

After the Lyme Bay tragedy, the Health and Safety Executive investigated the position of Health and Safety at outdoor activity centres (HSE 1996). It found that the HSE had "little contact" with such centres as standards "were considered to be acceptable" (p. 4). Yet one year after Lyme Bay, 40% of centres still had no safety policy; 17% had not carried out a risk assessment; 7% had no emergency procedure and 21% had no instructor training. It would appear that much of the Health and Safety legislation relies on there being an organisational need to apply it: without such monitoring, gaps start to appear. HELA (1998) reported that in 1997 there were, in England and Wales, 188,000 Consumer/leisure service premises enforced by local authorities; that only 66,000 visits were made to such premises; and that, on average, each officer is responsible for 800 premises, that overall visiting (to all premises) has fallen by a fifth since 1993.

In 1995 the Government felt that it could no longer rely on HSWA 1974 to secure safety at commercial outdoor activity centres and introduced the Activity Centres (Safety of Young Persons) Act 1995. This, like Sports Stadia and Public Entertainment, demanded that a licence be held before the activity could take place. Sadly, it required a tragedy and public outcry to bring forth the legislation against the wishes of the sector (Simmonds, 1996) who, at the time, were looking for more deregulation as per the Deregulation and Contracting Out Act 1994.

c)   Licensing

Until the Activity Centre Act of 1995 most licensing of sporting activities was concerned with protecting the spectator (e.g. Safety of Sports Ground Act 1975; Local Government Act 1982 -Public Entertainment Licences for wrestling etc.). There was no licensing of sport *per se*: local authorities could licence fairgrounds (Local Government Act 1976), license stables to protect the horses (not the humans!) and require public dancing venues to have a licence; and the possession of dangerous articles (e.g. guns) might require a licence. There is still concern that the licensing of activity centres may have gone too far (Trotter; 1994), even though it is limited to those dealing with minors on a commercial basis (so voluntary and educational groups are excluded). However, of those inspected in the first year of the scheme (1996–97), one third failed their initial inspection (Donne, 1998). There is also a concern that businesses may be operating illegally because of the costs and paperwork involved.

According to the HSE (Ives, 1999) 'only' two children have been killed in supervised outdoor activities since the tragedy. The HSC's Adventure Activities Industry Advisory Committee was due to publish a report in 1999 on accident rates and the success of the scheme, and this should assist in assessing how effective it has been. Some (Donne, 1998) want the licensing to be extended to voluntary groups. This raises a particular problem, in that, though the law may be likely to reduce the risk of accidents at licensed premise, it may well reduce opportunity to participate in controlled activities.

Civil Action

This area of the law provides a number of remedies for those wishing to claim damages for wrongful behaviour by sports organisers, officials, clubs and other bodies. One of the main actions is **Breach of Contract** — an implied term in business contracts (Supply of Goods and Services Act 1982, s.13) being that the service is supplied with due care and skill. This may be applicable to the professional coach. If an action is founded on contract law, the main impact is in terms of the extent of the damages.

Negligence (including Occupiers Liability and Negligent Advice) is the most common action involving those injured during sport and recreation and is the focus of most material on civil actions. Many actions brought against organisations are possible because of the principle of vicarious liability in which the employer is also liable for the employee's actions whilst they are acting in the course of their employment.

In 1996 the Court of Appeal found in favour of Ben Smoldon, an amateur rugby player (aged 17 at the time of the accident), against referee Michael Nolan for negligence. It was agreed that Nolan's negligence in refereeing the game had allowed a scrum to collapse, so causing Smoldon's injuries (Smoldon v Whitworth 1996). The case caused a great deal of concern and former England Rugby player Roger Utley (1996) spoke of a "sad state of affairs", and said "this sort of judgement makes it even more difficult for the organisers to find people to put themselves in the firing line" (p. 21). The Lord Chief Justice, though, stated "The judge ([n the High Court] had emphasised that his judgement in the plaintiff's favour was reached on the very special facts of that case. He had not intended to open the door to a plethora of claims by players against referees and it would be deplorable if this were the result".

A year later in the High Court, in Woodroffe Hedley v Cuthbertson (1997), Judge Dyson found against a mountaineering instructor whose negligent instruction had resulted in the death of the plaintiff's father. The Judge stated: "This decision should not be seen as opening the floodgates to claims against mountain guides whenever such accidents happen. Mountain climbing is extremely dangerous. That is one of the reasons why so many risk their lives each year on mountains. Anyone who climbs with a guide is, as a matter of law, treated as consenting to the ordinary dangers of mountain climbing".

The American experience of negligence actions has led Dougherty to state (1994: p. 247): "The threat of a lawsuit arising from an injury has had a major impact on sport and physical activity programs". Appenzeller (1998: p. 7) states:

> ... critics insist that lawsuits are out of control, and if allowed to continue, will inevitably change the nature of sport as we know it and eventually destroy sport. ... On the other hand, there are a number of proponents of litigation in sport who believe that courts are the sole vehicle to curb and control negligence in sport. These people accentuate the importance of the court and believe it safeguards the welfare of the participant and attempts to end violence and discrimination of every sort in sport. They insist that litigation or the threat of litigation makes sport better, as participants now enjoy the safest equipment, finest facilities and best medical care and coaching ever.

The willingness of American participants (and lawyers) to resort to the courts has forced these issues of responsibility out into the open and as a consequence organisers appear to be increasingly conscious of their potential liability. The law concerning negligence in America is very similar to our own, and so it is possible that in England the growth of litigation may follow the pattern in the USA.

The negligence action in England has developed, in its modern form, since 1932 when Lord Atkin considered the duty to one's neighbour in Donoghue v Stevenson 1932. The establishing of a duty of care, its breach and consequential damage form the structure of the action. Defences of *'Volenti non fit injuria'* (consenting to a particular risk), 'contributory negligence' and 'necessity' can be put forward. The areas which have caused most difficulty for the courts are reported by Moore (1997: p. 47) as:

1) whether a duty of care exists in the particular circumstance of a case;

2) if so, what the appropriate standard of care is; and
3) how the issue of consent affects both the nature and extent of the duty.

There is a body of cases (Condon v Basi 1985; Elliot v Saunders 1994; McCord v Swansea City AFC 1997) that demonstrate that the duty of care owed to participants may vary according to the circumstances of the activity. In Smoldon v Whitworth 1996 the court was heavily influenced by the Rugby Football Union's safety rules for Colts games that the referee was expected to follow, and said that there was a higher duty of care, in that respect, to the 17 year old player.

Consent to risk is all important in determining the extent of the duty. In the USA this is referred to as 'assumption of risk'. Champion (1993: 161) illustrates this by reference to the case of Ordway v Superior Court (1988) involving horse racing:

> Assumption of risk is more intransigent as a doctrine in the ultra hazardous sports of horse racing and car driving. In a case where a jockey was thrown and injured during a race as a result of the closing of two horses... the jockey assumed the risk of injury as a result of the negligence of another jockey even though the second jockey was in violation of the rules as long as that jockey's conduct was not reckless.

In the Smoldon case, the Lord Chief Justice stated that the "plaintiff had consented to the ordinary incidents of a game of rugby football of the kind in which he was taking part". In other words, the courts are influenced by the established rules and normal conduct of a game in determining when behaviour has gone beyond what is acceptable. It creates a difficulty for governing bodies if a sport tightens up its rules: it may then become easier for claimants to establish that responsibility for injury lies with the officials for not enforcing rules properly. As Griffiths-Jones (1997: p. 8) states, "... in Sport cases, decisions on the issues of liability are likely to be fashioned by the particular sporting context within which they fall to be judged".

The Cuthbertson case was determined on what was established practice. The Judge stated, "in reaching my conclusion that Mr Cuthbertson's [decision to use a single ice screw] was in breach of his duty of care, I have had to have regard to the expert evidence that I have heard". However, the Professional Guide Association, of whom Cuthbertson was a member, also held their own panel on the matter and found him to have acted reasonably. Roger Payne, secretary of the British Mountaineering Council (BMC), said "the reaction of the climbing world to the High Court judgment was 'utter disbelief'" (*Daily Telegraph*, 7 October 1997). Andy Macnae, National Officer of the BMC, felt that there were a "range of possibilities" open to Cuthbertson and that the judge had simply opted for "the more persuasive witness" (Macnae, 1999). The effect of litigation has certainly prompted many to consider insurance — though in the Cuthbertson and Nolan Cases both were insured, which may in itself have made it worth mounting the actions.

Liability for injuries to children

Another area which has caused much difficulty is that of injuries to children. Children are less able to appreciate risks than adults and so it is more difficult to establish consent. The Occupiers Liability Act 1957, s 2 (3), recognises that "an occupier must be prepared for children to be less careful than adults". Warnings of risk are clearly less likely to be understood by children and disclaimers are, anyway, of little effect because of the Unfair Contract Terms Act 1977.

Occupiers also need to guard against allurements: for example, equipment which may tempt children. The 1984 Occupiers' Liability Act also protects those who are trespassing, where injury is foreseeable, and clearly this impacts on children. There is a duty on the parents of *young* (not defined) children to ensure that they do not wander about on their own or that, if they do, they are only allowed to go to safe places (Phipps v Rochester 1955). Parents are expected to warn their children against obvious natural or man-made hazards (Simkiss v Rhonda Borough Council 1983). However, where the danger is concealed the duty is on the occupier (Bainham, 1993). Parents can consent to risk on behalf of the child, for instance the young child playing cricket, and as the child gets older so its ability to consent to risk grows (Titchener v British Railways Board 1983). Where an activity is aimed at children, the law is far more willing to place tougher duties on the provider. In Phipps v Rochester (1955) it was pointed out that "different considerations may well apply to public parks or to recognised playing grounds where parents allow their children to go unaccompanied in the reasonable belief that they are safe". In Linkin v Swale Borough Council (1987) the judge observed that a child should be expected to play "abnormally" with equipment and not always use it "correctly". Given the potential for accidents at playgrounds and the limited consent of children to risk it is not surprising that the equipment has become less exciting and more money has been spent on absorbent surfacing. There is also a greater willingness, when an accident does occur, to blame the provider rather than put it down to life.

One must also ask whether a willingness of the courts to identify responsibility for accidents involving sport and physical recreation is likely to improve safety standards. Atiyah (1993: p. 361) states:

> One of the most important of the suggested functions of personal injuries compensation law is deterrence of potentially injury-causing conduct and the prevention of injury causing incidents such as accidents.

However, in response to research in this field, the writer continues:

> Almost all writers who have considered the matter have come to the conclusion that there is no reliable evidence that liability to pay tort damages has any significant effect on the level of accidents or accident costs; although logically, of course, the absence of evidence does not prove that liability to pay the costs of accidents has no substantial deterrent effect. (Atiyah, 1993: p. 392)

It has also been argued that insurance can give organisations a buffer against the full impact of being sued.

Conclusion

The paper has sought to consider the extent to which the law has identified responsibility for risk in hazardous sport and physical recreation. There has been an understandable reluctance of legislators, enforcement agencies and those in the sporting world to see such interference and the law has, if anything, spilled over from other areas (e.g. Health and Safety). Courts have had difficulty in establishing clarity both in this country and America. There is an understandable reluctance to treat such an activity as comparable to other activities because of risk being an inherent part of it.

Sport is very diverse both in its participants and organisations — from highly skilled adult professionals to young enthusiasts; from corporate multinationals to local teams run entirely by volunteers. The diversity of activities and the inherent risks involved in participating in them do not allow easy clarification in this area.

The danger of intervention is that volunteers and non-profit bodies will not want to subject themselves to be scrutinised in the courts and blamed in public for their lack of care. Insurance may be a comfort, but it could also result in an action going ahead!

Health and Safety law does not appear to have created a water-tight environment for safety in sport, as demonstrated by the behaviour of some outdoor activity centres. Licensing has the advantage that it forces preventative behaviour to conform with safety standards, though it is less likely to bring about the Robens ideals of self-regulation. However, the present mass of safety regulations could be doing much the same, without any guarantee that all are conforming.

It is difficult to evaluate the impact of Civil actions, though there are plenty of advocates and critics. The problem with reliance on it as a system of policing is that it takes an accident to highlight a problem before it is addressed by the industry. A similar comment could be made with regard to the intervention of the Health and Safety authorities. In many respects there is a need to discover what determines safe practice in the sports sector and how far the public are prepared to accept the risk of accidents as part of sport.

The responsibility for safety in physical recreation is not clear: very often the particular circumstances of a case will determine who is seen as responsible. However, a high publicity case, for instance a child injured at a local authority playground, can cause great concern to those providing the activity. When the activity does not generate income and is not provided under a legal duty, as with playgrounds, then there is a great risk that providers will not want to run the risk or pay the extra costs in avoiding possible legal liability. We have begun to enter such an age.

References

Appenzeller, H. (ed) (1997) *Risk management in sport*. Durham (NC): Carolina Academic Press.

Atiyah (1993) *Accidents, compensation and the law*. Oxford: Butterworth.

Bainham, A. (1993) *Children: The modern law*. Bristol: Jordan Publishing.

Barker (1998) 'Sporting brief', *Health and Safety* (February): pp. 10–14.

Champion, W.T. (1993) *Sports law*. St Paul, Minn: West Publishing Co.

Consumer Protection Unit (1989) *Sensations and risk in sports. Pilot study*. Lucy MacCleary. London: Department of Trade and Industry.

Daily Telegraph (1997) 'Colleagues clear guides blamed for mountain death', 7 October: p. 8.

Dawson, S., Willman, P., Clinton A., and Bamford, M. (1988) *Safety at work: The limits of self regulation*. Cambridge: Cambridge University Press.

Donne, K. (1998) 'Against the tide', *The Leisure Manager* Vol. 16, No. 5: pp. 17–18.

Dougherty, N. (1994) *Sport, physical activity and the law*. Champaign, IL: Human Kinetics.

Dunning, G.(1996) 'Sporting negligence', *Solicitor's Journal* 19 (January): pp. 38–39.

Gardiner, S. Felix, A. James, M. Welch, R. and O'Leary, J. (1998) *Sports law*. London: Cavendish.

Griffiths-Jones, D. (1997) *Law and the business of sport*. London: Butterworths.

HASS (1998) *Leisure accident surveillance system*. Consumer Safety Unit at the Department of Trade and Industry. London: D.T.I.

HELA (1998) *Health and Safety Executive/Local Authority Enforcement Liaison Committee Annual Report*. London: HSE Local Authority Unit.

HSE (1996) *A report into safety at outdoor centres*. London: HMSO.

———— (1997) *Key Fact Sheet on injuries within leisure service industry*. Bootle. Unpublished.

———— (1999) *Managing health and safety in swimming pools*. London: HSE Books.

Ives, S. (1999) Safety Policy Unit, HSE, E-mail Correspondence with author.

Jones, V. (1998) 'Red is for danger', *The Leisure Manager* Vol. 16, No. 1: pp. 15–16.

McNae, A. (1999) British Mountaineering Council, Manchester. In conversation with the author.

Moore, C. (1997) *Sports law and litigation*. Birmingham: CLT Professional Publishing.

NPFA (1998) *Legislation and children's play*. London: NPFA.

Nell, V. (1998) 'Why young men drive dangerously', *The Safety and Health Practitioner* (October): pp. 19–23.

OPCS (1993) *Monitor on deaths*. London: HMSO.

———— (1998) *DH4 statistics on death*. London: HMSO.

Robens Committee (1972) *Robens Committee report on safety and health at work*. Cmnd 5034. London: HMSO.

Simmonds, B. (1996) 'Slow progress', *Leisure Management* Vol. 16, No. 6: pp. 22–23.

Trotter, S. (1994) 'Activity holidays and the law', *New Law Journal* 1 April: pp. 454–455.

Utley, R. (1996) 'A game referees can only lose', *The Guardian* 12 April: p. 21.

Williams, G. (1983) *Textbook of criminal law*. London: Stevens.

Zuckerman, M. (1994) *Behavioural expressions and biosocial bases of sensation seeking*. Cambridge: Cambridge University Press.

Sport and Leisure Planning: the Need for Assessment

Ari Karimäki

Department of Social Sciences of Sport,
University of Jyväskylä (Finland)

When developing the sport and leisure planning to more open, versatile and pluralistic directions, attempts at developing service quality and meeting the individual needs of the users must also be taken into account. The purpose of this paper is to examine the need for change in local and regional planning, in the framework of the Finnish welfare state. Public swimming pools, built as a result of the expansion of the welfare state, are taken as an example. The special characteristics of planning, decision making and utilisation are seen in the context of one modern leisure pool in Äänekoski, Central Finland. To fill the void left by traditional rationalistic planning rising from purely economic considerations, perspectives from impact assessment in promoting regional equality, are considered.

Introduction

The global economic and political changes of the last few decades have affected the organisation of public sport and leisure services. In trying to satisfy citizens' multiple needs the Finnish public sector now more than ever before offers services that are directed according to the private and voluntary sector (Heikkala and Koski, 1999). The increased autonomy of the municipalities has incited the central government to evaluate the changes made at local level, because the financial preconditions for arranging the public sport and leisure services vary from one region to another. From the point of view of the central government, the need for evaluation is apparent. However, at the local level it can be experienced as an external imposition if the local particularities are not taken into account as a starting point of the evaluation.

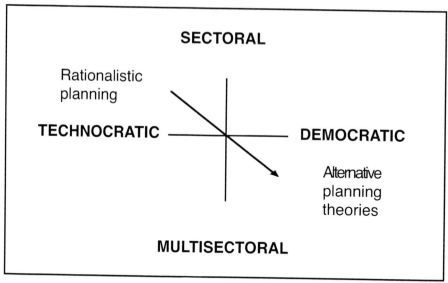

Figure 1   **Planning in transition in Finland (Linna, 1996, p. 26)**

The increased autonomy of the local authorities in Finland can be seen as a result of the institutional renewal during the 1990s. Finland was severely hit by the world-wide recession in 1991 and government was forced to make changes in the ways of providing public services (Kasvio, 1995). In the field of planning, this has meant a transformation from the centralised and institutionalised planning to more decentralised and open approach to planning (**Figure 1**). Traditional, rationalistic planning has emphasised normative planning, which produced standardised sport and leisure services. As an option, alternative approaches to planning have arisen. In the area of sport and leisure this has particularly taken the form of collaborative planning (Suomi, 1998: p. 12).

A wider approach, which also means crossing the lines of the traditional sectors in the local administration, is a consequence of a general *"argumentative turn"* in planning (Healey, 1995; Fainstein and Fainstein, 1996). This means that the planners and the users of services are coming gradually closer to each other, so the important starting point of the planning process is to identify the needs of the local citizens. These needs are real and they are independent of the administrative sectors. To catch a holistic view, one central feature of the planning process is a better understanding of the relation of the expert's technical language to public language and social questions (Fischer, 1996: p. 502).

My approach to planning is based on the way of thinking that the regional expert (that is, the planner) applies general knowledge in the local context, thus underlining the importance of identifying the specific local ways of life. As an example, I examine sport and leisure planning from the point of view of impact assessment by presenting some details of the planning of one modern leisure pool in the town of Äänekoski, in Central Finland. To give an extensive background for this local project, I will first describe public swimming pools more generally in a national welfare state context, which includes an international comparison with the utilisation of public swimming pools in UK.

Public pools have been very popular both in Finland and in UK, and they were constructed during the development of the national welfare state (Standeven 1992; State Committee Paper 1990). Leisure and recreation were added strongly to welfare services during the 1970s (Heinilä, 1977: p. 49; Henry, 1994: p. 18) and swimming has since then become one of the most popular forms of recreation in both countries. Although the Finnish welfare state is closer to the Nordic model (see Kasvio, 1995), where public provision of services has been larger and more stable longer than in the UK, it is apparent that the construction, supply and the utilisation of public swimming pools has been in line with the changes in UK. The historical development of the different types of pools, which vary from the traditional rectangular pools to refurbished pools and to new multifunctional leisure pools, also have impacts on public demand (Standeven, 1992: pp. 33–34; Karimäki, 1999: p. 76).

Public swimming pools as a Finnish welfare state project

In Finland, the construction of public swimming pools is connected to the development of a welfare state in the 1970s. Planning and construction of pools based on the needs for competitive swimming changed to a leisure-oriented view concerning the citizens' growing needs for leisure time participation. Local authorities built about a hundred public swimming pools, which were of the conventional rectangular design and were made for serious swimmers wanting to keep healthy and active (State Committee Paper, 1990: p. 52). Although it was uneconomic to maintain public pools, they were seen as important investments to citizens' wellbeing. They were seen to contribute to the individual and societal wellbeing and therefore should be supported by public money. In the 1980s, a much smaller number of new pools were opened, but the "leisurisation" of existing conventional pools by adding more water features and facilities for children and special groups started to take place (LIPAS, 2000; State Committee Paper, 1990: pp. 21-22; Vesanen, Paukkunen and Olin, 1983: p. 23).

In the early 1990s, the Finnish welfare state faced a dramatic economic crisis. The consequences to sport and leisure were unavoidable, and during the recession only a few new leisure pools were opened. Now, after the recession, more pools will be constructed, but the emphasis of the planning of swimming activities for the new Millennium is in the "leisurisation" of existing conventional pools, not in the construction of new leisure pools (Ministry of Education, 2000: p. 34).

The situation in the swimming market in Finland is similar to that in the UK (Gratton and Taylor, 1990: p. 44; Kenvyn and Johnson, 1993: p. 85; Standeven, 1992: p. 34, 36). The swimming market is segmented: while some customers want the traditional experience of serious lane swimming, others want merely to have fun in the water. The main reasons for visiting a leisure pool are pleasure and enjoyment, while swimmers in conventional pools primarily go for fitness (Kylpylämatkailun toimialatutkimus, 1993: p. 42; Standeven, 1992: p. 37). The users of leisure pools are younger than those in conventional pools, and the use is not dominated by a small number of regular users (Gratton and Taylor, 1990, p.44; Karimäki, 1999: p. 112).

The segmentation of swimming market becomes deeper with the "leisurisation" of the conventional pools and construction of new leisure pools. Segmentation challenges the planning and construction of swimming activities nationally: what types of pools do we need and where they should be located? When you take the existing regional pools into consideration in local and regional planning, it is possible to locate new pools as appropriately as possible. In spite of that, the threat of regional inequality is apparent, because some areas remain deficient in pool availability, while other areas face over-provision. In the next section, this argument is examined further.

Social impact assessment of a leisure pool

The method used in this case study was Social Impact Assessment (SIA). The types of impacts considered were social, demographic, economic and political, and both positive and negative impacts and their distribution to local people were taken into consideration (see Burdge and Vanclay, 1998; Finsterbusch, 1985; Freudenberg, 1986; Interorganizational Committee on Guidelines and Principles for Social Impact Assessment, 1998). Usually the Impact Assessment is the identification of future consequences of a proposed action and the aim is to become conscious of different point of views and attitudes towards the project. If successful, SIA is a method for creating a common language and knowledge so the different interest groups can compromise during the planning process.

This study includes examination of the planning, decision-making and utilisation of one modern leisure pool. The data gathered is composed of the

Table 1   Data gathered in Social Impact Assessment of Äänekoski leisure pool 1995-1997

Baseline conditions
— Statistics of local population, economics and politics
— Documents of planning and decision making of the pool (years 1986-1994)
— Local newspaper articles (years 1990-1994) n=199

Scoping
— SIA literature
— Swimming pool research papers
— Interviews for interest groups, n=15
— Survey for local citizens, n=350
— Questionnaire for pool users, n=583
— Interviews for pool users, n=6

surveys, questionnaires and interviews of the citizens and pool users, documents of decision-making, newspaper articles and statistics representing local population, economics and politics (**Table 1**). The heterogeneous information was encapsulated to describe the citizens' relationship to the project and furthermore to make an assessment of the different impacts that are experienced by local people. (Karimäki, 1999)

The total population in Äänekoski is 13,770 (1997). The majority of inhabitants (70%) live in the town centre. The rest live mostly in the western and northern remote areas, where the distance to the centre is from 20 to 40 kilometres. The new leisure pool was opened in February 1996 and turned out to be a success. During the first year there were 106,827 visitors, which is a large number compared to other towns of this size (Karimäki, 1999: pp. 107–108). One considerable factor is that there has been conventional swimming pools in neighbouring towns of Suolahti and Saarijärvi, from the beginning of the 1970s. The distance between Äänekoski and Suolahti pools is only 8 km and between Äänekoski and Saarijärvi 30 kilometres.

The comprehensive Impact Assessment too serves as a description of the local planning-process. One of the main problems is usually the placement of a project, because there are a lot of arguments for different alternatives and these arguments are rarely systematically examined. In the studied case, it was significant to determine the grounds for locating the pool. The planners' starting points were the location in the middle of the population centre, close to the schools and other services and with good transport connections. The popularity of leisure pools among young people was taken into consideration too: the pool was located next to the existing sports hall, where the local youngsters have visited regularly for years. When locating the new facility in connection with the sports hall, there was no need to change urban landscape either.

The placement seems to be very rational. The general standards regarding the construction of swimming pools were taken into consideration (State Committee Paper, 1985: p. 23). Yet this study *a posteriori* shows how standards missed the fact that in Äänekoski there is a noteworthy proportion of potential pool-users far away from the new facility. 30 percent of Äänekoski inhabitants live in the remote areas, but only 9 percent of the leisure pool users came from outlying villages (**Table 2**). The distance is clearly perceived as constraining: when asked for a reason why they did not use the new facility, "too distant" was the main reason given by responders in the survey (n=122).

Table 2   **Regional distribution of leisure pool users (n=583)**

Area:	%
Centre area	74 %
Other municipalities	18 %
Remote areas	9 %
Total	100 %

One of the questions in this decision-making process was how people in remote areas would be able to use the new pool. That dilemma can be found in the opinion of the village school teacher:

> "One point is this local unity. Will this be more of a uniting or isolating factor when comparing remote and central areas? We have found out that in the field of sport we are already outside some services."

Serving as a counterbalance to the village school teacher's point of view, the opinions of the inhabitants in the centre showed that they were quite happy to have the new facility in their daily catchment area:

"The closer the pool is, the lower the threshold to visit – enthusiasm for physical exercise will surely grow. The group of pool users is very extensive compared to many other sport facilities, which are being planned too, so a swimming pool is clearly better for the public good. Naturally pools in Suolahti and Saarijärvi would have been sufficient, but because of the distance many would have not started swimming at all."

Still, the regional division is problematic when we think about the planning and decision-making. It is even more complicated, when one realises that swimming pools already exist in the neighbouring towns. In a way, it is easy to understand the opinion of the village school teacher, because the distance from the northern areas to the new pool (as much as 40 kilometres) would not be significantly shorter than to the existing Suolahti pool, which is only 8 kilometres further.

Local authorities have got used to this dilemma. The interviewed local leisure manager reflects local circumstances, but on the other hand shows understanding towards the needs of the citizens in the remote areas:

"We have thought here that the equality is not realised. In the remote areas, there are services different from ours, but on the other hand, it is a certain choice from an individual to live in remote villages – nobody is obliged to move there. Naturally, the services exist in the population centre but the other side of the coin is that if we have there (in the remote area) some services we should come out of it quite creditably. I am sure we are not able to do that all the time, because we are getting some critics. These are matters of great importance for them."

The question is of regional equality. It is apparent that people in remote areas will not be able to use the new pool as frequently as those in the town centre. In the comprehensive Social Impact Assessment one cannot ignore this, because at the moment of decision-making you should consider the issue of access and opportunity. It looks as if these details concerning social impacts and their distribution have not been so much beyond our control (decision-making) as beyond our concepts (see Gramling and Freudenburg, 1992: p. 231). In the context of decision-making it seemed to be clear that economical fluctuations and costs were taken as central factors, but how people in remote areas would be able to use the new facility was not considered as important.

Toward a comprehensive Impact Assessment in sport and leisure planning

The experiments of the impact assessment are encouraging. The Social Impact Assessment based on the identification of consequences is a tool to create a holistic view of the project for the decision-makers. In the long run, the central function of the assessment is to anticipate the consequences of the proposed action. In the field of planning it means that more attention should be paid to the viewpoints of different interest groups and communication processes. Impact assessment is not about finding the "right" answers, it is about learning from planning and decision-making processes, so the procedures can be developed for the needs of the pluralistic society.

In the Social Impact Assessment, the general knowledge and viewpoints of citizens, decision-makers, authorities and planners form the information basis. The values of the interest groups are complex, but an essential part of the information. In the field of science this means accepting more relativist and pragmatist philosophy as a basis for planning (Leskinen, 1994: pp. 125–126). The researcher's (or evaluator's) role in the process is to be a *facilitator*, who serves not only one interest group, but creates common knowledge, which allows communication to flow from the group and process to another. My suggestion for the impact assessment process is provided in **Table 3**. It is based on the comprehensive model of Social Impact Assessment presented by Gramling and Freudenburg (1992: p. 218).

Table 3   Comprehensive view for the impact assessment

Process	Stakeholders	Researcher's role
Planning	Planners, authorities and citizens	Create common knowledge
Preparing decision-making	Local authorities	Anticipating alternative consequences
Decision-making	Decision-makers	
Follow up	Researcher	Evaluation of consequences; Development of assessment

The model is general, but the details of assessment take shape in accordance with certain prevailing circumstances and data available. For example, general facts on the use of swimming pools were useful in identifying specific usage features of the leisure pool. In the same way we can study sports-halls and multipurpose halls, but there is not as much data available on the utilisation of these halls. Because of this, comprehensive impact assessment put emphasis not only on communication but on reliable and versatile data collection, too.

Conclusions

As a background for a change of planning and re-organisation of the services, two trends can be identified. On the one hand, there is the traditional rationalistic planning with strong emphasis on standardised sport and leisure services. On the other hand, there is a need for taking regional and social equality into account. When, and if, the planning process is getting closer to the citizens, the opportunity for getting information based on local knowledge is increasing. Data enlightening the local processes is needed in order to apply the processed information in the local context immediately. Also, the skills of the local decision-makers in making informed decisions are evaluated more closely than before, because the inevitable conflicts and tensions between the rationalistic starting point and the realisation of equality often culminate when decisions are made.

In order to make the data on which the decisions are based as relevant as possible in the long run, the planning, the decision-making and the use of the services could be seen as a continuum. When developing planning methods, comprehensive Impact Assessment is one promising tool to create common knowledge which will be available during the whole process. An extensive examination lays proper foundation for successful communication, too. Then, the experiences and views of the planners, local authorities, decision-makers and citizens form the informative basis for the assessment. That underlines the extensive identification of impacts and their distribution in reliably predicting who will be benefiting and who will be losing by the proposed decision.

References

Burdge, R. J. and Vanclay, F. (1998) 'The practice and future of social impact assessment', in R. J. Burdge (ed) *A conceptual approach to social impact assessment.* (Revised edition) Middleton: Social Ecology Press, pp. 265–284.

Fainstein, S. and Fainstein, N. (1996) 'City planning and political values. An updated view', in S. Campbell and S. Fainstein (eds) *Readings in planning theory.* Cambridge. Massachusetts: Blackwell, pp. 265–287.

Finsterbusch, K. (1985) 'State in the art in social impact assessment', *Environment and behavior* Vol. 17, No. 2: pp. 193–221.

Fischer, F. (1996) 'Risk assessment and environmental crisis: Toward an integration of science and participation', in S. Campbell and S. Fainstein (eds) *Readings in planning theory*. Cambridge. Massachusetts: Blackwell, pp. 485–506.

Freudenburg, W. R. (1986) 'Social impact assessment'. *Annual Review of Sociology* Vol. 12: pp. 451–478.

Gramling, R. and Freudenberg, W. R. (1992) 'Opportunity – threat, development and adaptation: Toward a comprehensive framework for social impact assessment', *Rural sociology* Vol. 57, No. 2: pp. 216–234.

Gratton, C. and Taylor, P. (1990) 'Leisure vs. conventional pools'. *Leisure Management* Vol. 10, No. 1: pp. 42–45.

Healey, P. (1995) 'The argumentative turn in planning theory and its implication for spatial strategy formation', in T. Pakarinen, and H. Ylinen (eds) *Are local strategies possible? Scrutinising sustainability*. Tampere University of Technology, Department of Architecture, Urban Planning Publications Vol. 29, pp. 46–70. Tampere. Finland.

Heikkala, J. and Koski, P. (1999) *Reaching out for new frontiers. The Finnish physical culture in transition in the 1990s*. University of Jyväskylä. Department of Social Sciences of Sport.

Heinilä, K. (1977) 'Social factors affecting sports and recreation', in P. Vuolle (ed) (1998) *Sport in social context by Kalevi Heinilä. Commemorative book in honour of professor Kalevi Heinilä*. University of Jyväskylä. *Studies in Sport, Physical Education and Health* 50, pp. 47–51.

Henry, I. P. (1994) *The politics of leisure policy*. London: Macmillan.

Interorganizational committee on guidelines and principles for social impact assessment. (1998) 'Guidelines and principles for social impact assessment', in R. J. Burdge (ed) *A conceptual approach to social impact assessment*. (Revised edition) Middleton: Social Acology Press, pp. 93–124.

Karimäki, A. (1999) *Äänekosken uimahallin sosiaaliset vaikutukset*. Jyväskylän yliopisto. Liikunnan sosiaalitieteiden laitos. Tutkimuksia 64.

Kasvio, A. (1995) *Reinventing the nordic model. Can the nordic countries succeed in 21st century global competition?* University of Tampere. Department of sociology and social psychology. Laboratory of action research. Working paper 2.

Kenvyn, I. and Johnson, C. (1993) 'The importance of market awareness to successful management and performance: the example of swimming pool provision in UK'. Paper presented in the First European Congress on Sport Management, 23–25 September, Groningen, Netherlands.

Kylpylämatkailun toimialatutkimus. (1993) Matkailun koulutus- ja tutkimuskeskuksen julkaisu A: 46. Helsinki.

Leskinen, A. (1994) *Environmental planning as learning: The principles of negotiation, the disaggregative decision-making method and parallel organization in developing the road administration.* University of Helsinki, Department of Economics and Management, Land Use Economics. Publications 5. Helsinki.

Linna, T. (1996) Ympäristövaikutusten arviointi strategisen suunnittelun menetelmänä. *Yhteiskuntasuunnittelu* Vol. 34, No. 3: pp. 21–36.

LIPAS. (2000) *The National Databank of Sport in Finland.* University of Jyväskylä. Finland.

Ministry of Education. (2000) *Activities scheduled for 2001–2004.*

Standeven, J. (1992) 'Aquatic facility usage trends in UK and Europe'. *Official Conference Proceedings in Australasian Aquatic Recreation Centre Conference and Trade Show*, September 16–18, Melbourne, Australia.

State Committee Paper 1985: 5. The Ministry of Education. Helsinki.

State Committee Paper 1990: 52. The Ministry of Education. Helsinki.

Suomi, K. (1998) *Liikunnan yhteissuunnittelumetodi.* Metodin toimivuuden arviointi Jyväskylän Huhtasuon lähiössä. University of Jyväskylä. Studies in sport, physical education and health 58.

Vesanen, A., Paukkunen, L. and Olin, K. (1983) *Uimahalli sosiaalisena palvelulaitoksena. Jyväskylän yliopisto.* Liikuntasuunnitelun laitoksen tutkimuksia 27.

Best Value in Leisure Services: a Philosophy or a Quality System?

Christine Williams

Lancashire Business School,
University of Central Lancashire (UK)

Introduction

The recent introduction of the Best Value policy into public sector leisure facility management has seen a number of measurement tools to be developed or adapted. These include new performance indicators (Audit Commission, 1998) and the UK Quality Scheme for Sport and Leisure (QUEST) (Sports Council, 1996). The author investigates whether or not these techniques are capable of fulfilling the monitoring needs of Best Value (BV). The paper will considers whether the introduction of BV requires a change in organisational cultural more akin to the philosophy of Total Quality Management (TQM) (Oakland, 1993) or if it is just another service delivery monitoring device, needed on the route to achieving a TQM organisational culture.

An overview of quality in the UK public sector leisure services

The quality systems most utilised in local authority leisure services are Investors in People (Employment Dept., 1992), ISO9002 (Johnson, 1993), Citizen's Charter and Chartermark Award (Cabinet Office, 1991) (Walsh, 1998: p. 53).

Freeman-Bell and Grover's (1994: p. 559) research indicated that local authorities were obligating organisations to certificate to BS5750 (as then), if they won the management contracts. Walsh (1998: p. 69) found that in a minority of leisure management contracts this is still the case but that a range of quality systems have been indicated including QUEST.

Leisure service providers have also embraced the concept of performance monitoring as prescribed in the Citizen's Charter initiative but gaining the inter-related Chartermark Award has not been seen to be of value (Williams, 1997a: p. 125). As well as outlining service level agreements to their customers (i.e. the temperature of the water in the swimming pool), some charters include the customers' responsibilities when they use the facility e.g.

> Assist us to keep buildings clean and tidy.
> Be aware of the needs of other users.
> Adhere to booking times.　　(Williams, 1997a: p97).

The customers' fate if they do not adhere to these, however, is not stated.

Ravenscroft (1996: p. 168) argues that "meaningful" sets of performance standards cannot be found in public leisure services. Deakin and Walsh (1996: p. 38) suggest that this is due to the public sector's inexperience of target setting in advance and the fact that quantitative measurements dominate the service monitoring processes (e.g. monitoring of admissions rather than how effective the service has been). Effectiveness monitoring is the very requirement of the BV ethos. The present government has expressed continuing support to Citizen's Charter principles with a new initiative, "Service First" (Cabinet Office, 1998). The relationship between Service First and BV will be discussed later in the paper.

Performance measurement needs a clear set of objectives to be effective. The change of local government management culture, brought about by Compulsory Competitive Tendering (CCT) (Torkildsen, 1999: p. 259), means that these are now financial efficiency, customer needs, and social objectives (Williams, 1997b: p. 212). Of the three, financial efficiency is the main priority of public sector leisure services and is therefore constantly monitored, this has the effect of creating conflicts with customers' needs and social objectives. For instance, managers know what their customers' needs are but cannot always afford to provide it.

To summarise, the introduction of CCT meant that performance monitoring was inevitable as local authorities needed to check whether or not contractors were delivering the services to that stipulated in the tender documents. The inexperience of local authorities of carrying out this task resulted in the far easier system of monitoring being adopted. Only the processes and outputs were examined utilizing formal accredited quality systems (i.e. BS 5750).

BEST VALUE — Implementation

The BV policy is in the early stages of implementation being piloted by a number of local authorities. BV is considered to enable local authorities to continuously search "...to improve the quality, efficiency and effectiveness of all its services....." (ILAM, 1997: p. 1).

The Local Government Act 1999 requires that the BV regime applies to all local authority services unlike CCT. In BV the three "E's" (Economy, Efficiency and Effectiveness) of CCT, which are used to evaluate the service provided, have been supersede by the four "C's" of BV: Compete, Compare, Consult, and Challenge (Audit Commission, 1998: p. 5), these will be discussed on an individual basis.

The monitoring method of competition is still regarded as an appropriate measure. Although parts of the public sector are familiar with this due to CCT, a wider range of formats is possible under BV (see **Table 1**).

Whilst comparative analysis is the basis for a number of the methods to introduce competition into public sector service delivery, this is also part of the general monitoring regime of BV.

Table 1   **Alternative forms of Competition**

A. *Restructure the in-house service to match performance of the best private and public sector providers.* This requires the additional expense of independent benchmarking reports, especially from the private sector.

B. *Provide core service in-house and buy-in top up support.* This is said to improve performance of the internal service providers, but if contracting out follows existing custom and practice of the private sector, this may be confined to specific functional areas (i.e. information technology). Competition in this context is indirect.

C. *Contract out all the service, tenders only allowed from external organisations.*   The local community as well as the employees will not be happy at the sudden loss of jobs.

D. *Form a partnership with an external organisation.* This requires a competition to find a partner. The amount of competition generated by this method, will depend on the roles and responsibilities of each partner.

E. *Traditional CCT model of an open competition between internal and external organisations.*

F. *Dispose or sell off the service and its assets.* Again an issue the community may not be happy with.

(adapted from White Paper para 7.29 cited in Footitt, 1999: p. 15).

Monitoring services by comparing one local authority with another requires services to be audited and benchmarked (Dale, 1994: p. 362) against best practice, whether this is an appropriate method will be debated later in the paper. The third element of BV is the legal obligation in BV to consult the local community including other stakeholders (i.e. businesses located in the area). The difficulties of this task are discussed later. Finally "Challenge" comes from the Minister's statement on BV proposals " ... see local services improve every year ... at a price people are prepared to pay" (Armstrong, 1998: p. 1). This is continuing the notion that improvements can still be made within local government services which will generate savings.

The four "C's" management culture is embedded into a framework of twelve BV principles (DETR, 1998: p. 12). The monitoring of the service is highlighted in these principles and has to be carried out by reference to "The Family of Performance Indicators (PI's)" (Footitt, 1999: p. 8). This comprises of four sets of PI's, of which three are devised by central government or its agencies, these are (DETR, 1998: p. 11):

1. Nationally-set best value service indicators (including corporate health PI's)

2. Indicators set by government departments

3. Service specific PI's set by the Audit Commission

The first set (national best-value indicators) are not finalised at present.

Individual local authorities need to establish the fourth set of PI's, local indicators (DETR, 1998: p. 18), but these must have regard to the service specific PI's. Documentation required by this initiative is the production of annual performance plans. These will be audited yearly plus a periodic external inspection. The body responsible is the BV Inspectorate which comprises of the Audit Commission as well as existing service inspectorates (Audit Commission, 1999).

DETR (1997: p. 1) suggest that the "Best Value framework will be simple, straightforward, but challenging". (I would take issue on its simplicity.) Davies and Girdler (1998: pp. 30–31) have itemised seven possible consultative groups, although the "dedicated users" may be relatively easy to consult, "the whole of the electorate" will not. Wide scale consultation will not only be costly, diverting resources away from services but time consuming, a criticism levied at many existing quality systems (Robinson, 1996: p. 13).

Gaster (1992: p. 58) is an advocate of open, multi-stakeholder consultation processes. He sees it as a way of defining organisational objectives and setting performance standards. Beale and Pollitt (1994: p. 216) disagree, stating that public services dominated by professional providers, prefer informal, peer-validated standards with minimal user judgements. Recent research has shown that over 50% of responding leisure departments use a number of consultation methods and sample non-users as well as users (Guest and Taylor, 1999: p. 99).

Both these points of view are accommodated within the monitoring regime of BV, but conflicts may occur between locally determined needs and nationally imposed standards. The Local Government Association (1998: p. 1) and the Association of Direct Labour Organisations (Wakeley, 1998: p. 8) have expressed concern regarding the weighting given to local PI's against national ones. Wakeley (1998: p. 8) goes so far as to contextualise this in terms of centralised prescriptives against local freedoms. This is pertinent as leisure is a discretionary service.

If the alternative approach is taken and the balance is weighted in favour of the service required by the community, Sanderson (1996: p. 91) suggests that "best practice" will not emerge. This contradicts the dual notions, that service monitoring devised for BV are dedicated to meeting the local communities needs as well as allowing best practice to prevail.

Discussion

The underlying principle of BV is the placing of users and other stakeholders central to service provision and the delivery decision making process. Therefore, BV requires the monitoring of service effectiveness suggested by the 3 E's of CCT but not implemented. This primary objective should bring about an enhanced service. This seems to suggest that financial objectives take a lower priority but is not the case as the Audit Commission's proposed "national service specific PI's" (discussed later in the paper) concentrate on efficiency and economy.

Financial penalties are alluded to by Wakeley (1998: p. 8), suggesting that provision will be made to collate BV performance to allocation of capital funding etc. This is a repeat of funding "threats" to central government aided museums if they did not gain the Chartermark Award (Williams, 1997a: p. 135). As the author observed, winning the award becomes more important than improving service delivery. Improvements are a by-product rather than central to the organisational objectives.

Under BV's consultation strategy additional services may be identified having financial implications. This is contrary to the financially driven objectives of previous quality initiatives, where the main aim was the reduction of service subsidies.

Performance indicators

The proposed corporate health PI's (DETR and Audit Commission, 1999: p. 18) are generic to all local government services and are categorised into six sections: council management and performance; planning and measuring performance; customers and community engagement; partnerships; management of resources and staff development.

The DETR propose that these should act as "warning lights" of poor performance. For example, the counting of litigation claims is a prime indicator of the "warning lights" section, Gummesson (1994: p. 35) considers the collection of this type of information purely as a defence strategy and not related to service quality issues.

The Audit Commission (1998: p. 12) stated when turning their attention to leisure service specific PI's that "good indicators of the quality of outcomes remain elusive because of the nature of the service provided." This statement permits mechanistic processes and output monitoring to remain and is illustrated by their proposed National Service Specific PI's for leisure and recreation which have their foundation on the Citizen's Charter ones. For example: How many people visit swimming pools and sports halls? How much does this cost the council? How many playgrounds does the council provide? (Audit Commission, 1994: p. 23).

The proposed service specific PI's for museums are also indicative of monitoring economy and efficiency only. Whereas the monitoring of public sector libraries takes a different approach as a user satisfaction questionnaire is proposed. The number of questions is limited and the individual questions to be too vague, returning data that will be of limited use to those seeking a culture of continuous improvement (Audit Commission, 1998: p. 28).

The Audit Commission (2000 cited in ILAM, 2000: p. 1) acknowledges the difficulty in writing outcome related PI's for aspects of leisure provision and have asked for suggests from the industry. As the aims and objectives of leisure services providers will be different, a consensus amongst practitioners may be difficult to achieve. Sanderson (1998: p. 10) suggests that areas difficult to measure will be neglected and uses the health benefits from leisure services as an example.

Consensus may also be difficult to achieve when trying to co-ordinate the four different sets of PI criteria (Local Government Association, 1998: p. 2). These are in addition to Service First (Cabinet Office, 1998: p. 11) an overlapping public sector PI monitoring system. The aims of Service First mirrors those of BV; responsiveness, effectiveness, consultation, and best practice dissemination. Both government policies acknowledge an inter-relationship with each other but not the major overlaps (DETR, 1998: p. 18; Cabinet Office, 1998: p. 17).

The main difference is that all local government services must be managed under BV principles, whilst Service First monitoring is optional. The setting of the Service First PI's are at local level and external monitoring only takes place if the quality award is sought. The differences therefore are administrative rather than philosophical.

Benchmarking

As well as a comparison with the local and nationally set performance standards the BV regime requires that best practice should be disseminated throughout local government. One way to facilitate this is to make comparisons of similar services with another via a series of external benchmarking exercises. This can be less problematic than self assessment. Keehley et. al. (1997: p. 76) concurs that after going through a benchmarking process, "Public sector managers become better managers of limited fiscal resources by reallocating funds to higher priorities".

Benchmarking of an entire service rather than key processes is the most hazardous. The most beneficial, especially for discovering new ideas is when a partner from an unrelated industry is used, but BV does not advocate this. The principles of BV provide for a comparative analysis with other authorities but given that leisure relates to discretionary services, this may be difficult. Beale and Pollitt (1994: p. 206) when researching into PI's found that in general best practice may not be delivered. They consider that there are three service standards, the highest being "best practice" but they point out that the majority of organisations aim to perform to "the norm", and best practice becomes increasing rare.

Another difficulty is the lack of leisure or sport and recreation strategies in a minority of local authorities (Guest and Taylor, 1999: p. 99), judgements need to be carried out in terms of the organisation's objectives and without these it will be difficult to benchmark these services.

A combination of self and external assessments has been utilised by the commercial service sector. They are not considered individually but rather as quality tools integrated into a strategic quality management culture. These organisations tend to utilise the framework of a quality award as a basis into which other accredited quality management systems, tools and techniques can be integrated. These holistic quality awards are based on the business excellence model and its associated assessment criteria (EFQM, 1999: pp. 22–26).

In preparation for the BV legislation coming into force, the four UK Sports Councils commissioned a specialist monitoring tool based on the business excellence model, UK Quality Scheme for Sport and Leisure (QUEST) (Sports Councils, 1999).

QUEST

This is an industry specific quality award with statements applicable to leisure centre operations management, the Sports Councils perceive that it has a wider leisure related application. At present a health and fitness club model is being prepared.

The programme enables self and external assessment in four areas: facilities operations, customer relations, staffing, service development and review (*Quest News*, 1998: p. 3). The author is concerned that an over-emphasis has been placed on users' judgements of the service. This is the easiest group to consult in comparison to trying to monitor the views of other stakeholders from the community (e.g. council tax and unified business rate payers) as required by BV.

QUEST has also over looked the fact that in local authority leisure services, the ability to develop overall policies is not even within the power of client officers but rests with the elected members, who are often quite remote from the operational management of the service. This is different from managers of commercial organisations (Williams, 1997a: p. 227).

Although the original QUEST award (Sports Councils, 1999) has been revised to accommodate the Best Value framework, only 32 points out of an overall total of 632 are allocated to monitoring the effectiveness of a service (Sports Councils, 1999: p. 11). The minimum score to gain the award is 60%, therefore it would be possible to fail to score any points in this element and still receive it.

However, QUEST is evolving, and it will be interesting to observe whether or not effectiveness monitoring is adequately addressed in the future. Berry (1995: p. 22) when writing about quality awards noted that "... many companies that apply but do not win ... reported significant benefits none the less." It is better to monitor service and assess customers' requirements rather than do nothing, as long as the limitations of the monitoring systems are understood.

Conclusion

The management of facilities by BV regime suggests that the underlying philosophy is one of seeking continuous improvement and that customers' and other stakeholders' needs will be central to the decision making process. BV in theory appears to be an holistic approach more akin to the philosophy of TQM than an individual quality system.

This suggests that a change of culture is required for those services managed under the CCT ethos. Unfortunately the BV monitoring systems being made available to practitioners have an over reliance on adapting existing quality systems with all their inherent faults, rather than a fresh approach being taken. The Audit Commission's proposed PI's omit effectiveness monitoring, one of the most difficult elements of the BV regime. They are still concentrating on amending existing efficiency and economy PI's which have been criticised extensively. Local PI's proposals that are in the public domain seem to follow the same two E's pattern. Social objectives are being monitored in terms of percentage of school visits and opening hours (Scottish Museums Council, 1998: p. 6).

It appears that the aims and objectives encompassed in the philosophy of BV, are not being transferred into practice. From the early evidence available, the DETR and the Audit Commission appear to be driving a large part of the service delivery specification rather than customers and other stakeholders.

References — revision to house style requested from author Aug. 31

Armstrong, H. (1998) *Message from the Minister of Local Government. DETR Best Value Update 3.* Http: //www.local.detr.gov.uk/cct/bestval3htm

Audit Commission (1998) *Consultation on the Local Authorities performance indicators.* London: HMSO.

Audit Commission (1994) *Staying on course: The second year of the Citizen's Charter indicators.* London: HMSO.

Audit Commission (1999) *Best assured: The role of the Audit Commission in best value.* London: HMSO.

Beale, V. and Pollitt, C. (1994) 'Charters at the Grass-Roots: a first report', *Local Government Studies* Vol. 20, No. 2: pp. 202–225.

Berry, L. L. (1995) *On great service: A framework for action.* New York: Free Press.

Cabinet Office (1991) *The Citizen's Charter: Raising the standard, Cm 1599.* London: HMSO.

Cabinet Office (1997) *Charter Mark Awards 1998: Guide for applicants. Cabinet Office.* London; HMSO.

Cabinet Office (1998) *Service first: The new charter programme. Office of Public Service.* London; HMSO.

Dale, B (1994) *Managing quality* (2nd edition). Hemel Hempstead: Prentice Hall,

Davies, M. and Girler, D. (1998) 'First impressions', *The Leisure Manager* (December): pp. 30–32.

Deakin, N. and Walsh, K. (1996) 'The enabling state: The role of markets and contracts', *Public Administration* Vol. 74, Spring: pp. 33–48.

DETR (1997) *Compulsory Competitive Tendering: Changes to regulations and guidance.* London: HMSO.

DETR (1998) *Modernising local government: Improving local services through Best Value*. London: HMSO.

DETR and Audit Commission (1999) *Best Value and Local Authority performance indicators for 2000/2001*. London: HMSO.

Employment Dept. (1992) *Investor in people*. London: HMSO.

EFQM (1999) *The EFQM Excellence Model: improved model (final version)*. Brussels: European Foundation for Quality Management.

Footitt, J. R. (1999) *Preparing For Best Value: Letter to Local Authorities from Local Government Competition and Quality Division*. DETR. Http://www.local.detr.gov.uk

Freeman-Bell, G. and Grover, R. (1994) 'The use of quality management in local authorities', *Local Government Studies*, Vol. 20, No. 24: pp. 554–569

Gaster, L. (1992) Quality in Service delivery: competition for resources or more effective use of resources? *Local Government Policy Making*: Vol. 19, No. 1: pp. 55–64.

Guest, C., and Taylor, P. (1999) 'Customer Orientated Public Leisure Services in the UK. *Managing Leisure*, Vol. 4, No. 2: pp. 94–106.

Gummesson, E. (1994) 'Green service quality', in E. E. Scheuing, B. Edvardsson, D. Laciness and H. C. Little (eds) *Quality in services. Conference proceedings, International Service Quality Association*, pp. 33–35.

ILAM (1997) *Best Value: a definition and process, Fact Sheet 97/10*. Goring Upon Thames: ILAM.

ILAM (2000) *Leisure News*, 27 January – 2 February. Goring Upon Thames: ILAM.

Johnson, P. L. (1993) *ISO9000 Meeting the new international standard*. London: McGraw-Hill.

Keehley, P., Medlin, S., MacBride, S. and Longmire, L. (1997) *Benchmarking for best practices in the public sector*. San Francisco: Josey-Bass.

Local Government Association (1998) *Best value performance measurement and assessment: LGA's response to the Audit Commission on national P I's*. http://bestvalue.igmb.gov.uk/omnisite2

Maynard, R. (1995) 'Investors in people: Quality through people', *Quality World* October: pp. 697–702.

Oakland, J. S. (1993) *Total Quality Management: The route to improving performance* (2nd edition). Oxford: Butterworth Heinemann.

QUEST News (1998) 'Benefits for everyone', *QUEST News* December: pp. 1–4.

Ravenscroft, N. (1996) 'Leisure, consumerism and active citizenship in the UK', *Managing Leisure* Vol. 1, No. 4: pp. 163–175.

Robinson, L. (1996) *An investigation into the use of quality programmes in Local Authority Leisure Services. Conference Paper*, Cardiff: WLRA 4th World Congress.

Sanderson, I. (1996) 'Evaluation, learning and the effectiveness of public services: Towards a quality of public service model', *International Journal of Public Sector Management* Vol. 9, No. 5/6: pp. 90–108.

Sanderson, I. (1998) 'Beyond performance measurement? assessing 'value' in local government', *Local Government Studies* Vol. 24, No. 4: pp. 1–25.

Scottish Museums Council (1998) *Best value for museums: A corporate approach. Museums issues No. 8.* Edinburgh: Scottish Museums Council.

Sports Council (1996) *Quest: UK quality scheme for sport and leisure.* London: Sports Council

Sports Council (1999) *Quest: UK quality scheme for sport and leisure: issue 2.* London: England Sport.

Torkildsen, G. (1999) *Leisure and recreation management* (4th edition). London: Spon.

Wakeley, N. (1998) 'Direct Services, Best Value and the White Paper', *The Journal of Direct Labour Organisations* September: pp. 8–9.

Walsh, P. J. (1998) *The use of quality programmes and services in Local Authority sport and leisure centres.* Preston: Unpublished M. A. Dissertation.

Williams, C. (1997a) *Quality systems and service delivery in the UK leisure industry.* Preston: Master of Philosophy Thesis.

Williams, C. (1997b) 'Quality management: a means of meeting customers' needs'. Conference paper, Australian and New Zealand Leisure Association Conference, University of Newcastle, NSW, Australia: ANZALS pp. 211–217.

Fairness and Flexibility in the Scottish Leisure Industry

Anna MacVicar, Margaret Graham, Susan Ogden and Bernadette Scott

Department of Hospitality, Tourism and Leisure Management, Glasgow Caledonian University (UK)

Introduction

The last twenty-five years since the introduction of the Sex Discrimination Act 1975 have witnessed legal recording and recognition of gender inequality issues in the work environment. However it has been argued that, while the restructuring of work alongside more flexible forms of employment has enhanced women's visibility in the workplace, new forms of employment disadvantage have emerged (Huws, 1997). In particular, flexible contractual working arrangements have provided further benefits for those managers and employees at the core of the organisation, at the expense of job security for those on the periphery of the workforce (who provide numerical flexibility). Women's dual responsibility towards their domestic and paid work roles further increases their vulnerability to employment disadvantage at the periphery. The issue of 'fairness at work' has been in part addressed by the Employment Relations Act 1999 (DTI, 1999) which aims to encourage shared male-female responsibility towards work and family commitments. It is hoped that these initiatives will go further than the "add women and stir approach", highlighted by Wimbush and Talbot (1988: p. 5) based on the use of masculine models of improvements. As part of a wider study looking at flexible working within the Scottish leisure sector, this paper explores issues of fairness and flexibility. The growth of flexible employment patterns, pressure for flexibility in the leisure sector and arguments surrounding gender inequality at work are first considered. This is followed by a discussion of the research methodology and results of a case study analysis of 5 leisure organisations across the public, private and not-for-profit sectors.

The flexible workplace

The nature of work in the 1990s has become associated with more flexible employment opportunities as work schedules become more controlled by rhythms of demand than mass production processes. Golzen (1999) has suggested that post- modern living is based on a series of wants to be served and that night and day is of no consequence to the contemporary consumer. This is especially important for workers in the service industries who must satisfy these consumer needs. Kreitzman, cited in Golzen (1999: p. 5) states that "tourists operate on a seven-day, 24-hour clock" and therefore work patterns must change accordingly. Guest (1997) states that the "new flexible workforce" allows employer flexibility in contracts, hours, location, finance and function. However, for the worker, flexible employment tends to be associated with atypical non-standard employment contracts, job insecurity (there has been a 17% drop in employee perceptions of job security in the period 1990-97) (Maitland, 1997), low pay, and inequality of opportunity in terms of skills development and career advancement (Blossfield and Hakim 1997; Rueberry 1988 and Maitland 1997). In short, the insecurity of the periphery is accepted to provide security for the core workers (Atkinson, 1984). Rueberry (1988) argues that flexibility allows employers more control over staffing costs and the ability to fluctuate their human resources according to swings in demand. Consequently, Dickens (1992) argues that, as women are more active in atypical work than men, the growth in flexible employment serves to further marginalise their subordinate position in the labour market.

Development of leisure as flexible workplace

In the context of leisure, occupational structures have adapted to suit the needs of the emergent leisure democracy. Indeed the fact that the post-modern leisure facility user lives his/her life bound by modern industrial time patterns, means that flexibility is the answer to the industry's peaks and troughs of demand. Coalter (1989) argues that popular freedom of choice in leisure reveals a conflict of interest between the supply of public leisure services, based on societal needs and the real market demands of the leisure market. In terms of leisure policy, new parameters have been drawn widening the role of public provision at a time when funding is at its lowest ebb. As a consequence of this, the functional purpose of the public sector has diversified. Indeed commercial aspects of leisure provision are being exploited alongside social inclusion policies redefining the public sector's role in leisure welfare.

Efficiency policies like Compulsory Competitive Tendering, recently replaced by the regime of Best Value, has further narrowed the divisions between public leisure and commercial leisure. For the commercial sector, the utilisation of flexibility is geared towards serving high spend markets by achieving standards of excellence in service delivery with the primary objective of profit maximisation. The growth of the private sector according to Randall and Heath (1997) has contributed to these culture changes within the public sector, encouraging a more consumer led approach, in that they must be more efficient and financially driven.

A more recent development has been for local authorities to consider transferring public leisure facilities to Charitable Trust Status (CTS). The establishment of arms-length, non-profit making Charitable Trusts brings a number of financial benefits for leisure facility management — including exemption from the payment of value added tax on entrance charges and relief from 80% of national non-domestic rates (Randall and Heath, 1997). Another advantage is that charitable not-for-profit organisations can gain additional funding from sources such as the National Lottery and external sponsorship. The Trust is accountable to a Board of Directors, of whom up to 49% will be Local Authority (LA) members where the LA remains the main funder. Thus, the Trust management must submit business plans to the Board for approval as well as changes to aspects of operational policy — including human resource management policy.

A key HRM issue which arises in the transfer of public leisure facilities to Trust status is the extent to which employees' conditions of employment and pensions are protected under the Transfer of Undertaking Protection of Employment Regulation (TUPE) (Acquired Rights Directive) 1999 (DTI, 1999). Under CCT, it was initially argued by private contractors that the Directive only applied to 'commercial undertakings'. However, latterly it was accepted that it also applies to public sector employees who transfer to a commercial contractor. Despite protection at the time of transfer, evidence suggests that there has been slight reductions to terms and conditions of employment post-transfer. The main areas affected have been reductions in the number of staff employed, overtime, sickness and holiday pay (Adnett and Hardy, 1998: p. 43). Although, in most cases the decreases were modest — less than 5% — a concern relates to how the gap will further widen in the future.

Inequality and developments in the gendered labour market

The study of sociology of work up until the late 1970s did not consider gender to be an issue. Structuralists assumed changing inequalities at work derived from the decline in the number of full-time jobs in the manufacturing industry (Goldthorpe and Lockwood, 1969; Beynon, 1973). The major growth of the service sector has resulted in much greater increases in female recruitment than male, thus feminising the services labour market. Indeed, according to labour force statistics over 4.5 million women of working age are in paid employment with dependent children (Social Trends, 1998). Simultaneously women's involvement in the home has intensified with more women as single parents, primary breadwinner and head of household. Regardless, however, of whether or not they are involved in the public arena of paid work, women's work tends to reflect their domestic role having a negative impact on their occupational status, thus reproducing female disadvantage and occupational segregation (Dex, 1988). Franks (1999) reinforces this argument by stating that women are more likely to be nurses, cleaners or office workers who must work because they have chosen a family life and motherhood.

Balancing home and work

Radical feminists argue that since the 1970s, opportunities for women in the public arena of paid work has gradually marginalised them further. The patriarchal relationship women have with capitalism reproduces their subordinate role in paid work (Walby 1990). Johnson (1999) has indicated that things are not getting any better for women workers as they continue to lose out in the pay stakes, due to the drive to cut costs and keep shareholders happy. Research has also demonstrated, that women in flexible employment particularly are also less likely to be members of a trade union and suffer from weaker job security (En Gender, 1994, Walby, 1990).

Oakley (1974) was the first pioneering feminist to draw parallels between the process of female socialisation and the reproduction of domestic labour with male industrial apprenticeships. She argued that the female family socialisation was an "imitative activity", acting as an induction for their expected domestic role. Thus it is alleged that women with family commitments are synonymous with downward mobility (Dex, 1988). Even dual career families with male and female partners in symmetrical career roles, continue to involve women in a higher proportion of domestic responsibility (Rapoport and Rapoport, 1971). Reserve army theorists argue that women become pulled into the labour market in mass only in times of economic crisis to help bolster capitalism.

Key arguments put forward by radical feminists centre around the limitations by which women can achieve upward mobility and career advancement.

Although more women than men in the UK are active in the service sector, vertical segregation in the top three managerial categories is greater than in France, Germany and Denmark (Equal Opportunities Commission,

1992). Sex role stereotyping has been blamed for placing limitations on female ambition and restricting female career advancement. This is despite the fact that women are thought to bring a special set of female skills to the workplace, namely sensitivity, the "humanisation" of situations and highly attuned people skills (Cassell, 1996). Unfortunately, many areas within the service industries play on "other" stereotypical aspects when employing females, namely physical appearance and sexual attractiveness.

Cassell (1996) has stated that employers often divide the work on gender lines based on questionable perceptions and that they use positive customer feedback and competitive edge to legitimise the process. She argues that jobs women undertake are subordinated to the male equivalents basically because of the perceived relationship with the domestic arena of unpaid work. However, Cooper (1984) argues that women tend to lack the confidence to maximise their potential in terms of career development, thus hindering their maximum utility of career opportunity. O'Leary and Ickovics (1992) argue that although the glass ceiling is beginning to crack with women becoming more visible in top managerial positions, they tend to receive fewer rewards when compared to male equivalents. Given that one survey suggests that seventy-three per cent of managers have reported that long hours seriously encroach on the time they spend with their children (Worrell and Cooper, 1998), women may be deliberately choosing not to break through the glass ceiling.

A recent Mori poll (People Management 1999: p. 11) has stated that only "eight per cent of parents work for employers who help with childcare". The parents in the survey felt that they required more flexible working hours and some help with contributions to nursery fees. Most women take career breaks whilst their children are young, primarily due to a lack of affordable childcare (Burchell *et al.*, 1997). During the 1990s, the availability of childcare for the under five's has risen, however, Burchell *et al.* (1997) argue that this growth has been inconsistent and often involves informal child care arrangements. More pressing is the issue of after school care for children. As women participate more in full time work their domestic responsibilities become more difficult to juggle. Thus legislation is currently seeking to address the work-life balance.

Legislating for fairness

The public policy agenda has, however, recently been directed more towards issues surrounding the quality of working life and the relationship between working life and home life. The Employment Relations Act 1999, with its Parental Working Time and Part-time Work Directives, is aimed at helping to create a competitive society which is also socially cohesive and caring, thus changing the culture of employment relations (Department of Trade and Industry, 1999). The measures aim to increase both the rights of the individual and their collective rights, and press employers to take account of their employees' dual responsibility to both their market and family roles (Blair, 1998).

As well as reducing inequality among part-time workers, parents, women and men will have more opportunity to combine paid work with family life.   The Parental Leave Directive, effective from 15th December 1999, allows expectant fathers and mothers to take up to three months leave after the birth or adoption of a child. It is thought that this option will prove popular, particularly with fathers even if unpaid, although it seems that few companies have actually considered implementation of such a scheme. MacErlean (1999: p. 79) has suggested that "some employers still have to get used to the idea of men wanting to spend time with their children".

Given the ongoing debate about the need to address these issues legislatively, this paper aims to offer some insight into the extent to which the flexible working practices prevalent in the leisure industry are promoting fairness or perpetuating inequalities between males and females in the workplace. A particular issue to be investigated is the extent to which the public leisure sector is the "leader" in terms of employment family friendly policies and practices or, in the face of ongoing competitive pressures has become the "follower" of private sector practices.

Research methodology

The methodology for this study is based on a multiple case study research design, applying a replication rather than a sampling logic (Yin, 1991). Thus each of the five organisations studied — two public sector, two Charitable Trusts and a private sector leisure organisations — were selected to "serve a specific purpose within the overall scope of inquiry" (Yin, 1991: p. 53). Applying theoretical replication logic, differences in ownership was the first selection criteria applied as this was anticipated to produce "contrary results for predictable reasons" (*ibid.*: p. 53) since the literature suggests that public sector organisations generally speaking have both a wider access to flexible working and family friendly working arrangements (Cully *et al.*, 1998). A second public and trust case study were also selected in order to build in an element of literal replication, thus if ownership is important, similar results are predicted for these case studies. Unfortunately a second private leisure organisation of comparable type in terms of range of facilities could not be accessed. **Table 1** details the breakdown of the data collection methods utilised for each case study.

Table 1   Case Study Data Collection

CASE STUDY	FOCUS GROUPS	STAFF INTERVIEWS	MANAGEMENT INTERVIEWS
PUBLIC 1	1 male and 1 female focus group (5 staff in each)	None, as focus groups allowed	3 HQ and 1 male centre manager (no female managers at the Centre)
PUBLIC 2	No focus groups	12 staff interviews (3 male and 3 female) in two facilities	3 HQ, 6 managerial (2 male and 2 females at Facility I and 1 male and 1 female at Facility 2)
PRIVATE	No focus groups	6 staff interviews (3 male and 3 female)	5 interviews (2 male and 3 female interviews)
TRUST 1	1 male and 1 female focus group (4 staff in each)	None, as focus groups allowed	2 male and 2 female managers interviewed
TRUST 2	No focus groups	11 staff interviews (3 males and 3 females in Facility 1 and 2 males and 3 females in Facility 2	1 HQ, 6 managerial interviews (2 males and 1 female at Facility 1 and 1 male and 2 females at Facility 2
Totals	2 male and 2 female focus groups	29 staff interviews (14 male and 15 female)	29 managerial interviews (11 males and 11 females at Facilities)

Case study characteristics

Across all case studies, the aim was to study the working practices of broadly comparable leisure centres in terms of range of facilities and activities. Thus all centres had swimming pools, gyms, crèche or soft play room, and a café and/or bar. In addition Public 2 (facility A) and the private facility also had a considerable number of outdoor activities, such as tennis. In total, six out of the seven facilities were flagships, i.e., relatively new or recently refurbished centres which offered the most up-to-date facilities in the local area. Within Public 2, both facilities studied had been operational for 4 years or less. The facility studied in Trust 1 had been set up as a Trust 7 years ago. In contrast, both centres studied in Trust 2, Public 1 and the Private facility had been established for some time. Trust 2 had only been operational as a Trust for approximately one year, following the transfer of all leisure facilities from local authority control. Opening hours ranged from a minimum of 347 days (Trust 2) to a maximum of 363 days per year (Private). The Private sector facility had the longest daily opening hours (7 am — 11.30 p.m.). Across the facilities a range of shift patterns and cycles were in existence. For example, within facility B, Public 2 the hours of a full time leisure attendant were:

- early shift 6.30 a.m. — 2.30p.m.;
- late shift 2.30 — 10.30 p.m.; and
- the mid shift — 10 hours on a Saturday, 14 hours on a Sunday and the remainder of the 15 hours to be made up in the working week.

Flexible working practices

A wide combination of flexible working arrangements were found across the case studies. The most numerically and functionally flexible facility was found within Trust 1. Here, a large contingent of casual staff were relied upon throughout the year, supported by a core of functionally and structurally (e.g. very team based) flexible full-time staff. In contrast, within the facilities which had recently transferred to Trust status (Trust 2), although there was a long-term commitment to develop "cross-skilling" and "flexible job descriptions", they were still reliant primarily on full-time and part-time permanent staff. This was particularly an issue at the larger facility:

> There is not as much flexibility as we would like as regards delivery of services. If certain people call off sick if can be difficult to move staff around to cover that specific area. (General Manager, Trust 2, facility C — flagship facility)

Within the smaller facility at Trust 2, functional flexibility was at a further stage in its implementation, although it was felt that further flexibility was still required:

> We have to become more flexible as an organisation and not before time, ... we are not giving value for money and we are not open the times people want. There's working mothers who can't come in at the

times that we open the crèche. They want to come in the afternoon — we have the crèche in the morning — we don't have the crèche in the afternoon, therefore we have to bring in part-time staff to manage this. We have now come to the realisation that as a customer led service, it is the customer that leads and not the politicians. (Duty Manager, Trust 2, facility D, dryside)

Trust 2, which had only recently transferred from the public sector, shared many similarities in terms of employment practices with the two public sector case studies. Similar to Trust 2, the largest contingent of staff in Public 2 were on full-time or part-time permanent contracts, rather than employed on a casual basis. Corporately, the HRM policy for leisure is that because of:

The diversity of the service and the overall service requirements, staff at all levels must be flexible to carry out any duties to ensure the maintenance of an effective and economic service. (Personnel, Public 2).

All operational staff were described as "peripatetic", meaning that they can be requested to work in any facility within the local authority. (In Public 2 an HRM specialist indicated that the Department was aiming to encourage what was termed Corporate Work Application, which was described as a more functionally flexible, team based approach to working.)

Public 1 also relied mainly on a combination of full and part-time staff but, in contrast to Public 2 and Trust 1, they had 'designated' staff for 'designated areas', with staff only crossing over into other functional areas to gain experience for career progression. The private sector facility adopted a similar approach to functional flexibility; although unlike all other facilities, they had a strong preference for full-time staff, with two-thirds of staff working full-time. Both senior male managers at the Private facility centre stated that they preferred full-time staff because they "gave more commitment". They did not even use casual staff for coaching activities. Their overall approach to staffing appeared to be due to the fact that all customers paid by monthly or annual subscription and, therefore, management were better able to forecast the peaks and troughs in demand from their customers than their counterparts in the public and trust sector.

The issue of using overtime to cope with fluctuations in demand also varied between the case studies. Management within Trust 2 were paying from flat-rate to double time for over-time, depending on when employees had started (prior or post transfer to Trust status). Particularly within the flagship facility at Trust 2, management were aware that their over-time budget was excessive. It was felt that this could be alleviated through "a pool of relief casuals" available all year round – they appeared to aspire towards the model followed in Trust 1. This was currently an issue subject to trade union negotiation. Public 1 also paid enhanced overtime rates after 39 hours were worked (the normal working week 35 hours). In contrast, Public 2 offered a flat rate payment for overtime (the same as the normal hourly rate) in order to meet economic imperatives. This had led to some difficulty in getting volunteers to work extra hours. The Private facility also offered operational staff extra hours but only at a flat rate. However, managers regularly worked an extra 10–20 hours per week with no additional financial reward. This appeared significantly different to the other organisations where management working hours averaged 35 per week, rising to 39 hours for line managers. In public 2, although many senior managers worked "all hours worked" contracts, they were entitled to time-off-in-lieu where they had worked excess hours.

Lifestyle policies

Significant differences were found in the level of sophistication of lifestyle policies between the case studies. Currently within the Public 1 and 2, there are a number of lifestyle policies (including the implementation of current maternity leave and pay provision) which assist employees 'to juggle' their lives. These policies are a deliberate strategy of the Councils to help regenerate the depressed local economy because as one personnel manager in Public 1 put it: "flexible working patterns allow people to return to work ... only a stick of dynamite would convince senior HRM specialists that any job could not be job shared."

In Public 1 and 2, Maternity Support leave is granted to anyone supporting a mother and this does not necessarily have to a parent. Public 2 also have a policy for Adoption Leave and are considering a policy of leave for foster parents. Within Public 2 they additionally have allocated places at two nurseries in the area, with payment on a sliding scale dependent on income. They also have two schemes designed to encourage unemployed people to gain work experience: one specifically targeted at lone parents under 25, and one targeted at people over 25 years of age (the funding arrangements for both schemes were different hence the two categories). The majority of participants are women. Support mechanisms, such as crèche facilities and an allowance for suitable work attire, have been provided to ensure the success of these projects.

In addition to these policies both Public 1 and 2 have:

• flexible working time policy whereby all full-time permanent employees can, with agreement, vary their arrival and departure times to suit their personal circumstances, within the guidelines set to protect the service requirements of the customers;

- job sharing, which is the voluntary sharing of a full-time post; part-time working;

- paternity leave (or maternity support leave) of 5 days, in addition to the statutory maternity leave provisions;

- special leave (paid or unpaid) and unpaid career breaks which must be a minimum of one year up to a maximum of four years.

However, notably, employees in the public facilities did not have access to a workplace nursery on-site. This was the situation in all the case studies, although informal arrangements existing in Trust 1, whereby employees could use the soft-room crèche to fill a childcare 'gap' for an hour or two. In the private facility, employees were given a 10% discount to the franchised on-site crèche.

The managers in Public 1 were well aware of how useful flexible working could be for managing employees' changing lifecycles, particularly for women. One quoted a very good example of how the internal labour market of the Council had allowed one married woman to continue working and effectively balance her childcare commitments with her husband's work pattern. She had worked in the evenings at a facility when her husband came home from his job but was about to move to a day job within the local authority central offices now her child was starting school.

Trust 2, which had only recently transferred from local authority control, had a well established job sharing scheme with female returners job sharing throughout all areas of the facilities. They also had 5 days paternity leave and a policy allowing maximum of 10 days per annum dependency leave (5 days paid and 5 days unpaid). This serves to limit the effect of the 25% attendance bonus on the income of carers. However there was some concern from management about the abuse of the dependency leave policy. It was felt that the attitude of some employees was, that it was part of their annual leave. Trust 2 also have a 2 year career break for childcare and a 1 year break available for any other reason (both subject to 5 years service). Male fathers highlighted the fact that shift patterns had made it easier for them to share their childcare responsibilities and as a consequence minimise the expense of childcare. However a downside to this was:

> ... we don't normally have time when the three of us are together an awful lot.

In Trust 1, where the facility had been established as a Trust since it opened, there was a recently approved job sharing scheme, enhanced maternity benefits for those with two years service, which were further enhanced after five years service. Staff could also informally use the facilities soft room for two to three hours at a time if required for childcare purposes, which the staff looked on as "a perk of the job". It was expected that Trust 1 'contracted' employees were very flexible about changes in shift pattern and this could be very difficult for females with children. One female employee interviewed who had found the shift patterns of her reception job unsuitable, had transferred to an administration job where she was able to work a day shift, 3 days part-time. It may well be that the shift patterns worked by female leisure workers, allows them to combine their paid work and other commitments more successfully than in other occupations with more traditional 9.00a.m–5.00p.m hours of work. One full-time female leisure attendant found her work patterns allowed her to juggle the "second shift" quite well. For example on a late shift she quite happily fitted in the domestic chores before coming to work because it was easier for her (her partner was a 9.00 a.m.–5.00 p.m. employee).

Within the Private case study there were no additional benefits available to employees outwith the statutory ones. Although staff did have access to the franchised crèche and if they needed a day off, whether it be to cover some caring or domestic responsibility they could swap shifts or use some of their annual leave entitlement. The only female managers who complained about balancing work and life were located at the Private facility. Here there was a general atmosphere of a lack of family friendliness.

Gender segregation, employee development and career progression

An element of occupational gender segregation was found within the case study evidence. In Public 1, Trust 1 and the Private case studies there was an all female team of reception staff and crèche/soft play workers. However in Trust 2 and Public 2, a minority of full-time male receptionists were employed in 3 out of the 4 facilities surveyed. These males were highlighted by management as being excellent in this role. The Private case study had an all male team of chefs and kitchen staff.

Analysis of the managerial staff showed that the only facility without female managers was Public 1. (However in another facility run by the same council there was an all female management team).

All managers expressed a commitment to ensuring that staff were trained properly for their jobs. All managers carried out induction and training took place to meet job and legislative requirements and customer care training. In some facilities (Public 1 and 2, Trust 2), training was scheduled into the weekly work cycle and this was reflected in the opening hours. In Public 2 there was a weekly rolling training programme which ensured staff on all shift patterns whether full-time or part-time received the training. Management also open up the training to casual staff and insisted, "if they don't attend training courses, if they are not trained, then they won't get phoned to work" (Manager, Public 2).

Performance Appraisal or employee development was fairly well established in Public 1 and 2, Trust 1 and in the Private club. Trust 2 were in the early stages of implementing a newly devised performance appraisal scheme. In Public 2, there is an Employee Development and Review scheme in place which is carried out annually for APTC workers. However, it has not yet been cascaded down to the manual workers, e.g., the leisure attendants and maintenance staff. Similarly in Public 1, casual staff and 'manuals' do not receive career progression (EDP), access to information technology training or secondment because they are needed at work.

Staff who teach aerobics get an all inclusive rate of pay, which is to allow them individually to cover any additional updating they may require. If however the Public 1 facility required a new class on 'body pumping', the manager would fund a course for one of his part-time aerobics instructors (if there is nobody trained and available in the local labour market to teach it).

In both focus group discussions in Public 1 and Trust 1, the male staff tended to be more focused than the female employees about their career progression. One had negotiated his working pattern to fit around a post-graduate course he was studying and personally funding; another male participant was about to commence a part-time degree following his HND. In Trust 1, one male employee had been given time off to pursue further external training opportunities. Most of the men in Public 1 and Trust 1 were adamant that they did not want to be "wearing a green shirt and blue shorts for ever" and if they did not already have it they "wanted a shirt and tie". However at the same time, many had entered the leisure industry because they were attracted to the sporty lifestyle associated with the job: "I lived most of my life in gyms anyway". Employee interviews conducted in Public 2 and Trust 2, revealed similar sentiments. In Trust 2, both male and female leisure attendants expressed a desire for career progression as there was dissatisfaction with the level of pay which was described as inadequate unless overtime, and allowances for weekend working were also obtained. However, part of the impetus was to progress to the higher grade in order to get the better shift pattern with more weekends off and fewer late finishes.

In the female focus groups undertaken in Public 1 and Trust 1, these issues were not so apparent, partly due to the fact that the groups were skewed by female administrators or receptionists who were more focused on the nature of the job, rather than the leisure context. As one remarked. "I could be doing the job anywhere". In public 2, the incentive to remain working for the organisation was partly due to the perception that maternity conditions were superior to what would be provided doing reception work for a private sector employer.

In the Private case, none of the staff interviewed had primary responsibility for caring for children or elderly relations. They tended to view the leisure context of their jobs favourably — liking the social contact with the guests and the security of working within leisure which was perceived as a major growth industry. There were limited internal career progression opportunities because there was only one club in the Chain within Scotland. Nevertheless, staff who had career expectations in leisure/hospitality felt they had been encouraged/supported by the Private club management .

Conclusions

In conclusion, the case studies confirm that a wide range of flexible working practices are prevalent in Scottish leisure centres. Men and women leisure workers in the Public 1, Trust 1 and Private case studies participated equally in the full range of flexible working practices, with equal numbers in the core managerial, peripheral and casual workforce. Trust 1 was significantly more functionally, numerically, structurally and financially flexible than the other facilities. Trust 2 and Public 2 aspired to this model in a number of ways, both had where possible flat-rate overtime. Public 2 and Trust 2 generally operated or aspired towards functional flexibility. The Public 1 and Private facilities expected the least amount of functional flexibility.

In Public 1, male and female leisure employees had greater opportunity to choose working patterns to suit their personal needs and the opportunity, through a large pool of internal vacancies which existed out with the facility, to change their job in order to better balance unpaid work and paid work commitments. This is consonant with the preliminary findings of the Workplace Employee Relations Survey (Cully *et al.*, 1998). In Public 2, again both sexes generally had access to part-time work patterns which allowed them to balance their life-work commitments. In Public 2 significant efforts had been made to encourage women returners back to work. Trust 1 and 2 also had women returners in job sharing positions. Women employees in the Private club tended to conform to the patterns of work which best suited their employer's needs. A universal finding is that shift working is used by both sexes to better manage the financial burden and parental responsibility of childcare.

Despite the variation in flexible working and family friendly policies across the case studies, female employees had equally pursued career development opportunities. However, an element of role-segregation persists in relation to more generic, non-leisure jobs such as reception duties, although women workers with significant domestic responsibilities were present in senior management roles. This had clearly emerged due to role-segregation existing beyond the leisure industry. However, even here, examples were found of male 'leisure' attendants who had taken jobs in reception areas. Their motivation to enter these roles was partly due to the realisation that these positions had a higher pay rate than other jobs within the facilities. Arguably where facilities have functional flexibility, such gender-segregation should be less prevalent, however within the case study with the most flexibility, this did not extend to the reception area (i.e. there were still mainly female staff working in reception).

In some facilities, receptionists did not perceive themselves as leisure-specific workers, and consequently had opted not to actively seek career development opportunities within the leisure sector. Younger female leisure-specific workers, even where they were employed on a casual basis, had ambitions to progress within their organisations, as did their male counterparts. The training for most levels of staff appeared to be extensive in all facilities. Those on the periphery of the workforce, however, were less likely to be included in performance- or career-review initiatives and were normally excluded access to non job-specific job training.

In summary, the Scottish leisure industry can be regarded as 'feminised', in that women have entered the industry in equivalent numbers to men. In general, role segregation is reduced partly due to the fact that traditional feminised 'domestic' work, such as cleaning, is normally undertaken as part of the job descriptions of a Leisure Attendant. However, there is an element of segregation between leisure specific and non-leisure specific jobs. Employees — whether full-time, part-time or casual — with a sporty lifestyle, are most likely to put themselves forward for promotion in the internal labour market. The general lack of career opportunities is an issue for these workers. Employees in non-leisure specific jobs — like receptionists — appear to have less opportunities for advancement.

The public sector leisure employers appear to offer the most advanced family-friendly policies. However, in a climate where the option of transferring leisure services to Charitable Trust Status is gaining serious consideration, it is possible that, despite the new national legislative policies currently being introduced, the well-established family friendly policies in the public sector may be diluted in the future. The indicators are that, post-trust formation, organisations are likely to fully re-evaluate the HRM policies previously followed.

References

Adnett, A. and Hardy, S. (1998) 'The impact of TUPE on Compulsory Competitive Tendering: Evidence from employers', *Local Government Studies*, Vol. 24, No 3: pp. 36-50.

Atkinson, J. (1984) 'Manpower strategies for flexible organisations', *Personnel Management* Vol. 16, No. 9: pp. 28-31.

Beynon H (1973) *Working for Ford*. Harmondsworth: Penguin.

Blair, Tony (1998) 'Foreword: Fairness at Work White Paper: A Review of the Proposed Legislation', http://www.dti.gov.uk/IR/fairness.fore.htm 14.5.99.

Blossfield, H.-P. and Hakim, C. (1997) 'Comparative perspective on part-time work', in H.-P. Blossfield and C. Hakim (eds) *Between equalization and marginalization*. New York: Oxford University Press, pp. 1–17.

Burchell, B., Dale, A. and Joshi, H. (1997) 'Part-time work among British women', in H.-P. Blossfield and C. Hakim (eds) *Between equalization and marginalization*. New York: Oxford University Press, pp. 210–246.

Cassell, C. (1996) 'A fatal attraction? Strategic HRM and the business case for women's progression at work', *Personnel Review* Vol. 25: pp. 51–66.

Coalter, F. (1989) 'Leisure policy: 'An unresolvable dualism?', in C. Rojek (ed) *Leisure for leisure*. London: MacMillan Press Ltd., pp. 115–129.

Cooper, C. L. (1984) *Women in management*. London: Heinemann Ltd..

Cully, M. *et al.* (1998) *The 1998 workplace employee relations survey*. London: DTI. [www.dti.gov.uklemar]

Department of Trade and Industry (1998) 'Fairness at Work White Paper: A Review of the Proposed Legislation', http://www.dti.gov.uk/IR/fairness/part5.htm 14/5/99.

Department of Trade and Industry (1999) 'The Employment Relations Act 1999 Fairness at Work', www.dti.gov.uk/IR/erbill.htm.

Dex, S. (1988) 'Gender and the labour market', in D. Gallie (ed) *Employment in Britain*. Oxford: Blackwell, pp. 281-309.

Dickens, L. (1992) *Whose flexibility?*. London: The Institute of Employment Rights.

En Gender (1994) *En Gender Audit*. Edinburgh: En Gender.

Equal Opportunities Commission (1992) *Women and men in Britain*. London: HMSO.

Franks, S. (1999) 'We thought we'd found the answer, but it isn't working', *The Scotsman* (Nov. 1): p. 10.

Goldthorpe, J. H. and Lockwood, D. (1969) *The affluent worker in the class structure*. Cambridge: Cambridge University Press.

Golzen, G. (1999) 'Comment', *Human Resources* (April): p. 5.

Guest, D. (1997) 'Motivating The Flexible Workforce', IPD Conference 1997.

Huws, U. (1997) 'Flexibility and security: Towards a new European balance', *Citizen's Income Trust Discussion Paper No. 3* (December). London: Institute for Employment Studies, p. 52.

Johnston, R. (1999) 'Equal opportunities slips down the list of priorities', *People Management* Vol. 5, No. 11: p. 2.

MacErlean, N. (1999) 'Family affairs', *Human Resources* (April): p. 79.

Maitland, R. (1997) 'Motivating the Flexible Workforce', IPD Conference 1997.

O'Leary, V. E. and Ickovics, J. R. (1992) 'Cracking the glass ceiling: Overcoming isolation and alienation', in U. Sekaran and F. Leong (eds) *Womanpower*. London: Sage Publications, pp. 7–29.

Oakley, A. (1974) *The sociology of housework*. Oxford: Martin Robertson, pp. 113–20.

People Management (1999) 'Employers lag in childcare', Vol. 5, No. 11: p. 11.

Randall, S. and Heath, S. (1997) *Charitable trust status for local authorities: Key legal and practical issues*, third edition. London: Lawrence Graham.

Rapoport, R. and Rapoport, R. (1971) *Dual career families*. London: Penguin.

Rueberry, J. (1988) 'Employers and the labour market', in G. Duncan (ed) *Employment in Britain*. Oxford: Blackwell, pp. 251–280.

Social Trends (1998) 'ONS — Labour Force Survey', p. 28.

Walby, S. (1990) *Theorising patriarchy*. Cambridge: Blackwell.

Wimbush, E. and Talbot, M. (1988) *Relative freedoms: Women and leisure*. Milton Keynes: Open University Press.

Worrell, L. and Cooper, G. (1998) 'Managers begin to draw the line on long hours culture', *Professional Manager* (November): p. 42.

Yin, R. K. (1991) *Case study research: Design and methods*. London: Sage.

Part II

ETHICS

Sport, Leisure and the Ethics of Change

Alun Hardman

Department of Physical Education and Sport,
State University of New York (USA)

Introduction

Change is a phenomenon constantly present in the broad domain of sport and leisure activities. It occurs in practices that range from top level sporting competition to senior citizen fitness classes. Given that change is a ubiquitous experience, at issue is how change impacts existing social practices and what we are to make of such events. Much will depend on who is impacted by change and how. In the realm of sport, for example, when Dick Fosbury jumped over the bar backwards to win the gold medal at the 1968 Mexico Olympics, he split the high-jumping community. For the North American's, Fosbury's efforts were a revolutionary change, and an expression of 'west-coast individualism'. To the European purists, plying their craft with the more traditional Western Roll and Straddle technique, his revolutionary style represented a vulgar abomination, typical of the non-conformist attitudes of sixties radicals. History informs us that the Fosbury flop became the predominant technique in high-jumping while other techniques became redundant.

Changes in the field of leisure provision too, have a significant impact on different social groups. Local authority decisions on facilities and programme provisions, for example, all impact leisure opportunities for various interest groups. These decisions and the ensuing changes involved become more significant when a reallocation of resources and funding is involved. Though an economic rationale may provide the overriding justification for the majority changes implemented by various leisure providers and sports governing bodies, many changes in sport and leisure require justifications of a qualitatively different kind. The growing business of eco-tourism, for example, adds to its bottom-line ecological concerns with the pleasurable experiences offered to paying customers. As a result, developmental changes implemented in this area must weigh carefully the competing, and often conflicting demands that each rationale places on those who provide such services.

In this paper, I will suggest that the concept of change in sport and leisure provision is a broad complex one, and that at its core, change can be as much an ethical issue as it can be an economic or a technological one. Traditionally, however scholars in the area of sport and leisure have analysed change from a sub-disciplinary approach. As a result physiologists can tell us the best ways to improve our conditioning, biomechanists how to improve skill, psychologists how to maximise our competitive potential, leisure managers how to improve administrative policy, while ethicists deal with problems of sporting behaviour. Few theorists however, have attempted to assess change in the area of sport and leisure from a more comprehensive perspective — one that takes into account a number of competing evaluative rationales.

There are four parts to this project. The first part of the paper briefly identifies some of problems associated with defining and evaluating "change" in sport and leisure practices. The second part identifies important substantive elements of sport and leisure based on Alasdair MacIntyre's conception of a social practice. It is argued that these elements of sport and leisure are analogous to MacIntyre's concept of an "internal good" and that they can be used to establish the starting points, or a set of constraints, around which debates on change in sport and leisure should take place. In the third part of the paper, I develop an overarching paradigm expresses as a "pyramid of constraints" that consists of the various internal goods identified in part one. The "pyramid of constraints" aims to provide a normative scheme for evaluating the overall significance that change has on sport and leisure's internal goods, and in particular, the means to evaluate changes that appear to be both positive and negative. Finally, in the fourth part of the paper, I will examine one significant examples of change to assess the efficacy of the pyramid scheme.

Problems in defining and evaluating change in sport and leisure

As the main purpose of this article is to present ideas on evaluating change, a number of significant preliminary conceptual discussions, for practicable reasons, are omitted. At the outset, it is important to recognise that these debates are required to establish a number of substantive premises that sustain a number of claims made later in the paper. The conceptual discussions omitted here principally involve defining the concepts of sport, leisure, and change (with particular reference to sport and leisure). Extensive work on the first two concepts has been conducted, with a number of significant contributions cited frequently in philosophic literature on sport and leisure. The main arguments will not be reported, and for the purposes of the discussion, the two concepts of sport and leisure, though markedly different, will, except where necessary, be addressed together for the remainder of paper.

The concept of change, however, requires greater attention, particularly with respect to understanding its impact on sport and leisure. Unlike the concepts of sport and leisure, change is a process rather than a thing of substantive content. Change is something that occurs to activities such as sport and leisure, and therefore identifying the substantive content of such activities and how they can change is a pre-requisite to any evaluation that may follow. In the case of sport and leisure, some important substantive elements subject to change include the various formal rules and regulations associated with participation, and the penalties and proscriptions that occur when rules are broken. In addition, substantive change may occur in the way the rules are interpreted, and to which participants the different rules and regulations apply. Change also occurs with respect to regulations on equipment, training protocols, pre-, in-, and post-game procedures, strategies, and skills. While a thorough taxonomy of those substantive elements of sport and leisure subject to change is possible, the previous list should provide an effective description.

A more controversial conceptual issue is that of determining exactly when change in sport and leisure occurs. A number of important considerations are relevant here. In particular, deliberations on the magnitude, the direction, the speed, the duration, and the frequency of change are necessary. An even more fundamental discussion must explain if it is even possible to evaluate change when it seems that no fixed frame of reference is possible. The argument here suggests that the individual or individuals making an evaluation on change may need to take into account that they too are subject to change over time, and therefore their evaluative standards are contingent with history. I recognise that certain philosophical problems associated with such issues are curcial and address them, albeit briefly, in the concluding remarks.

Sport and leisure as a changing social practice

The ensuing discussion on an evaluative scheme for change in sport and leisure is based on the work of Alasdair MacIntyre, and in particular his concept of a social practice developed in his seminal work *After Virtue,* published in 1984. MacIntyre's critique has been well received and extensively utilised in critical discussions on the moral, social, and political status of sport and leisure pursuits and provides an effective platform from which to generate discussion on change.

According to MacIntyre, debates on the conflict between and within rival moral traditions including those of a sporting and leisurely kind, can be resolved by objective and impersonal standards of rationality once the concept of a *telos* has clearly established the purpose of such practices. The central constraint on change within his account revolves around the continuing cultivation of certain virtues necessary for living the good life. They are acquired within a moral framework made up of three interrelated concepts – a social practice, a narrative unity of human life, and a tradition. The following discussion focuses on how these concepts contribute to a critical understanding of change in sport and leisure practices.

The individual cultivates fulfilling sport and leisure pursuits with others through the development of key virtues such as justice, courage, and honesty. These virtues, MacIntyre argues, are not only central to meaningful social and political co-operation, but are necessary to live the good life and also partially define it[1]. They are acquired, cultivated, and exhibited through engagement in a number of activities that are themselves constitutive of, and situated within, wider cultural traditions. The notion of a social practice and their internal goods is vital for MacIntyre's account. He describes a practice as:

> ...any coherent and complex socially established co-operative human activity through which goods internal to that form of activity are realised in the course of trying to achieve those standards of excellence which are appropriate to, and partly definitive of, that form of activity, with the result that human powers to achieve excellence and human conceptions of the ends and goods involved are systematically extended. (MacIntyre, 1984: p. 187)

The crucial component of MacIntyre's critique is the distinction between a practice's "internal" and "external" goods. MacIntyre uses the example of a young child learning to play chess to illustrate his point. He suggests that at the beginning, the child may only be motivated in so far as she is offered candy to play. For her to play well and try to win, the payoff may need to be increased. While candy remains the foremost reason for her participation, the child has every reason not to heed the rules of chess and every reason to use the most expedient means possible. The particular ludic enterprise does not yet provide a sufficient motivation for the child because valuing chess intrinsically is not part of the child's way of thinking. Over time however, MacIntyre argues that with careful nurturing the child may come to recognise, appreciate, and value the unique kinds of analytical strategies and competitive skills that the game involves. These features are goods internal and specific to the game of chess. Once initiated into the kinds of delights that chess has to offer, she has reason to seek and preserve them. If the child then plays in a frivolous way, or uses illegal strategies to deceive her opponents rather than attempting to do her best using the analytical skills positively constituted by the rules of the game, she deprives herself of those internal goods.

MacIntyre's example illustrates that there are both goods internal and partly definitive of social practices, as well as goods external and contingent to them. In the chess example, candy serves as an external motivation for the child's behaviour. Elsewhere, external goods may take the form of power, prestige, status, or wealth, and can be achieved through engagement in many activities. In contrast to the excellences of a specific sport or leisure pursuit, they are not tied to any particular social practice. When external goods are the primary motivators, and constitute the greatest value for practitioners, they may be sought through a number of different means with greater or lesser degrees of success. As a result, when practices become only a means to provide external goods, many people may engage in them, but they are likely to regard their internal goods with indifference. For this reason, MacIntyre concludes that external goods stand in an instrumental relation to practices where their main purpose should be to bolster and sustain the pursuit of goods and virtues internal to them.

The distinction between internal and external goods of a practice has a number of important implications for change in sport and leisure activities. It suggests transformation should prioritise the pursuit of goods internal, rather than goods external to them, because internal goods are the defining quality of, and cannot be obtained except by, direct engagement in such practices. This reinforces the view that a social practice requires practitioners to recognise the importance of evaluative standards and paradigms that already operate in a practice. In reality what this means is that novices unfamiliar with a sport and leisure activity need to familiarise themselves with that activity's standards of excellence, heed the criticism and advice of veteran participants, officials, and coaches in order to purse the practice's internal goods. In other words, in order to be successful in the practice, a participant must defer (at least at times) to the existing shared standards and communal authority that currently defines an activity.

While MacIntyre argues that the initiation of individual practitioners into practices requires deference to established standards of excellence, the process does not require inductees to replicate, without question, every virtue, skill, strategy, and judgement currently in place. In fact, MacIntyre's scheme anticipates that opinions will constantly differ as to the ways practices should best precede and that out of such disputes practices evolve, due in part to practitioners' changing perceptions of its basic paradigms and standards, or in other words, its internal goods. Nevertheless, such disputes as to how change occurs within sport and leisure practices take place around a key set of internal goods that help differentiate such practices from other social activities. A brief outline of the unique goods internal to sport and leisure practices, therefore, is necessary, for they establish the benchmark for evaluating subsequent change.

The internal goods of sport and leisure practices

One possible method for differentiating the key internal goods that form the basis of a normative account of change in sport and leisure practices involves identifying a number of universal and significant (a) structural, (b) aesthetic, and (c) moral elements of such practices. Unfortunately space does not allow these internal goods to be presented in detail, but each is listed below followed by an example that aims to clarify the issues at stake when each element is subject to change.

Structural goods of sport and leisure practices

At the structural level the normative constraints of change in sport and leisure practices draw heavily on four underlying principles. They include problem solving, contesting, skill, and physicality.

(1) Sport and leisure as problem solving activities

Example: The development of oversize titanium drivers and other composite metal golf clubs together with more resilient and aerodynamically manageable balls continues to increase diving distances in golf, thereby eliminating many of the fairway hazards previously in play. In some cases, repositioning tees or moving hazards is impossible. Furthermore, with prospects of further technological improvements, doing so would provide only a temporary way of preserving the testing difficulty of golf. Diminished tests provide a weaker resource for exhibiting contesting differences and superior performances.

(2) Sport and leisure as contested activities

Example: Recent rule changes implemented by the International Triathlon Federation to allow "drafting" in the cycle portion of a race, a practice that previously resulted in a time penalty, has changed the relationship between the means and ends of the sport. Under the new rules, contestants who are strong swimmers have less of an advantage because, by working as a group, other contestants can conserve energy during the swim, and catch up to the good swimmers during the cycling portion of the race, even though they may be mediocre swimmers and cyclists. As a result many practitioners recognise that the race really begins with the running portion of the event. While the change makes for good television and increases the drama content of the event, it has been criticised for diminishing the overall quality of triathlon contests.

(3)   Sport and leisure as skilful activities

Example: In the past table-tennis players used the technique of flipping their paddle under the table between shots so opponents would not know which side of the bat contacted the ball on each successive hit. The strategy effectively eliminated an opponent's ability to read the spin on the ball and respond skilfully. The International Table Tennis Association banned this practice in the late 1980s with a rule that required the paddle sides to be covered with differently coloured pieces of rubber. The rule eliminated the need for an opponent to guess which side of the bat, and consequently what kind of spin producing surface, would be used in the stroke. Without the rule, returning service adequately in particular, had become a fifty-fifty proposition.

(4)   Sport and leisure as physical activities

Example: The use of a cart provides less physiologically demanding means for completing a round of golf than does walking 18 holes. The Professional Golf Association's dilemma is whether or not the physical demands of walking are an important part of the game or if the change significantly alters the game test. The issue emerged as an element in the Casey Martin debate where, because of his disability, he was granted an exception from the PGA no-cart rule in 1998.

Aesthetic goods of sport and leisure practices

The structural constraints of sport and leisure activities outlined in the previous section are effectively neutral with regard to the vitality of the experience. While sport and leisure structures are valued in that they establishes a problem to be solved and provide broad guidelines for the skills and strategies contestants should or should not use, they are impartial as to what elements are the most effective, impressive, exciting, beautiful, pleasing, or dramatic. Sport and leisure activity structures lack the life and verve that come only when the animation and spirit of human culture provides poignancy and expressive significance. These qualities are determined for the most part by the values, meanings, and kinds of significance that individuals or groups of practitioners give to, or find in, their participation in sport and leisure activities. Not surprisingly the range of values may vary considerably. Nonetheless a number of core elements are good candidates for the aesthetic goods of sport and leisure practices.

(1)   Sport and leisure as graceful activities

Example: In recent years a number of competitive ice-dancers have become increasingly critical of the ever-greater emphasis on athletic moves such as quad-twisting and combination jumps. Their complaint is that rewarding such moves allows more athletic, less graceful competitors to dominate the sport.

The sport's governing bodies argue that the viewing public is more interested in seeing moves of a complex athletic kind than those that are less spectacular and more resemble dance.

(2)   Sport and leisure as dramatic activities

Example: The "Golden Goal" rule introduced into soccer overtimes in 1996 has had a mixed reception. Initially seen as a less one-dimensional tie-breaker than a penalty shoot-out, many are uneasy with the manner in which it impacts the dramatic tension of the game. Advocates of the penalty shoot-out method argue that it allows for the formal development of tension where one can anticipate and pinpoint the precise event that determines the outcome of the contest. Advocates of the golden goal rule argue that the tension of the shoot-out is too great and that it allows an isolated event and specific individual to decide the outcome of a team game.

(3)   Sport and leisure as character developing activities

Example: The introduction of most valuable player (MVP) awards in many sports at all levels, but particularly the professional ranks, tend to emphasize individual members of a team rather than the cohesive unity of the team itself. Furthermore, as most MVP awards go to players with the most impressive statistics, certain players whose contributions are no less impressive or significant to the overall success of the team (such as the play of an offensive lineman) spectators tend to be less knowledgeable or appreciative of team play.

(4)   Sport and leisure as ritualistic activities

Example: In recent years, particularly at the professional level, the duration and intensity of the regular season has led many to question the extent to which a large number of games are particularly competitive or significant. Many have suggested that more than enough games exist to determine regular season champions and that the majority of the games are catered to television audiences. Furthermore, as regular season play only results in a play-off berth, few tangible rewards exist for exerting one's efforts consistently or maximally in early season play.

Internal goods and the morality of sport

Central to a moral understanding of sport is the narrative history that locates an individual's actions in a particular social practice and its institutional setting. A tradition is formed by the unification of practices around common goals and shared meanings that enable practitioners to appreciate the broader social importance, integrity, worth, and meaning of that practice. Traditions become the basic setting for a narrative life, which in turn are the basic settings in which virtues are exercised. In this way, traditions provide the resources for making rational decisions on what the quest for "the good" specifically involves. At the same time the evaluative standards that traditions sustain also become the normative standards by which individuals attempt to uphold and live a good life of their own.

(1) Narrative unity of sport and leisure traditions

Example: While the issue of maturity and performance readiness is a generic one in sports, it presents a particular problem for women's sports such as gymnastics, ice skating, and swimming where maturation often impairs performance. To dissuade an overemphasis on highly competitive training at an early age, the International Olympic Committee recently elevated the competitive minimum to age sixteen. Once again, institutional policy changed, in part, in response to the concerns raised by practitioners most familiar with the internal excellences (in this case, ones related to the well-being of competitors) of a practice.

A pyramid of constraints

The previous list of internal goods and examples of issues affected by change in sport and leisure activities suggest no indication of their relative significance. In this section of the paper I will suggest one method for adjudicating the kinds of change that take place at the three evaluative levels. At the heart of the evaluative scheme connecting the structural, aesthetic, and moral rationales together is a pyramid of constraints (see Figure 1). The figure provides a visual representation of the way in which change in sport and leisure can be evaluated.

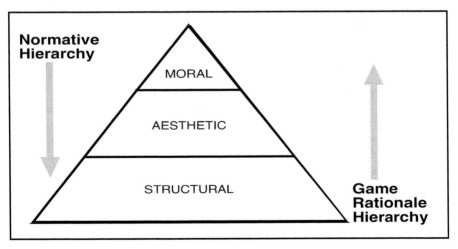

Figure 1   **The Pyramid of Constraints**

According to the scheme, any substantive change can be evaluated according to the structural, the aesthetic, and the moral constraints characteristic of sport and leisure. The constraints identified at each level work independently of the other two and may be involved in judging any change under consideration on their own. Some changes may have more of an impact on sport and leisure's structural principles, others on sport and leisure's aesthetic core, and others yet on sport and leisure's moral codes.

In many cases however, deciding whether a specific change should be endorsed may be difficult because evaluative judgements made at the three different levels may be in conflict. Some changes may be acceptable in structural terms, but violate certain aesthetic or moral criteria. Others may enhance the aesthetic or moral aspects of a sport but diminish its structural qualities. Still other changes may be acceptable on moral grounds but violate key structural and/or aesthetic elements of sport and leisure practices. Given that changes in sport and leisure practices may produce contrary evaluations at the structural, aesthetic, and moral levels an overall procedure is needed to resolve those cases that lead to contrasting conclusions.

The pyramid of constraints attempts to reconcile the evaluative differences between competing rationales. Involved are two principles that are crucial to understanding how the structural, aesthetic, and moral constraints of sport and leisure are related and function when evaluating change. The first principle argues that the three conceptual levels of the pyramid, when viewed as a whole, and understood in a broad way, exhibit a distinct, compelling, and logical relationship that places limitations on change. The second argues that the different evaluative principles operating at each level must fall within overall morally acceptable boundaries. Ethical constraints therefore, may place further limits on change than could conceivably take place at each evaluative level if such concerns about change were unimportant. These two aspects of the pyramid of constraints will now be explained in more detail.

Elementary to the logic of the pyramid, and suggested by its shape, is the view that key basic structural principles of sport and leisure cannot be violated at either of the progressively "higher" aesthetic and moral levels. According to the pyramid of constraints therefore, narrower more specific issues of change presuppose a base that consists of relatively more stable and settled issues that can be debated independently from sport and leisure's aesthetic and moral qualities. In other words, the structural elements of sport and leisure are the most fundamental and can be examined apart from aesthetic and moral considerations. In reality, of course, sport and leisure is never truly free of aesthetic or moral content, but in an important logical sense, the structural principles, can be formulated without regard for aesthetic and moral concerns. At the structural level then, it is possible to describe sport and leisure without reference to its aesthetic or moral content.

The key issue is change in sport and leisure, and so aesthetic and moral constraints fall within more basic structural ones. As the stepwise logic proceeds, sport and leisure's aesthetic constraints fall within structural limits and in turn, sport and leisure's moral constraints fall within aesthetic limits. A logical relationship exists whereby moral constraints reside within the constraints imposed by aesthetic considerations which in turn reside within those constraints imposed by structural considerations. This means that while the evaluative standards operating at the moral level, for example, guide change in an indefinite number of ways, they must operate within the conceptual boundaries of sport and leisure's aesthetic standards. In turn, changes based on an aesthetic evaluation of sport and leisure can occur in an indefinite number of ways, but logically speaking, they too must honor the standards on which sport and leisure activities *per se* are judged.

The logical order among the three evaluative levels is not inviolable, for aesthetic goals could be used to argue for a change that transcends the structure of sport and leisure pursuits. One could, for example, stipulate that a goal in soccer counts only if players perform an elaborate celebration with appropriate dramatic quality in front of a panel of judges who then determine if the score stands. The pyramid allows one to see why, in this case, writing a new constitutive rule to that effect is likely to be regarded as ludicrous and that debate over such a structural change would be fruitless. This however is not to say that at times significant aesthetic issues may not be in conflict with structural issues where the decision may not be so clear-cut.

Nonetheless, the pyramid's depiction of sport and leisure activities as ones that involve broader to narrower constraints does suggest that, at least for changes in physical games and pastimes, where evaluative issues conflict, priority should reside with foundational criteria that explain the basic charac- teristics of the activity itself. Without this ranking it would be difficult to make the argument that some changes can threaten the central rationale of sport and leisure activities in significant ways. A failure to give priority to basic principles that demarcate sport's and leisure activities from other social practices makes it impossible to adjudicate the relative value of one change from another, particularly changes that have their parentage in aesthetic or moral standards.

The second key principle argues that the pyramid scheme and the logical relationship between levels must reside within acceptable moral limits. In addition to the logical constraints that work from the bottom up or from the broadest to the narrowest level of constraint, change in sport and leisure is also constrained from the top down, or from the narrowest to the broadest level. Without precedence given to the ethical, an activity that was classified sport and leisure according to the criteria developed at the structural level but led to the senseless death of its participants could only be modified by later moral input — say to guarantee that these deaths were as painless as possible[2]. Nevertheless, as it is desirable to eradicate games of this kind, the greatest weight should be given to moral concerns — even to the point of trumping structural and aesthetic concerns, and sending gamewrights back to their drawing boards.

In the fast paced world of adventure sports such moral concerns are central to the progress of a number of contemporary leisure pursuits. Health and safety issues involved in activities such as canyoning, base-jumping, eco-challenges and escorted mountain ascents bring into question the very existence of the activity, particularly given the spate of highly publicized catastrophes that have dogged their recent past.

The preceding analysis of the pyramid of constraints suggests two possibly incompatible principles are involved in monitoring change in sport and leisure. The first argues that change, at least in logical terms, should prioritize the pyramid's structural base. The second proposes that, in ethical terms, the apex and moral concerns take precedence.

On closer inspection, the two principles (in the majority of cases) need not contradict each other. Logically one should begin the analysis of sport and leisure by considering change in broad terms. By doing so, it becomes apparent that an infinite number of physical tests could be discovered or invented. Beyond the structural level there exists a smaller pool of artificial physical tests that produce aesthetically pleasing activities. Beyond that, there is an even smaller pool of artificial physical tests that produce aesthetically pleasing activities that are also morally supportable. As a result, for a majority of cases, if a change is incompatible with structural features that constitute an attractive and interesting artificial physical test it will be a waste of time to then look further to examine how the change impacts the activity's aesthetic and the moral features. At the same time, there is a sense in which higher level concerns trump lower ones. Moral criteria carry more weight than aesthetic and structural changes even if it means we must eliminate crucial elements that explain an activity's appeal. For this reason, moral concerns may limit the range of aesthetically interesting changes in sport and leisure activities, which in turn limit acceptable structural possibilities. In short, we have little duty to preserve any particular artificial physical test, but have a considerable obligation not to murder.

Evaluating examples of change in sport and leisure practices

In this final section, changes in the activity of golf will be briefly examined to assess the usefulness of the pyramid model.

In structural terms is increasingly evident that advances in golf technology are altering the game. Improvements in club design, particularly with drivers, have altered the average hitting length of reasonably skilled golfers. In addition, the designs of some golf balls limit the amount of flight deviation that results from a hook or slice. As a result of technological advances, a number of stationary hazards on many courses positioned to penalize under-hit and off-line shots have become redundant. In many cases, the only way to bring existing bunkers trees and water hazards back into play is to lengthen the hole. While this may be possible in some cases, in the majority of cases, few courses can expand in this fashion.

The response of a number of greenkeepers has been to increase the difficulty of the course in other ways, primarily by reducing the width of the fairways, thickening the rough, increasing the difficulty of pin placements, and in a few cases, changing short part five holes into long par fours. The result is that the difficulty of the test has been preserved in other ways despite technological advances.

Even so, other problems remain, for now the test of golf has changed to favour golfers who can hit long and straight, rather than players who have a full range of skills, or a good "short game" on and around the green. In other words, the skill requirements of golf, due to technological efficiency, have changed to a narrower band of abilities. This change has more of an impact on the qualitative aspect of golf contests, favouring power hitters, rather than touch players.

The changes in the range of skills and abilities noted above have probably more of an impact at the aesthetic level, and in particular, affect the quality of the golfing spectacle. Arguably, what gives golf its spectator appeal, is a finely balanced contest on a course that allows for players of contrasting styles and abilities to be equally successful through counter-balancing strengths and weaknesses. Contests between one-dimensional driving specialists diminish the range of appreciative skills, and make the outcome more predictable. As a result fewer opportunities will arise for the kinds of dramatic confrontations that presently exist between the game's personalities as golfing styles become more uniform and predictable.

At the moral level, a relevant distinction appropriate to this issue is whether the individual golfer is engaged in the practice as a private or a public setting. In other words, it seems that an individual golfer's decision to embrace technological help is a matter for each individual golfer to decide when such decisions impact the individual alone. In the case of a golfer playing a round on their own, there appears no good reason to limit technology. But in situations where play is organized the issue is more complex. One can envisage a continuum of cases where the kind of technological advances permissible varies according to the level and bearing of the competition. In the majority of cases, golfing contests are low-key affairs, primarily between weekly pairs and foursomes where golf rules are applied relatively loosely. As it is unlikely that technological help will improve the deficiencies of the weekend hacker significantly, the integrity of the test will remain. At the elite level of play, however, technological advances may significantly affect the severity of the test and the relative competitive standings of the players. It seems reasonable, therefore, for organizations such as the Professional Golf Association to implement appropriate technology standards to avoid further technological advances that limit the range of testing skills and erode the ambiguity of the test. At the recreational level however, it seems reasonable for sports goods manufactures to take advantage of the innate difficulties of the activity and continue to meet the demands of everyday participants. The reduction of a few strokes for the average player, after all is unlikely to threaten the integrity of the whole test. On this basis the preceding analysis suggest that on structural ground, care is needed when assessing technological advances at the elite level, but at the recreational level, such concerns are insufficient to justify the complete prohibition of technological improvements preferred by the recreational golfer.

Conclusion

Upon reflection, the underlying rationales within the pyramid should not be considered as something fixed or inviolate. Instead the pyramid system provides one method of capturing the different kinds of social and contingent rational propositions which give sport different kinds of meaning and life, and the ways in which we might think of the relationships between them. The pyramid allows individuals and groups to assess change in a way that does not reduce what is right and proper to whatever the prevailing social thinking of the day may be. It drives a wedge between the way we think about change in sport, and what the popular, commercially orientated, mainstream perspective has to say about it.

Notes

[1] Mike McNamee (1995) suggests a more 'catholic' account of the virtues that takes into account both their different natures and function in sport avoids the reductivism to which MacIntyre is prone. Drawing on the work of Edmund Pincoffs (1986) he suggests that different moral and nonmoral virtues are located in functional settings rather than within practices. Pincoffs's two broad classes of virtue — instrumental and noninstrumental — suggest that virtues may also be found within non-practices, such as

fitness activities, and in within institutions that allow practices to prosper and flourish through careful nurturing.

2   A vision of such a sport is portrayed in William Harrison's 'Rollerball murder' (Harrison, 1985). In this fictional game, the potential for death is integrally woven into the structural logic of the game such that its elimination on moral grounds effectively ruins the game's skill and tension.

References

Harrison, W. (1985) 'Rollerball murder', in D. L. Vanderwerken and S. K. Wertz (eds) *Sport inside out*. Austin, TX: Texas Christian University Press, pp. 31–42.

MacIntyre, A. (1984) *After virtue*. Notre Dame, MI: University of Notre Dame Press.

McNamee, M. J. (1995) 'Sporting practices, institutions, and virtues: A critique and restatement', *Journal of the Philosophy of Sport*, XXII: pp. 70–73.

Pincoff, E. (1986) *Quandaries and ethics*. Lawrence, KS: University of Kansas Press.

Just Leisure, Ethical Fitness, and Ecophilosophical Perspectives

Karla A. Henderson

Department of Recreation and Leisure Studies,
University of North Carolina at Chapel Hill (USA)

> The paradox of our time in history is that we have taller buildings, but shorter tempers; wider freeways but narrower points of view ... more money, but have less quality things to show for it; we buy more things, but enjoy them less ... more conveniences, but less time ... more experts and more medicine, but less wellness ...
>
> We've learned how to make a living, but not how to have a life; we've added years to life, but not life to years ... we've cleaned up the air, but have neglected and polluted our soul ... more time for leisure pursuits, but less fun doing them... [Author unknown]

These paradoxical ideas provides a framework for examining "just leisure". As socially conscious researchers, we cannot afford to avoid examining the meanings of social justice. In the new Millennium, the discussion of leisure requires a continuing focus on ethical dimensions. The examination of leisure and ethics began long ago, but today the discussions have moved beyond philosophers only. The nature of ethics as the study of right action continues to preclude tidy and unthinking answers to complex and difficult problems.

Just leisure

'Just' leisure does not mean 'mere' leisure that connotes a devaluation of the contribution that leisure can make to people's lives. Rather, it relates to the notion that leisure and recreation contribute to social as well as environmental justice. Fain (1991) suggested, "every act of leisure has moral meaning" (p. 7). Therefore, leisure researchers and managers ought to examine how leisure in the outdoor environment is also a manifestation of choosing how one "ought

93

live" as well as to help others make choices regarding leisure. Foregrounding
Fain's questions, "When we are free to do as we please, what do we do, why
do we do it, and what do our actions portend?" (1991: p. 12), the purpose of
this paper is to address ethical fitness, defined as the capacity to recognize
moral challenges and respond to them, related to environmental and social
justice in the contexts of leisure.

Just leisure has its roots in the notion of justice. Justice refers to fairness
and morally right action. Fairness, rather than sameness, is required to
achieve justice. Further, justice relates both the social and environmental
concerns. Social justice includes a vision of society where the distribution
of resources is equitable and all members are physically and psychologically
safe and secure. In this society individuals are both self-determining and
interdependent. It involves a sense of one's own agency and a sense of social
responsibility toward and with others and for society as a whole (Adams *et
al.*, 1997). Social justice refers to an understanding of present and historical
social inequities and a recognition of how these inequities continue to influence
attitudes due to the pervasiveness of oppression in society. These definitions
of social justice depend on people thinking that they make a difference in
the world. Social justice, as juxtaposed to social diversity with its emphasis
on recognizing and celebrating differences, focuses on the disparity of power
that different groups have historically or presently been accorded.

Environmental justice is an outgrowth of social justice with a focus on
how the environment impacts on people's lives and *vice versa*. It goes beyond
hegemonic environmentalism that emphasizes species and land preservation
(Warren, 1996). With its roots in problems resulting from environmental
racism, environmental justice proposes that individuals and communities
practising just leisure cannot abdicate their responsibility to examine the
impact of any encounter with the environment from ecological and social
perspectives. The goals of both social and environmental justice are reflected
in social movements and "radical" approaches that allow individuals, and
communities, to go from best interests to choices, from paternalism to self-
determination, and from invisibility to visibility (Rioux, 1993). Social justice,
environmental justice, and ethical fitness are processes as well as goals.

Any kind of de-privileging, discrimination, or inequity is, of course, *prima
facie* an ethical issue. Therefore, any leisure researcher committed to quality
of life issues should also be committed to the fundamental values of justice,
equity, and empowerment (Henderson, 1997). Further, leisure should be an
intentional act deliberately designed to bring about positive outcomes in
individuals. If equity is to occur, then we must intentionally frame the ethics
and aims of leisure, and not leave matters to fate. As Singh (1989) suggested,
to be a member of a community of moral persons is to be concerned as much
with the actions of others as with one's own, and "learning to act justly and

fairly towards other people, races, sexes, etc., cannot be left to chance" (p. 230). Equity is embodied in demonstrating an interest in the protection, growth, health, and well-being of people as well as of environments.

Ethical fitness

The presence of the "still small voice" (Quinnett, 1994) is an idea that professionals and participants must recognize for just leisure to occur. How do people make choices that reflect personal and professional ethics of caring about themselves, each other, and the environment? Personal and professional ethics provide a way of finding the best course to enable a sense of right and just living in a complex world and what the relationship between people and the environment should be. Leisure researchers have an obligation to analyze how people develop the sensitivity to recognize a situation as posing personal or professional ethical considerations. They also need knowledge of what responses are ethical, a willingness to act, judgment to weigh considerations, and humility to seek additional knowledge to guide actions (Quinnett, 1994). For example, when a leisure opportunity is proposed, people need to think how this behavior might affect others whether it is related to the impact on the environment and/or the impact on diverse groups.

Developing ethical fitness is similar metaphorically to developing physical fitness, and provides a basis for making sound choices about the personal, professional, or environmental dimensions of leisure. Kidder (1995) described ethical fitness as a capacity to recognize the nature of moral challenges and respond with a conscience, a perception of the difference between right and wrong, and an ability to choose what is right and live by it. Ethical fitness may be just as important as physical fitness when the focus of the field's work is on "just leisure". Ethical people base their actions on reasoned knowledge and attitudes and their actions reflect what is in their hearts. Further, ethical fitness is not only a dimension for individuals, but also for managers of leisure opportunities. This ethical fitness can also contribute to developing practices that benefit nature.

Ecophilosophical views

The intersection between social and environmental concerns provides an important philosophical underpinning for understanding just leisure. The availability of the environment for leisure, sport, and tourism means that leisure researchers or managers have more, not less, responsibility for environmental issues than might otherwise be thought. A number of ecophilosophies exist that provide a belief system for assumptions about the environment and, some radical ecophilosophers would even add, our survival as a planet. In the late 1960s we saw the first photographs of earth from space and realized how the earth occupied a small space that appeared fragile and confined. This new consciousness and the activism of the New Left, as well as the feminist and student movements, sparked the contemporary environmental movement (Seager, 1993). Since that time, ecophilosophies such as ecofeminism (Plant, 1989), deep ecology (Duvall and Sessions, 1985), and social ecology (Merchant, 1992) have focused on a deeper human relationship with the earth.

The value of any ecophilosophy, however, lies in the questions raised, not the answers provided (Henderson, 1999). Ecophilosophies make the connections between humans and nature visible (Fox, 1994). Talk about leisure and the connection between humans and the environment is normally absent except in discussions about outdoor or countryside recreation. Even in writings about the outdoors, the environment is often only a backdrop and not central to the discussion. Seldom do we question the very morality and socio-environmental consciousness of supporting valued leisure activities. Perhaps if we did, we would not even use the outdoors as a leisure venue. Each time we go into the outdoors, we make an environmental impact. Therefore, an ecophilosophy is most useful in evoking critical theory about leisure and concomitant impacts on social and physical environments. Ecophilosophies are further lenses whereby researchers and managers can examine the potential and the pitfalls of just leisure related to people and the environment.

Ecophilosophical perspectives provide direction concerning how just leisure might be manifested relative to outdoor activities. Although many people are more aware of the need for social justice related to leisure and the impact of race, class, and gender on what people do and how they feel, an environmental ethic for leisure has not emerged. Fox (1994) suggested that leisure involvement must be assessed on our ability to protect the environment or leave it for future generations, to sustain communities and cultural identities, and to nurture a relationship between humans and nonhumans. All consumptive leisure pursuits should be evaluated using criteria that acknowledge the impact on ecosystems, social systems, and relationships.

Most policies concerning outdoor recreation have not focused on ecophilosophical principles. For example, in the United States, wilderness protection generally is based not on dedicated environmentalist tenets but the overall political structure of domination and the rationalist concept of controlling nature (Vance, 1997). The hegemony that mitigates leisure and ignores ethical fitness relative to the outdoors and the environment are rarely discussed. To examine just leisure, this essay will focus briefly on three ecophilosophical views that might provide some guidance for our discussions: ecofeminism, ecotourism along with sustainable tourism, and social ecology.

Ecofeminism

Feminist ethics provides one way to understand the social and environmental dimensions of just leisure. A question that becomes prominent in this perspective is "what is good for women?". Humberstone (1998) and Vance (1997), however, suggested that feminist perspectives have been all but silent on environmental issues.

The primary discourse of ecofeminism is the belief that the oppression / domination of women is connected to/with the oppression/domination of the earth (Henderson and Bialeschki, 1991; Plant 1989; Warren, 1990). Ecofeminist beliefs go beyond liberal feminist issues of equality to integrity and dignity related to human and environmental concerns. By tying ecofeminist perspectives to the meaning and conduct of leisure, connections are made regarding human rights and the environment that challenge previously held ideas and practices. Ecofeminists ask questions about why women and nature are subordinated in some leisure activities. Ecofeminist views provide us with a global view that embraces the value of all people and the ecology of the land pertaining to leisure.

No one form of ecofeminism exists, but all the views share a common commitment to making visible the ways that patriarchy dominates women and nature. Ecofeminists embody this commitment by developing practices aimed at ending the exploitation of women and of nature. Vance (1997) argued that related to wilderness, the rationalist policy of controlling nature is the same one used to control women (and others). Ecofeminists propose that all acts should focus on respect for, and the diversity of, human beings and the life enhancement of natural environments. Applying aspects of ecofeminism can help us consider what we do, why we do it, and how it contributes overall to ending the domination of people *and* of nature.

Ecofeminism provides a critical theory for examining just leisure. Ecofeminism, however, is not without shortcomings to note. Some people dislike the dualities suggested in the subject/object and male/female propositions put forth (Fox and McAvoy, 1989). Critics also question the proposition that a nonsexist society would imply an ecologically benign society. Still others believe that ecofeminism does not address the class, race, and Westernization issues that have led to environmental destruction. Ecofeminists sometimes are criticized for "scapegoating" men and for suggesting that it is women's role to "clean up" after what males have done. Another criticism of ecofeminism is that it is essentialist. Women and girls may not be inherently and naturally closer to the earth. Further, not all women experience a closeness to nature even through ecofeminism suggests a nature/culture dualism and in essence a reinforcement of the idea that biology is destiny. Similarly, a controversial shortcoming of ecofeminism described by Seager (1993) relates to assumptions regarding the "earth as mother". The earth as mother as a sacred and honored female life force is a powerful icon. Ironically and on the other hand, the earth is not our mother; it does not take care of just because we are human beings. Further, according to Seager, "The complex, emotion-laden, conflict-laden, quasi-sexualized, quasi-dependent mother relationship ... is not an effective metaphor for environmental action" (p. 219). If the earth is our mother then we are children and have less responsibility for accountability. It also suggests a benign relationship. For radical environmentalists, the greatest criticism of ecofeminism often has to do with the implicit assumption of ecofeminism that human issues are more important than nonhuman aspects of the environment.

Nevertheless, ecofeminism provides a philosophy that links the human and environmental worlds. Assessing leisure from the standpoint of what it means to women and nature, as well as questioning power relationships, would be one way of establishing ethical fitness for how we live out lives out of respect for ourselves, others, and for living and non-living entities that have no voice.

Ecotourism and sustainable tourism

Leisure and tourism are often linked as tourism is a principal leisure activity. Tourism's multifaceted function as a socioeconomic and politico-cultural phenomenon is a complex industry having its own rules and codes of ethics. Yet, tourism is almost wholly dependent on the environment. If the environment is degraded, many forms of tourism are diminished. Hultsman (1995) argued that just tourism refers to acting in a fair, honorable, and proper way. He noted that tourism has become more important as an economy than as an experience. Thus, ethical fitness as environmental consciousness is important to consider within the contexts of ecotourism and sustainable tourism. Sustainable tourism and ecotourism are not the same concepts because not all ecotourism is sustainable, and not all sustainable tourism has to be in natural areas. They both, however, often have similar eco-philosophical goals.

Ecotourism, nature tourism, appropriate tourism, ethical tourism, and responsible tourism are some of the tourism descriptors emerging in recent years that have overlapping and imprecise meanings, but might be grouped under the heading of "alternative tourism". The appeal of ecotourism is the opportunity to see and possibly become connected to endangered cultures, lands, and animals. Properly practised, ecotourism is multifaceted with its low impact, small-scale nature that educates the traveller. Ecotourism can also provide funds for conservation, help empower local communities, and foster respect for different cultures and human rights. Further, people who earn their living from ecotourism are more likely to defend natural resources against destructive activities. The most remote corners of our delicate planet are easily accessible by modern transportation so they might be protected by making people aware that they exist through ecotourism. Ecotourists often fight to keep the wild places wild because they have seen these areas and have been touched by their beauty.

Sustainable tourism development is a model that can have impetus for structural change within society by moving away from a strictly socio-economic focus toward not compromising the future (Fennell, 1999). Sustainable tourism relates to not consuming natural resources at a higher rate than they can be replaced, maintaining biological diversity, recognizing and valuing the aesthetic appeal, following ethical principles that respect local cultures, and involving and consulting local people (Williams, 1998). Mass tourism is typically not sustainable. In a world where some humans are perpetually valued more than other life forms, the principles of ecosystem management and human ecology embodied in sustainable tourism can help us to better understand the place of humans in the natural world (Fennell, 1999). Sustainable tourism centrally embodies an ethical dimension.

Although ecotourism offers a practice that can lead to sustainable development through its low impact, non-consumptive, and locally controlled nature, it is not without ethical problems. Fennell (1999) noted that although ecotourism began as a concept designed by ecologists to actively prevent the destruction of the environment, it also has become a marketing term for tourism developers. Unfortunately, the models of ecotourism have evolved to define the phenomena not in terms of relationships, but novelty, movement, benefits, economic revenues, and commodities. For example, what is marketed as environmentally responsible travel may really be "ecotourism lite" or a new name with some environmental add-ons. Even the ecotourism motto of "leave nothing but footsteps, take nothing but memories" can be environmentally destructive. Further, ecotourism can interrupt indigenous people's ways of life. It is not possible to visit an environment and not have some deleterious effect. Similarly, the term sustainable tourism has been a mixed blessing. It has been adopted to promote a clean and green image but often it, too, is a marketing gimmick.

If researchers and managers care about the future of leisure, it is necessary to adopt a greener agenda. Fennell (1999) illustrated that perhaps the most important aspect facing tourism planners and managers is not to insert small numbers of environmentally aware people into pristine environments, but to improve the sustainability of ethical and responsible mass tourism. A role may be to demonstrate the ability of the industry to become more ecologically accountable. Sustainability should be the philosophy and cornerstone of the development of the tourism industry since the natural environment constitutes most of its primary resource base. New forms of tourism bring with them new environmental challenges and more demanding standards for sustainable development. Tourism in all parts of the world will need to face more stringent conditions on growth and development. The industry must look at and manage change to address the ethics of environmental concerns.

Ethical fitness concerns how the tourism industry can put the environment first by controlling capacity, developing tourism with dignity, fostering a culture of conservation, and helping to solve environmental problems. Ecophilosophies behind ecotourism and sustainable tourism can provide the basis for addressing emerging issues of just leisure and can insure that tourism development monitors its own ethical fitness.

Social ecology

A variety of ecological perspectives could be applied to just leisure (e.g., deep ecology, green politics) but I would like to describe a bit about social ecology. Social ecology addresses the imperatives of models of development and suggests there are no innocent victims (Seager, 1993). Social ecology confronts how humans relate directly to the environment. In other words, it incorporates humans and their interdependence with nonhuman nature (Merchant, 1992). In an ecological society, dominance and hierarchy could be replaced by equity and freedom. Social ecologists have a deep commitment not only to reversing the domination of nature, but also to removing social domination and to questioning whether capitalism and ecology have anything in common (Merchant, 1992). The ecophilosophy of social ecology provides a way to question issues of social and environmental justice. The implications of social ecology calls into question the ambiguous relationship between how people use the environment and environmental protection.

Social ecology is concerned with not "others" but "anothers" in relation to a moral consciousness to, for, within, and about the environment. It addresses the situated knowledge of the lived experience. Humberstone (1998) suggested the need to examine the philosophies and ideologies embedded in organizations that make any leisure in the outdoors a possibility. It is, however, a giant leap from social research and social explanation to generate large scale democratic political movements to halt environmental degradation. Social ecologists might ask what role leisure plays in this larger movement if it does not focus on fulfilling basic human needs through an economic restructuring that is environmentally sustainable.

Just leisure, from a social ecology perspective, cannot occur without acknowledging the power of privilege and the diversity among people. Just leisure requires that "gender inclusivity", "race inclusivity", "class inclusivity", and "ability inclusivity" rather than "neutrality" related to any of these diverse situations ought to be a part of an environmental and outdoor consciousness. Arguing that no differences exist denies actual differences in power and resources among groups (Rhode, 1990). Affirming the similarity between women and men, black and white, gay and straight, or any groups may inadvertently universalize or validate norms of the dominant social groups. These norms often have not addressed diverse interests, experiences, and perspectives for groups participating, or not participating, in outdoor activities and environmental protection.

Summary

Just leisure calls for ethical and moral discussion and debate. These discussions might involve analyses of social identities and the practices of groups that use natural environments to convey values. The discussion must occur at the practical and theoretical level. These discussions ought to synthesize ecological approaches, be sensitive to a plurality of voices, identities, and practices, and be underpinned by a concern for social as well as environmental justice.

Any one ecophilosophical view is not going to sustain us in providing socially and environmentally responsible leisure or just leisure. Any ecophilosophical critique of leisure begins with the recognition that too much will be lost though the exclusion of any perspective. All aspects of leisure point to the cultural, political, and economic roots of societal problems addressed from many perspectives.

Several summary points may help to recount the usefulness of ecophilosophies in addressing just leisure and ethical fitness. First, the recognition of the limits to environment has fueled the search for solutions. As women and men address these issues, the relationships between the domination of nature and of people provide insights. Second, we must explore multiple levels of truth if we are to understand leisure. Ecophilosophies may give some new insight. Third, the transformation of the society is not a product but a process. We are not sure what the products will resemble but minimally hope that it eliminates subordination on the basis of gender, race, ethnicity, and class, and stops degradation of the environment. Fourth, many positions on leisure and environmental reform have failed to take into account people's interests and needs. Ecophilosophies represent a practical movement for social change arising from the struggles of people to sustain themselves, their families, and their communities in the face of maldevelopment and environmental degradation. The idea is not just to change who wields power but to transform the structure of power. Radical ecophilosophers might suggest that the domination of the environment is bound up with class exploitation, racism, colonialism, and neocolonialism. The basic issues regarding social and environmental justice require many approaches.

The transformation to a broader based view of nature and culture interactions and from ecophilosophy to praxis to fundamental social change is far from complete. The challenge to leisure researchers and managers is to address how leisure has an impact on culture and environment. We need a variety of models to understand the meanings of leisure and how people *and* the environment matter. A critique based on ecophilosophical views may not change the course of action but it might change attitudes, thereby raising consciousness and eventually promoting change.

References

Adams, M., Bell, L. A., and Griffin (eds) (1997) *Teaching for diversity and social justice*. New York: Routledge.

Duvall, W., and Sessions, G. (1985) *Deep ecology*. Salt Lake City: Peregrine Smith.

Fain, G. S. (1991) 'Moral leisure', in G. S. Fain (ed) *Leisure and ethics: Reflections on the philosophy of leisure*. Reston, VA: American Association for Leisure and Recreation, pp. 7–30.

Fennell, D. A. (1999) *Ecotourism*. London: Routledge.

Fox, K. M (1994) 'Negotiating in a world of change: Ecofeminist guideposts for leisure scholarship', *Journal of Leisure Research*, Vol. 26, No. 1: pp. 39–56.

Fox, K. M., and McAvoy, L. H. (1989, April) 'Environmental ethics: Strengths and dualisms of six dominant themes', Paper presented to the *Leisure and Ethics Conference*, Boston, MA.

Henderson, K. A. (1997) 'Just recreation: Ethics, gender, and equity', *Journal of Park and Recreation Administration*, Vol. 15, No. 2: pp. 16–31.

——— (1999) 'Ecofeminism and the human/environment intersection', *Environmental Papers Series*, Vol. 2, No. 1: pp. 8–14.

Henderson, K. A., and Bialeschki, M. D. (1990–91) 'Ecofeminism: Recreation as if nature and woman mattered', *Leisure Information Quarterly*, Vol. 17, No. 1: pp. 1–5.

Hultsman, J. (1995) 'Just tourism: An ethical framework', *Annals of Tourism Research*, Vol. 22, No. 3: pp. 553–567.

Humberstone, B. (1998) 'Re-creation and connections in and with nature', *International Review for the Sociology of Sport*, Vol. 33, No. 4: pp. 381–392.

Kidder, R. (1995) *How good people make tough decisions*. New York: William Morrow and Co.

Merchant, C. (1992) *Radical ecology*. New York: Routledge.

Plant, J. (ed) (1989) *Healing the wounds: The promise of ecofeminism*. Philadelphia: New Society Publishers.

Quinnett, P. (1994) *Pavlov's trout*. Sandpoint, ID: Keokee Co.

Rhode, D. L. (ed) (1990) *Theoretical perspectives on sexual difference*. New Haven: Yale University Press.

Rioux, M. H. (1993) 'Rights, justice, power: An agenda for change', in M. Nagler and E. J. Kemp (eds) *Perspectives on disability* (second edition) Palo Alto, CA: Health Markets Research, pp. 515–523.

Seager, J. (1993) *Earth follies*. New York: Routledge.

Singh, B. R. (1989) 'Neutrality and commitment in teaching moral and social issues in a multicultural society', *Educational Review*, Vol. 41, No. 3: pp. 227–242.

Vance, L. (1997) 'Ecofeminism and wilderness', *National Women's Studies Journal*, Vol. 9, No. 3: pp. 60.

Warren, K. (1996) 'Educating for environmental justice', *Journal of Experiential Education*, Vol. 19, No. 3: pp. 135–140.

Warren, K. J. (1990) 'The power and promise of ecological feminism', *Environmental Ethics*, Vol. 12: pp. 125–146.

Williams, S. (1998) *Tourism geography*. London: Routledge.

"Sorry Ref, I didn't see it" — The Limitations of Shields and Bredemeier's Model of Moral Action

Carwyn Jones

School of Social Science, University of Teesside (UK)

Introduction

In this paper I provide a critique of recent social science research into moral action in sport. I argue that even the most complex and well-developed theoretical model, namely Shields and Bredemeier (1995), is problematic in its explanation of moral action on at least two grounds. First it is committed to a narrow conception of moral goodness. Secondly, moral character is primarily defined in terms of moral judgements that exemplify moral goodness. These commitments are problematic because they narrow the scope of moral evaluation and marginalise the role of virtue. In order to exemplify my critique I will employ a recent controversial incident in professional football in Britain.

Unfair play in sport

In order to contextualise my discussion, I refer to an incident that occurred on Saturday the 13th of February, 1999. During a fifth round English Football Association cup-tie, a newcomer to Football in Britain initiated an unprecedented sequence of events that lead to the replay of the tie between Arsenal and Sheffield United.

With fifteen minutes left in the game and the score one each, one of the Sheffield United players sustained an injury. The Sheffield United goalkeeper kicked the ball into touch, as is common practice so that the injured player could receive some medical attention. The injured player, however, failed to recover sufficiently from the injury and was substituted during the stoppage. Following the substitution, an Arsenal player restarted the match by throwing the ball deep into the Sheffield United half of the pitch intent on returning

105

the ball to the opposition goalkeeper. (We cannot be certain of his intention, however, his action reflected the custom in such circumstances, namely returning the ball to the opposition who were in possession prior to the injury.) Apparently unaware of his team-mates' intentions and the accepted custom in such circumstances, a young Nigerian player Nwankwo Kanu gave chase and collected the ball unopposed.

With the Sheffield United defenders caught off guard, Kanu centred the ball where his team-mate Marc Overmars scored, despite the best efforts of the goalkeeper and one of the defenders. With no *official* rule broken, the referee, having consulted a fellow official, awarded the goal. The Sheffield United players protested at the apparent injustice, voicing their anger toward the referee and the Arsenal players. The Sheffield United manager attempted to halt the game by withdrawing his team. Meanwhile, one of his team-mates explained to the bemused Kanu the cause of all the problems. With no precedent to guide the referee's action, the game continued and concluded with Arsenal winning by two goals to one. The protestations of the Sheffield United players continued after the final whistle and the injustice of the result was clear to most football supporters and followers.

Soon after the game, the Arsenal manager, in a conciliatory gesture, offered to replay the game, recognising the serious breach of the unwritten rules, or ethos of soccer. He also apologised for Kanu's actions, suggesting that they were attributable to naivety rather than to any unsporting intentions. The English FA, in an unprecedented move, agreed to the replay even though technically no rule had been broken. Following a discussion by FIFA, the game's world governing body, a rematch was sanctioned (which Arsenal again won).

In the next section, I discuss the Shields and Bredemeier theory of moral action and examine its utility in describing and/or explaining Kanu's actions.

Shields and Bredemeier's theory of moral action: a failure in judgement

Brenda Bredemeier and David Shields have researched the moral behaviour and attitudes in and towards sport for a number of years. Working predominantly in the strong competitive culture of North American high school and collegiate sport, often with other co-workers, they have commented widely on the relationship between sport and morality. To this end they initially employed Kohlberg's (1981) groundbreaking theory of moral development. Their methodology however, has evolved and produced a complex and comprehensive model of moral action that differs significantly from Kohlberg's original work. As Kohlberg's work spanned a range of research literature, only a short overview will be given here.

Kohlberg (1981), following Piaget (1932), outlined a comprehensive description of the nature and direction of moral development. He argued that moral development is essentially a species of cognitive development. In line with Piaget's identification of developmental stages, Kohlberg outlined a six-stage sequence through which moral development occurred. Moral development was essentially a process whereby, given the right environment, simple cognitive structures capable of immature egocentric judgements slowly gave way, and were supplanted by, complex and differentiated cognitive structures capable of mature autonomous moral judgements. Unlike the Aristotelian tradition of ethics, Kohlberg's account of morality is not couched in terms of substantive or thick moral concepts like cruelty, kindness, honesty and courage.

Central to Kohlberg's theory, and in keeping with the "deontological" tradition in moral philosophy, is the view that moral judgements are centrally important. Furthermore they are mature in light of their form rather than their content. It is not the particular issue addressed by a judgement that gives it its moral status, but rather the form the judgement takes. Kohlberg argued in a deontological fashion that moral judgements are universalizable and impartial. They conform to the requirements of Kant's categorical imperative, 'do unto others as you would have them do unto you'. Warnock (1983: p. 33) summarises thus:

> Such a judgement as 'you ought to pay the money' is (...) universalisable; that is, if I commit myself to this judgement in your particular case, I thereby commit myself to the view that anybody – including, most importantly, myself - in the circumstances in which you now are, ought to act in that way. I cannot, without logical impropriety, issue a different judgement in another case unless I can show that other case to be different in some relevant respects.

Given Kohlberg's epistemological commitments, any person's moral maturity is purportedly accessible by examining the form of their judgement. Kohlberg induced moral judgements for analysis using moral dilemmas. Shields and Bredemeier in their early research employed a similar methodology to compare and contrast athletes and non-athletes moral reasoning. Using both sport specific and non-sports moral dilemmas Bredemeier and Shields (1984) found that judgements made in response to sport dilemmas were characteristically egocentric and less mature than reasoning in response to non-sports dilemmas. By way of explaining these results, Bredemeier and Shields (1986a: p. 18) argued in line with prevailing sociological beliefs about the nature of play (in particular Huizinga 1950), that "... play is removed cognitively and emotionally from the instrumental concerns that permeate most of our existence". Moreover, in sport which is a particularly codified form of play, "the typical concerns and moral restraints of everyday life are temporarily set aside"(Bredemeier and Shields 1986b: p. 7)

Coining the phrase "moral atmosphere", they concluded that sport is peculiar with its own values and norms. Typically, in sport everyday morality is suspended or temporarily set aside in order for the game to be played. Games in virtue of their logic require a kind of self-serving or egoistic attitude whereby the personal or team good not only conflicts with, but trumps the goods of the opponents. It is claimed, therefore that the underlying logic is conducive to, or perpetuates an ethic or moral atmosphere that is more egocentric and less mature in character. Their research suggests that the particular features of the context which they label 'the moral atmosphere', affect moral reasoning. In line with many of Kohlberg's critics they report that moral judgements vary between contexts and do not ubiquitously reflect the cognitive complexity of a subject's moral stage. Their observations in sport further support the belief that moral maturity is not reducible to stage specific cognitive capacities. A model of moral action must therefore include more than stage specific reasoning abilities. Shields and Bredemeier's (1995) model informed by these observations incorporates numerous other psychological constructs and processes thought to be involved in moral action. The model also attempts to identify and account for the effects of external factors such as 'moral atmosphere' and explain their effect on both the consistency and maturity of moral reasoning. Importantly and problematically moral judgement remains a necessary if not a sufficient condition of moral action.

As I have suggested, Shields and Bredemeier's (1995) model of moral action attempts to integrate the psychological and contextual concepts involved assuming that 'moral maturity' is a more context-sensitive phenomena than Kohlberg believed. To this end they construct a more eclectic account of moral character. In the model, influenced by Rest (1984), the psychological primacy of moral judgement in moral action gives way to four processes which form the foundation of moral character: 'interpretation', 'judgement', 'value selection' and 'implementing action'. These processes are not definitive psychic processes nor do they necessarily occur in this temporal sequence. They are more of a heuristic or analytic sequence. Shields and Bredemeier (1995: p. 85), however, argue that "... there is a kind of logical progression among the processes so that it makes sense-for purposes of analysis – to divide the processes leading to moral action in the manner described".

1. 'Interpretation' is the process whereby a person recognises the important moral cues present in the situation. Certain manifest features frame, define or characterise the given situation. These cues identify or delineate the injustice invoking some kind of moral response. Clearly not all

situations require moral responses; certain situations can be interpreted as requiring a tactical response, or a technical response of some kind.

Fundamental to the current argument is a disagreement with the model's apparent commitment to *(a priori)* criteria for moral situations so defined with reference to moral principles. Moral situations, it will be argued, arise not only in breach of abstract principles, but for certain persons in certain concrete situations. There is an important difference here that will be highlighted when discussing the example.

2. The second process commences if, during the first process, the situation has been designated a moral situation. The second process is the cognitive process of moral judgement — for example 'I should act so as to rectify or ensure moral correctness in this situation'. The kind of moral judgement one makes depends on ones moral maturity. The more morally mature a person is, the better the quality of moral judgement offered.

3. The third process of value-selection requires a choice that reflects the moral judgement and guides action. In sport there is often a value conflict between self-regarding and other-regarding values, namely winning and fairness. If, during the judgement phase, a mature moral judgement is made, then a moral value will be selected to guide action.

4. The final process is the implementation of a moral response, to act in a way that is appropriate and reflects the judgement made and the value chosen.

These four processes are in the tradition of a model forming only the first of three tiers. It describes the thought processes of any given person *qua* person in any given situation. The second tier aims to encapsulate the numerous contextual and psychological capacities that impact each of the steps in moral action. To this end, they tell us something about the particular person and are classified in one of the following categories: the *'context'*, *'personal competencies'* or *'ego processes'*. *'Contextual'* factors refer to the qualities of the given situation, for example the composition of the team, the perceived goals, the prevailing 'moral atmosphere' and so forth. *'Personal competencies'* refer to the qualities of the agent that influence the quality of their inter-pretation, judgement, value selection and action. The personal competencies to which Shields and Bredemeier refer are the cognitive schemes or structures that undergird general maturity and complexity of moral understanding and judgement. Finally, the *'ego-processes'* are a psychoanalytic feature first seen in Haan's (1978) theory of morality.

Haan's theory, although heavily influenced by Kohlberg, differed in certain important ways. She argued that moral maturity was characterised by the ability to construct fair and impartial solutions in a process of moral dialogue and not, as suggested by Kohlberg, to deduce such solutions impartially. Moreover, Haan argued that the maturity of moral judgements was significantly more context sensitive than Kohlberg argued. She believed that it was to be expected that intersubjective moral maturity scores would vary between experiments depending on the context. Haan explained the difference in the maturity of a person's moral judgement with reference to certain psychic capacities or *'ego processes'*. Haan argued that different situations, especially unfamiliar or new situations, might lead to stress. The *'ego processes'* describe the way in which contextually induced stress is managed or mis-managed and its effect on moral judgements. Stress is managed either by employing *'ego defensive'* techniques or *'ego coping'* techniques. Both techniques are employed in order to preserve, maintain and sustain one's self-image and/ or ego. *Coping strategies* are conducive to morally mature judgements, whereas *defensive strategies* such as denial and repression often result in less-adequate moral reasoning: one who remains in control, or is 'coping', is more likely to reason consistently, unhampered or unhindered by the contextual factors.

Shields and Bredemeier similarly adopt the *'ego processes'* explanation of inconsistency, agreeing that they play an important role in the consistent and mature display of morally mature action in sport. *'Ego processes'* are therefore incorporated into their model of moral action.

To summarise, then, the second tier is a categorisation of the factors distinct from, but including cognitive capacities involved in moral action.

The last tier is peculiar, inasmuch as it further deviates from the traditions of cognitive developmentalist theory. It does so by outlining a supplementary account of mediating traits or dispositions that determine or influence the outcome of the model. So far the only attributes or qualities of persons which have been discussed are the cognitive potentialities on a general level (i.e. second tier of the model.) The *mediating capacities* or virtues are qualities of a particular person. They have predictive qualities that tell us something about what a particular person might do. The main function of the virtues in the model is to facilitate mature moral action by positively influencing the processes already described. A person possessed of these virtues also has an increased chance of acting in a morally mature way, despite all the possible distractions — i.e. problems and factors presented previously. Somewhat worryingly, to this end only four virtues are thought to be sufficient — namely 'compassion', 'fairness', 'sportspersonship' and 'integrity'. Shields and Bredemeier take their definition of 'virtues' from Erikson (1964) and define them as strengths that animate moral principles. If present, these four according to Shields and Bredemeier (1995: p. 192) " ... facilitate the consistent display of moral action".

This model forms the basis of Shields and Bredemeier's (1995 p. 192–193) account of *character* and its development. Character, they argue, is "...the possession of those personal qualities or virtues that facilitate the consistent display of moral action". The model is a significant shift away from Kohlberg's reductive cognitivism. He did not favour of a description of character in terms of certain virtuous dispositions.

In fact, Kohlberg believed that *virtues* — commonly defined as fairly stable dispositions to think, feel and act in a certain way — did not exist. He cited Hartshorne and May's (1928) research into character traits in children as evidence for this belief. He disparagingly rejected an account of character in terms of a collection of virtues, referring to it as a relative, 'bag of virtues' approach. Instead he argued in a reductive vein (following Plato) that 'virtue' was one, and that its ideal form represented the principle of Justice. Moral concerns, he argued, are by definition coterminous with issues of justice. The truly virtuous live by the requirements of the principle of justice in all circumstances, thus displaying a fully mature and faultless moral character.

Prima facie, Shields and Bredemeier's model rejects such monism and opens the door to a variety of character virtues. Unfortunately, however, their role is merely that of instrumental facilitator of morally mature action. Their model retains and relies upon an implicit commitment to the notion of 'moral maturity' entailed in Kohlberg's formalistic predilections: namely that mature moral action is impartial and universal. Virtues breathe life into moral principles and allow their requirements to be enacted. The four virtues, if present, help us achieve these standards consistently in moral action. To a great extent the display of these virtues is praiseworthy only insofar as they facilitate mature moral action — virtue, as they say, is not its own reward.

In the next section I aim to develop some of these issues raised in relation to the soccer example cited earlier.

A contextual application of Shields' and Bredemeier's (1995) model of moral action

The first issue I wish to discuss is the player Kanu's own particular thought processes in this situation, and not Kanu *qua* human being or *qua* football player. Certain personal and contextual factors influence his choices and actions. Shields and Bredemeier (1995) provide a list of these — ego processes, role taking ability, moral maturity and so forth. These factors are fairly contextually sensitive and stress or situational ambiguity may effect the process in which they are involved. Kanu's action, according to Shields and Bredemeier (1995) is the outward manifestation of the interaction of these factors. Moreover, morally praiseworthy action is more likely to occur if Kanu also possesses the four virtues of compassion, fairness, sportspersonship and integrity.

Before developing my critique, the efficacy of Shields and Bredemeier's (1995) model in describing and evaluating Kanu's behaviour will be examined. To do this I make two fairly uncontroversial assumptions. The first assumption is that it is clear what Kanu ought to have done in this situation. The norm is to concede possession to the opposition. The second assumption, one that I have alluded to earlier, is that Kanu's actions were not calculated to exploit one of the accepted norms of football in order to score a goal.

To use Shields and Bredemeier's terminology, this situation was one that called for a moral response rather than the tactical response supplied by Kanu. In cognitive development terms, Kanu's actions were indicative of an *immature moral judgement*. Consequently, he did not implement in action the requirements of the principle of fairness that characterises mature judgement.

The first process in the model is interpretation. Kanu had to identify the nature of the situation and decide whether or not a response was required. According to Shields and Bredemeier's model, Kanu's interpretation was effected by certain 'contextual influences', 'personal competency influences' and 'ego-processing influences' (identified in the first tier of the model above).

'Contextual influences'

Kanu was likely to have experienced what Shields and Bredemeier call *situational ambiguity*. More time than usual passed between the injury and the resumption of play and this may have contributed to Kanu's subsequent action. Increasing ambiguity of context is negatively correlated with maturity of moral judgement in that context. Shields and Bredemeier suggest that time pressure, others' motives, rules and norms are particular contributors to ambiguity in the context of sport. With the benefit of hindsight, it is clear that Kanu misread his team-mate's motive in throwing the ball down the line, and/or failed to understand the conventions and norms of soccer in relation to this situation. Shields and Bredemeier (1995 p. 95) argue that:

> When perceptions of moral meaning are confused, distorted, or unclear, decisions about rights and responsibilities may be tentative or based on erroneous assumptions.

It is reasonable to suggest that for Kanu the situation was ambiguous. He may have misread the situation and thus failed to recognise his team-mates intentions. His eventual moral failing may therefore be attributable to a failure to appreciate fully the nature of the situation because of its ambiguity.

'Personal competencies'

In this case Kanu's own 'personal competencies' may have contributed to his moral failing. Shields and Bredemeier suggest that morally mature action requires the actor to see things from others' points of view (*role-taking*) and through co-ordination of these other views to construct a third person perspective of the situation (*perspective-taking*). Role-taking is both cognitive and affective inasmuch that Kanu needed to understand how others saw the structure of the situation and, in addition, how they felt about the situation. Perspective-taking is the process through which Kanu attempts to equalise or relate his own perspective on the situation with the other parties involved. Again, viewing the incident from the outside and at the same time rejecting any pre-meditation on Kanu's behalf, there seems to be a significant absence, at least for this particular incident, in role-taking and perspective-taking competency.

'Ego-processing'

Shields and Bredemeier (1995) identify two 'ego-processes' that primarily facilitate interpretation: *'tolerance of ambiguity'* and *'empathy'*. The former is given short shrift and is described only in terms of being able to 'cope' with the ambiguities of sport described earlier. This limited explanation of the nature of the 'ego-processes' is problematic. It is in response to, and in support of, such a limited account that the four virtues play a significant and important role. Empathy, on the other hand, receives more satisfactory analysis. Empathy is given the role of moral motivator; its task is to move a person from their 'take' on the situation to a moral response. Shields and Bredemeier (1995: p. 105) argue that empathy is critical to the interpretative process "...because it engages the person in the context, motivates further moral processing, and ultimately provides a check on the more cognitive forms of guidance to moral action". Here again, Kanu failed miserably: he seemingly failed to 'tolerate' the ambiguity of the situation, and in lay terms he 'read it the wrong way'. It seems therefore that 'empathy' would not have helped him here, because he actually misread the situation. In fact empathy, taken as a motivating capacity, would only move him to act inappropriately.

It is possible to develop these remarks further to discuss the role of 'judgement', 'value selection' and 'action' in Kanu's behaviour. I believe, however, that examination of the first process, namely *interpretation*, is sufficient to highlight its flaw in relation to this example. I have described, using the model, how such a failure may be attributed to incorrect interpretation. Correct interpretation is fundamentally important for moral action; in fact it is a necessary condition for its occurrence. For Shields and

Bredemeier (1995), morally mature action cannot proceed in the absence of correct interpretation. Moreover, a moral intention is a necessary but not sufficient condition of morally mature action. Action can only be considered morally mature if it meets both of the following:

1. it is informed by a mature moral judgement.

2. it is intended to reflect the requirements of moral principles.

A failure to correctly interpret the situation necessarily rules out morally mature action because such action cannot meet both of the above require-ments. For Shields and Bredemeier, Kanu could be praised on moral grounds for refraining from taking advantage of the situation *only* if he fully understood that taking advantage transgressed the principle of fairness. Inaction does not count as morally right if the reason behind it is physical incapacity, ineptitude or apathy. Given the theoretical foundations of this model, it is clear that inadequate interpretation counts as a moral failing because correct interpretation is a necessary, but not sufficient, condition for mature moral action.

There are two issues that I want to raise in relation to the foregoing discussion. First, "character" is not helpfully reduced to the instrumental nature of Shields and Bredemeier's account. Dispositions and virtues have a central rather than a peripheral role in moral action. A person's action is a reflection of their character, they tend to behave in a characteristic fashion, we describe them according to their characteristics and their character is partly predictive of their actions. Character determines what they see, how they feel about things and what action they may take. Knowing something about their character tells us about the sort of person they are. The question concerning Kanu is whether he behaved characteristically or out of character. If he behaved uncharacteristically, then why?

The answer may be revealed in light of a less systematic account of character. The second issue raises some questions about the development of character itself. Insight into Kanu's actions may be provided through examining of the way one comes to learn and adopt certain conventions and values in particular cases – in this case football.

Re-describing character

Blum (1994: p. 30) argues that "one of the most important differences between people is between those who miss and those who see various moral features of situations confronting them". This difference is one attributable to a difference in character. It is not that certain people see moral situations and others do not, that some see injustice and others are blind to injustice. It may be true that some are more sensitive to injustice than others but some may be more sensitive to cruelty, love, compassion, courage, dishonesty and recklessness. Either way, it depends on the kind of person they are, the values they hold, the dispositions that form their character as well as the situation they are in. Pincoffs (1986: p. 21) makes the point clearly: moral problems, he says, arise only in opposition to any standards or ideals that one has — 'No standards or ideals no problems'. In the model there is a failure to recognise the role of a person's character or virtues in this sense in moral action. Far from a peripheral instrumental role, character virtues have a central and definitive role.

Shields and Bredemeier's account of 'interpreting a situation' as their first process is problematic. The situation I described previously is a fairly common one in football matches all over Britain and the world. Indeed, it is a kind of occurrence that may happen numerous times within a particular game. Almost invariably, though, the usual conventions are followed. It is an empirical question whether or not Kanu behaved appropriately, and it is clear that he did not. The fact that Kanu failed to act in accordance with convention reveals some kind of failure on his behalf. The most logical explanation according to Shields and Bredemeier's model is that Kanu failed to interpret the situation correctly. He did not deduce from the sensory cues available the nature of the situation unfolding. The ambiguous cues (normally one throws the ball to a team-mate and not to the opponents when returning the ball to the field of play) militates against the right course of action. Kanu, might have been able to morally recover the situation if he had been able to 'see things from a different perspective' — to 'take the role' of one of the other opponents or to muster some 'empathy' for his opponents, therefore inhibiting him acting against the convention in this case.

At issue here is what Kanu, as a player in the situation is faced with: what values shape his perceptions of the situation and subsequently guide his action? Character is involved in construction of situations, and not only action in them. Shields and Bredemeier pay lip service to this idea by discussing 'empathy' and 'ego-processing' influences such as 'tolerance of ambiguity' that would collectively facilitate mature interpretation. The problem however, is that the description given by Shields and Bredemeier suggests that when a person arrives in, or is confronted by, a given situation and proceeds to react to it, the quality of the reaction depends on certain other factors like 'role taking ability' and 'empathy'.

A more convincing description is given in reference to Pincoffs (1986). It is likely that there was no moral problem, no dilemma, no issue here for Kanu; and not because he failed to interpret maturely, make a mature judgement, choose the right value to guide action or implement his moral judgement. Conversely, it is not having failed to identify the salient cues as having moral significance that prevented Kanu from making a moral judgement, choosing a value and acting accordingly. Kanu simply did not see that what was unfolding in front of him called for a different response to what is the normal tactical response demanded in soccer. It is essentially a 'character flaw' on Kanu's part. He really should know the conventions and recognise what should be done when such a situation arises.

But before I discuss Kanu's character flaw, I want to reiterate that the nature of the moral failing was not an inability to recognise a situation where he ought to have acted impartially rather than selfishly. Neither was it a result of immaturity of moral judgement or retarded moral judgement brought on by the contours of the situation.

Kanu, having been shown the error of his ways was remorseful and apologetic. He was described as 'bemused', and the significance of the situation had to be explained to him by his team-mates. His Manager later suggested that Kanu was new to the country and simply did not know what was going on. If it was possible to intervene and explain the situation to Kanu at the moment it occurred, I believe that he would have acted fairly. He would not, with full knowledge of the situation, have attempted to take advantage and act in an apparently devious and unfair way. It may be helpful to re-state my main objections as a kind of 'working summary'. The first is that that moral failings are not all attributed to a failure to make mature moral judgements, a fact that I have illustrated in the course of this example. Secondly, I have suggested that certain situations or moral problems arise for certain people, and the breadth and depth of the moral mire depends partly on their character and identity.

The central question for Shields and Bredemeier (1995), and one that dominates rule-based ethical theories, is why a person fails to apply the requirements of a certain moral principles. Shields and Bredemeier have illustrated, through their model of moral action, certain possible reasons for his failure. They have also, albeit briefly and inadequately, suggested how the possession of certain virtues will reduce the chance of such moral failure. Their focus, however, remains on 'right' action determined by moral principles. In this case 'fairness rules', and Kanu's own personal qualities or characteristics are instrumentally important if he is to recognise a moral situation and come to act morally in response to it.

An alternative description casts the moral agent in terms of character as a collection of certain virtuous dispositions. Audi (1997: p. 160) suggests that:

Moral character is largely an interconnected set of traits, such as honesty, fairness and fidelity, which in turn, are largely deep-seated dispositions to do certain things for an appropriate range of reasons.

These virtues — honesty, fairness, fidelity — names are familiar to most. It is both their number and centrality in moral action that is disputed. A person who possesses a certain kind of virtue is a person who not only acts in accordance with that virtue, but must also firstly recognise a certain situation and be motivated to act in the situation. To this extent, Rorty (1988: p. 316) describes virtues as dispositions which "...organise perceptions and interpretations of situations in such a way as to elicit appropriate habits and actions". Moreover, as Flanagan (1991) argues, and reinforcing the earlier virtue-criticism from Pincoffs and Blum, the nature of the situation one faces is partly designated or defined theoretically by the kind of dispositions one has and the kind of person one is.

A person's character partly determines the kinds of moral problems and situations he or she may come across. As for Kanu, he failed to act correctly in this situation because of a character flaw. The exact nature of his character flaw is uncertain, but one would suggest that his flaw may be partly attributed to the new and unfamiliar situation in which he found himself. Kanu might have lacked concentration, attention, sensitivity or even knowledge of convention. These may not at first sight count as *moral* qualities, particularly for Shields and Bredemeier (1995), because they lack the required universal or impartial content. However, if Kanu is characteristically inattentive, a quality that characteristically prohibits him form acting in an appropriate way, it is right to suggest that this is a character flaw. Blum (1994) is particularly informative on this point. He argues that *moral perception*, seeing the moral contours of the situation, is a good in its own right. Conversely then, a failure to do so is a flaw, one of which Kanu is guilty.

More must be said here about how Kanu comes to act in accordance with convention in this case. This is a point about how one learns how to do the right thing at the right time and in the right way. Rorty (1993: p. 38) argues that virtues are "like other habits and dispositions, developed by practice and imitation". Furthermore, as Alderman (1997: p. 156) suggests, using football as an example:

> ... one learns to be virtuous the same way as one learns to cook, dance, play football and so forth, and that is by imitating people who are good at those sorts of things. Since being moral means learning how to do the right thing, it seems to me not at all logically odd to argue that learning how to be moral is strictly analogous to all other cases of *learning how to*. Rules, then are secondary in the first place insofar as they are not necessary to learn how to be moral. ... moral agents learn best when they act like people who exemplify what is expected of them.

It is not inconceivable that Kanu had not yet experienced this situation. His failure might be that he simply was not aware of the convention. It would take only a few occasions of observing what is normally done in this or similar kinds of situation for Kanu himself to note the convention and follow it. This may be an alternative explanation to his character flaws.

It might be objected that Kanu *must* have known the convention, that he could not have reached his age and experience without coming across such a situation before. Kanu *should* have known what was the appropriate thing to do. He acted inappropriately because of a character flaw — not injustice or immature reasoning, but lack of sensitivity or impatience or failure to concentrate. Such failings are not morally neutral if they lead to morally inappropriate behaviour; neither is their absence simply instrumental.

There is another reason why we should look to the convention of football and to Kanu's appreciation of them. It is observation, familiarisation and imitation of the norms and conventions, rather than abstract principles, that will inform Kanu about appropriate action. Knowing and understanding the principle of fairness alone will not help guide action in this situation. Being morally mature is similarly insufficient on the same grounds. Football is a rule-governed activity and these rules, as well as the way football is conventionally played, create moral situations. It is the rules and conventions of football, therefore, that define the fair and right course of action in each context. Abstract principles will not tell Kanu that he should leave the ball alone until the opposition has regained control of it. It is knowledge of *football* conventions that allow and direct us to act fairly and tell us how to act fairly *in football*.

Conclusion

I have attempted to illustrate how the most comprehensive and sophisticated model of moral action in the psychological literature, that of Shields and Bredemeier, is flawed with reference to its utility in describing moral actors and their moral actions in sport.

In contrast to Shields and Bredemeier, I argue that character virtues define the kinds of moral problems a person will see, and treat their role is not simply instrumentally connected with the facilitation of mature impartial moral judgements. This instrumental view of the virtues is partly attributed to an account of morality that identifies moral problems *a priori* as continued to those that raise questions of justice and fairness and demand impartial and universal responses. The methodology employed inherits the epistemological commitments of the deontological ethical theory on which it is based. The fairness or just qualities of the agents' actions are what counts. As such, moral concerns are reduced to fairness and justice. The result is that disposition to act honestly and compassionately is re-described as instrumental in ensuring just and fair action. Consequently, differences in moral personalities are ignored so long as each person exhibits morally mature action.

I have argued that moral character begins and ends with virtues. They are neither peripheral nor instrumental, but definitive of moral action.

References

Alderman, H. (1997) 'By virtue of a virtue', in D. Statman (ed) *Virtue ethics. A critical reader*. Edinburgh: Edinburgh University Press.

Audi, R. (1997) *Moral knowledge and ethical character*. Oxford: Oxford University Press.

Bredemeier, B. J. and Shields, D. L. (1984) 'Divergence in moral reasoning about sports and everyday life" *Sociology of Sport Journal* Vol. 1: pp. 348–357.

Bredemeier, B. J. and Shields, D. L. (1986a) 'Athletic aggression: An issue of contextual morality', *Sociology of Sport Journal*, 3: p. 15–28.

Bredemeier, B. J. and Shields, D. L. (1986b) 'Moral growth among athletes and non-athletes: A comparative analysis', *Journal of Genetic Psychology*, 147: pp. 7–18.

Blum, L. A (1994) *Moral perception and particularity*. Cambridge: Cambridge University Press.

Flanagan, O. (1991) *Varieties of moral personality. Ethics and psychological realism*. London: Harvard University Press.

Haan, N. (1978) 'Two moralities in action contexts: Relationship to thought, ego regulation, and development', *Journal of Personality and Social Psychology*, 36: pp. 286–305.

Hartshorne, H. and May, M. A. (1928) *Studies in the nature of character*. New York: MacMillan.

Kohlberg, L. (1981) *Essays on moral development. Vol. 1, The philosophy of moral Development*. San Francisco: Harper and Row.

Kohlberg, L. (1984) *Essays on moral development. Vol. 2, The psychology of moral development*. San Francisco: Harper and Row'

Pincoffs, E. L. (1986) *Quandaries and virtues, against reductivism in ethics*. Kansas: Kansas University Press.

Piaget, J. (1932) *The moral judgement of the child*. London, Routledge and Keegan Paul.

Rorty, A. M (1988) *Mind in action, essays in the philosophy of mind*. Boston: Beacon Press.

Shields, D. L. L., and Bredemeier, B. J. L. (1995) *Character development and physical activity*. Champaign, IL: Human Kinetics.

Warnock, G. J. (1983) *Contemporary moral philosophy*. London: Macmillan.

The Ethos of the Game:
Representations of the Good Game and the Good Player among Junior Football Players in Sweden

Matz Franzén
Department of Sociology, Uppsala University

Per Nilsson
Department of Curriculum Studies and Communication, Stockholm Institute of Education (Sweden)

Tomas Peterson
Department of Sociology, University of Lund

Introduction

Discussions relating to the characteristics and expressions of good sport are carried on in both the private and public sphere and the basis for them varies considerably. The dialogue may, for example, centre around the nature of good competition; that a special match or competition was particularly even, exciting and entertaining; that the outcome of the fight was for a long time uncertain, perhaps swaying back and forth; that the result was unexpected or that the performances were of an unusually high standard. Talk of good sport may further refer to what may be called taste in sport, and concern national stereotypes; whether French finesse is preferable to British fighting spirit, German efficiency or Scandinavian coolness. Questions concerning the existence of good sport therefore are many and varied.

The fact that these (and probably still more) discussions are in progress about what is to be regarded as good and first-rate sport is interesting in itself. This shows that people are convinced something that might be designated good sport can be identified, furthermore that this good sport is also considered to be worth arguing, struggling and fighting for. We also see how people (viewed as individuals or groups) and institutions (for example, scientific institutions, voluntary organisations, government and municipal authorities, companies, media) in our society take positions on the issue of what is good sport. Together, they form a social world — the world of sport — in which battles are fought for market shares, preferential rights of interpretation, prestige, power and, not least, the favour of the practitioners.

Theoretical framework

The theoretical platform for this paper will be the French sociologist Pierre Bourdieu's theory of practice, and in particular his notion of the social field. As a society becomes highly differentiated, a number of relatively autonomous microcosm, or fields, develop. A *social field*, in terms of Bourdieu, can be defined as *a system of relations between positions occupied by specialised agents and institutions that struggle over something they all find important* (Fornäs, 1995: 96).

According to Bourdieu, however, a social field is not only constituted of opposing positions, struggling agents and differing wills, but of shared presuppositions as well. Within a social field there are particular tacit understandings about what the practice within the field is about, as well as beliefs that make people feel their actions and efforts are worth while. These implicit commitments to the game of sport are collectively shared, and together they will produce a social definition of sport and a logic of practice. Hence, within the world of sports (and certain spheres in this world) there are hidden, non-verbal, understandings of the game that are taken for granted, agreements which the participants have to follow if they want to play the game, i.e. a *doxa* accepted by all as self-evident (Bourdieu, 1998: pp. 66-67).

To talk about a logic of practice is to talk about those historically determined regularities of the game — written into the game as possibilities and objective demands — that impose themselves on people who enter the field and that have dispositions as their basis (Bourdieu, 1998: pp. 133-34). The good player's habitus (i.e. the dispositions of the socialised player's body) directs (in the double sense of the word) his or her practices and thoughts like a force ("it is stronger than I"), but without mechanically constraining him or her; it also guides his or her action like a logic of necessity ("there is nothing else I can do", "I can do no differently") (Bourdieu, 1998: pp. 133-34). This means that practice has a logic, which is not that of logic, or of the logician (Bourdieu, 1998: 82). In other words, then, the ethos of the game can be described as a practical sense, a feel for the game. The ethos of the game is what gives the game its sense. It is the notion of the socially constituted (the conquered, constructed and confirmed) views of the good game and the good players.

When these properties specific to the field are perceived and recognised by social agents — i.e. social agents which are endowed with the categories of perception and appreciation permitting them to perceive, know and recognise them — the properties become symbolically efficient within the field. In fact, one can say that the properties become a *symbolic capital* that responds to socially constituted "collective expectations" and beliefs (Bourdieu, 1998: pp. 102-04) within the field. Therefore, connected to this doxa there is also a *symbolic violence*, i.e. the violence which is exercised upon a social agent with his or her complicity (Bourdieu and Wacquant, 1992: pp. 167).

The present study

The main purpose of this paper is to analyse the ethos of the football game. More precisely, the aim is (1) to describe socially constituted views of the good game and the good player among young football players in Sweden, and (2) to examine present gender differences in this respect.

In an attempt to clarify a number of issues concerning the role of football in young people's lives, a nation-wide longitudinal study was carried out. The population covered a total of 1,000 football playing girls and boys at the age of 13. Data were collected chiefly with questionnaires and have in this paper been analysed with factor analysis.

Results: The Good Footballer (Matrix 1)

The purpose of the analysis of factors is to find reasonable and relevant simplifications of three major batteries of attitudes[1] in the study. The first of these asks what characterises a good football player (Matrix 1: Pl 003—Pl 019, a total of 17 items).

A previous study of the correlation matrix in question, carried out item by item (Pl 3-19) showed the occurrence of a very complex pattern. The factor analyses confirm this conclusion. Seventeen items produce five factors. That is to say, the material can be reduced to five dimensions that are independent of each other.

The rotated factor analysis (varimax) is considerably easier to interpret in this context than the primary factor analysis, and for this reason we start from the former. As stated, five factors can be identified. Together they represent more than half of the variance in the material. Factor 1 is in a class of its own, having almost 25% of the variance, in comparison with 30% for the other four.

Can the factors be interpreted in a meaningful way? Is it possible to capture the characteristics that distinguish a good footballer from the young person's point of view?

Factor 1 as such is particularly interesting. Naturally on account of its central position in the complex of attitudes, but also because only two of the four items included have strong factor loadings. It is a question of being a good team player, never giving up and doing one's best all the time. The two items with a weaker factor loading refer to agreement with the claims "to be persistent and prepared to train" and "to manage the task given". Hence, all in all, it is very much a question of *loyalty to the team*. Naturally never giving up concerns will power, however it appears to be for the sake of the team one should do one's best all the time. This item has the strongest factor loading of those included in Factor 1. A good footballer is thus first and foremost a team player, which furthermore is more a matter of attitude than technical football skill. It could be generally designated *the team play factor.*

Table 1   The good footballer
                 (Matrix 1: PI 003 — PI 019, a total of 17 items)

Item	F1	F2	F3	F4	F5
Pl 003	.62	-.07	.30	.22	.14
Pl 008	.48	.40	-.15	-.04	.27
Pl 009	.46	.29	.16	.40	.04
Pl 014	.74	.24	.07	.02	.07
Pl 017	.23	.66	.18	.09	-.02
Pl 018	.06	.71	.26	.06	-.03
Pl 019	.10	.58	.19	.08	.24
Pl 005	.14	.23	.77	.00	.10
Pl 010	.05	.27	.76	.14	.02
Pl 016	.50	.18	.51	.08	.06
Pl 006	.17	.07	.29	.64	.06
Pl 011	.07	.02	.00	.75	.02
Pl 012	-.03	.38	-.07	.65	.10
Pl 004	.29	-.11	-.20	.20	.54
Pl 007	.27	.03	.17	.31	.65
Pl 013	.20	.05	.08	.04	.65
Pl 015	.08	.24	.09	.22	.50
Eigenvalues	4.16	1.53	1.44	1.05	1.02
Variance-%	24.5	9.0	8.5	6.2	6.0

However, pure will power should not be over-emphasized regarding Factor 1. The item implying agreement that a good footballer is ingenious, sees openings in the game, and is good at passing the ball — all technical football skills — are equally strong loadings in the factor as two of the items included in it. However, this has been moved to Factor 3 since it has a somewhat stronger factor loading there than in Factor 1.

In *Factor 2*, three items have stronger factor loadings (Play 017-019). The factor clearly concerns will power and could be aptly called *the will factor.* Compared with Factor 1 more individual qualities are involved (in turn): to be capable of running a lot on the field, to be "best when it really matters" and also "to help oneself" on the pitch. Will power further points in the direction of the will to win. Will power without an objective is rather meaningless.

In other words, it could be said that if the will factor points to fostering for competition, the team spirit factor has more to do with fostering in an association.

At the same time, to keep to the direct question here, both constitute components of what is a good football player for our young people — and, of course, not just for them. The result suggests that young people — with different variations and emphasis, which remain to be analysed — have taken on board a great deal of adult opinion about the meaning of football. The plausibility of such a conclusion is underscored by what emerges in connection with an examination of the remaining five factors. The conclusion is interesting because it is at the same time based on a result showing that what constitutes a good footballer is rather complex.

Factor 3 has three strong factor loadings. Two of them are very strong (at least seen from the variations of the present material). Both concern technical proficiency that is furthermore usually associated with a footballer player's individual skill, namely to have good and skilful control of the ball as well as a more specific proficiency: to be good at dribbling. The latter skill may be considered a subset of the former, which also concerns being able to trap, head and pass the ball. The factor may be christened *the ball skill factor.*

Hence, imaginative play — which is what item 16 captures — has a strong factor loading in both Factor 1 and Factor 3. At the same time, this characteristic might be considered the bridge between the game's more collective and individual aspects, that is to say what the team play factor and ball skill factor are about. In any case, together these two factors capture the skill the game of football requires and promotes but as if it were played without an opposing team. Given the existence of the opposing team, it becomes essential to take note of the will power factor, Factor 2, both for the researcher and the trainer. All in all, these three factors capture a great deal of what we intuitively associate with a good footballer.

What then do the two remaining factors concern? Although they are less central, even so they capture aspects of the game of football that are interesting. Three items have strong factor loadings in *Factor 4*. They concern characteristics that are not directly — that is to say immediately — of importance but are of importance in the long term for a football team to function. It is namely a question of being a good "mate", of being honest and fair on the field and also of taking responsibility for one's teammates there. We could nostalgically (in best 1950s style) christen the factor *the fair play factor*.

What then remains for *Factor 5*? A collection of characteristics that can be summed up as *the toughness factor*. Just as Factor 2, Factor 5 reflects the fact that football is played against an adversary, and also that a *direct fight* for the ball is built into the game. Agreement about the importance of being "rather nasty" on the field and "not to step aside when tackled" (Pl 007 and 013) give really strong factor loadings in this context. Two characteristics that open onto the mental aspect of toughness give slightly weaker factor loadings: not losing one's temper, nor to flare up or whine is one, whereas to be able to withstand "psyching out" on the field is the other — two factors that are, not unexpectedly, closely related.

All in all, our young footballers show they have a remarkably mature — that is to say differentiated — picture of what constitutes a good footballer. First and foremost it is a case of being a good team player, the truly central factor in our young footballers' view regarding what is required of them. After that they have to be skilful with the ball, preferably skilful at the game also, and also have the will to win. Finally, it is a case of being both fair and tough.

Of course we can expect to find variations among our young people concerning what are the most important characteristics for them. For instance, an examination has not yet been carried out regarding those for whom toughness is of central importance. We can expect interesting differences depending on the sex of the player, the position of the team in the league system, the aims of the trainer, and so on. The results of the factor analysis have prepared the way for such an analysis.

Different trends by gender

In the continued analysis it is fitting to initially disregard the importance of gender difference for what constitutes a good footballer, that is to say to start from the most cohesive picture the material demonstrates. But that is easier said than done. The fact that the material is fundamentally characterised by gender imbalance — the proportion of boy players is double that of girl players — points towards this: the material as a whole is not gender neutral even in its basic statistical distribution. Even though the aggregate material can be said to give the most cohesive picture and to that extent may be the basis for the continued analysis, it is fitting already at this point to carry out an introductory examination of gender differences in the perception of a good footballer.

To capture the gender differences to some extent, the aggregate result here will serve as a yardstick. The results of the same factor analysis for the respective sexes will simply be compared on the basis of what we have reported above. In order to limit the comparisons to real essentials and not be long-winded, the results are not reproduced in tables. Instead, we bear in mind the factors that are distinguishable and their respective ranking. Regarding identification of the factors' content, we limit further attention to items with really strong factor loadings. A procedure of this nature should suffice to capture differences in trends by gender and, at the same time, facilitate the actual comparison.

If the material is then divided by gender, an interesting difference emerges. The pattern in the boys' ideas of a good footballer is less complex; it can thus be summed up in four dimensions as opposed to the girls' five. However, it is worth considering first, the material as a whole.

Boys

The factor analysis distinguishes not five but four factors underlying the boys' perception of the good footballer. This shows arbitrariness in the actual analysis procedure that is connected with the convention of only fully reporting factor loadings for factor items with a lowest value of 1.0. It is ultimately this convention that makes us obtain four factors to work with on the part of the boys.

The contribution to the variance of the four factors distinguished is almost 50%, at the same time as the first factor represents more than half the contribution. The factor **F1b**'s value is also 4.49 while the remaining factors are at a much lower level, or in downward order: 1.46, 1.44 and 1.05 (F2-4b).

What does F1b represent? Its content largely tallies with what we found in F2 above. Thus, for the boys, *ball skill* was the most important characteristic regarding what constitutes a good footballer. It is worth noting that this factor carries at least as great weight as the other three. If we then take a look at F2b it chiefly resembles F1 above, but without being really equivalent to it. They have in common agreement concerning the importance of never giving up, doing one's best on the field (Pl 014). Agreement about being persistent and willing to train gives a really high factor loading. **F2b** concerns the importance of a strong will in the individual player, both in training and during a match. In brief: a *will factor*. It tallies in fact to a large extent with F2 above, and for this reason the will factor designation can also be used here. (Pl 017 and Pl 019 that are included in F2 are also to be found in F2b, albeit with weaker factor loadings.) The third factor for the boys (**F3b**) tallies to a considerable extent with the *fair play factor* F4. Finally, the fourth factor (**F4b**) largely corresponds to F5 above: the importance of *toughness* in a good footballer. The boys follow the general pattern in the material with two important exceptions. On the one hand they strongly *overemphasise* individual skill, on the other hand they *underemphasise* even more strongly the game's collective element, that is to say what emerged above as the team play factor (F1).

Overall, boys distinguish themselves first and foremost through the relative position of importance given to the factors. With them, there is primarily an emphasis on individual skill, and also on the will power and toughness of the good footballer — clearly at the expense of team play. Regarding the importance of playing fair, there is on the other hand no difference in relation to the survey material as a whole.

Girls

As has already been mentioned, five factors can be distinguished for the girls. Taken together they represent almost 55% of the variance. In relation to each other they are not as strongly separate as in the case of the boys (or as for the whole material), which the following series of eigenvalues shows: 3.68, 1.65, –1.1, 1.18 and 1.15 respectively (F1—5b). What do the factors concern when we look at those for the girls only?

The pattern that emerges surprises by deviating in important respects from what is obviously expected. The strongest factor for the girls tallies more with the strongest factor for the boys than generally applies in the material. On the part of the girls also there is reason to mention ball *skill* (Pl 005 and 010 have strong factor loadings), although perhaps not as a factor, because **F1g** also includes the item of being "best when it really matters" with a very strong factor loading (.72). If we take a look at **F2g** we see an item with a very strong factor loading, namely agreement with the importance of a good footballer never giving up, giving of his/her best (.80). A quality closely related to common sense has a relatively strong factor loading, that of being persistent and willing to train (.57), which points to a will factor, except that the characteristic of being ingenious, seeing openings in the game and being able to make good passes, have equally strong factor loadings (.54). Thus, the girls couple *persistence with some creativity* as though will power was not sufficient in itself. So far the girls in contrast to the boys show a qualitatively different profile of the good footballer in that the factor loadings differ. What to call the factors is not self-evident; nor is it perhaps as important as to point to the significance of gender differences in the perception of the good footballer.

However, in F3g we recognise one factor that largely tallies with *the fair play factor* (F4), albeit without a strong element of being a good mate within that factor. Instead, it is primarily a case of being honest and fair on the field and taking responsibility for one's teammates there. The girls continue to surprise us in **F4g** by stressing characteristics of the good footballer that are in no way usually associated with any form of girl culture. The following two characteristics have strong factor loadings: to be able to withstand "psyching out" on the field and also to be "rather nasty" (.64 and .67 respectively). The characteristic of neither losing one's temper, flaring up nor whining (.61) can be added to the strong emphasis on the value of both giving and taking on the field in the girls' image of the good footballer. *Toughness* is clearly valued by the girls in the ideal player. F4g resembles very much the toughness factor F5. Lastly, **F5g** in the girls' perception of the good footballer. The factor has only one characteristic with a really strong factor loading: to be a good mate (.77). There is also a factor loading for the characteristic of being a good team player in the factor (.53). This factor could perhaps be called *the solidarity or collective factor.*

In general, the girls demonstrate a perception of the good footballer that is partly the opposite of the general perception and the boys' perception. Strangely enough, the team play factor is not evident in the girls' perception either. Technical skill and will power are important characteristics of the good footballer for them too, followed by the moral qualities of being fair but also tough. It is not until after these characteristics have been ranked that a characteristic slightly resembling the team play factor appears, namely the solidarity factor, which, however, more clearly concerns being a good mate than a good team player.

The fact that the team play factor is the most important when we examine the whole material, but is hardly identifiable at all when the material is divided by gender, must be considered an unexpected result. The more exact importance of the team play factor is something for future analyses to discover.

Conclusions

To summarise, the data show that images of the good game and the good football player are constructed in an ongoing contest between struggling agents and differing wills. The findings indicate that requirements and preferences of the senior game are incorporated into a physical preparedness for action. These ideas, however, are represented very differently among girls and boys.

Notes

[1] If we should speak of representations, value patterns, attitudes or anything else in the context — this is a theoretical issue that is not discussed in this paper. The question of attitude, attitude matrix and corresponding designations for attitudes in continuation primarily have a technical-methodical meaning.

[2] It should be noted that the attitude pattern in the individual case may be and probably is simpler than that of the aggregate level, where it is more a question of the collective representation of (here) the good football player of the whole group. The factor analysis is a first step towards — a preparation of — a study of how attitudes vary among young people/ players.

References

Bourdieu, P. and Wacquant, L. J. D. (1992) *An invitation to reflexive sociology*. Cambridge: Polity Press.

Bourdieu, P. (1998) *Practical reason. On the theory of action*. Cambridge: Polity Press.

Fornäs, J. (1995) *Cultural theory and late modernity*. London: Sgae Publications.

Appendix

The rotated factor analysis (varimax)

Factor 1	The team play factor
Factor 2	The will factor
Factor 3	The ball skill factor
Factor 4	The fair play factor
Factor 5	The toughness factor

Different trends by gender — Boys

Factor 1	The ball skill factor
Factor 2	The will factor
Factor 3	The fair play factor
Factor 4	The toughness factor

Different trends by gender — Girls

Factor 1	The ball skill/best when it matters
Factor 2	The persistence/ creativity factor
Factor 3	The fair play factor
Factor 4	The toughness factor
Factor 5	The togetherness factor

Ethical Leisure: The 'Dark" and the 'Deviant" Disambiguated

Heather Sheridan

Cheltenham and Gloucester College of Higher Education (UK)

Introduction

Much of the literature on the conceptualisation of leisure has focused on its positive benefits (Driver *et al.*, 1991). Nevertheless, some writers have considered the more negative aspects of leisure: Becker (1963, cited in Dorn and South, 1989) on the marijuana user; Young (1973, in Taylor and Taylor, 1973) on drug sub-cultures; Downes *et al.* (1976, quoted in Bruce and Johnson, 1992: p. 204) on betting as a form of "safe deviance"; Stebbins (1997: p. 20) on the "thrills of deviant activity" such as vandalism and shoplifting. In a conference presentation entitled "The significance of serial killing for leisure studies", Rojek (1996) suggests that leisure theorists should study what he refers to as the "dark side" of leisure. In addition to serial killing, the kinds of activities, experiences and behaviours that Rojek characterises as the "dark side" of leisure, or "dark leisure", include substance abuse, illegal sex rings, domestic violence, paedophilia, trespassing and graffiti.

In response to this challenge to study "dark leisure", the aim of this paper is to see whether conceptual sense can be made of "dark leisure". Rojek (1988: p. 31) suggests that there is a dearth of research on "deviant leisure" even though we live in societies where there is widespread leisure-related illegal behaviour such as drug-use, home cassette taping, shoplifting, and participating in illegal sexual activity. Rojek (1995) claims that although society does acknowledge deviant leisure behaviour it is only to castigate and renounce it. "Normal" leisure is not associated with taking mind-altering drugs, theft, trespass, vandalism or sadistic sexual behaviour. Rojek (1988: p. 31) explains why studying deviant leisure is important:

Through studying what society defines as unlawful, disorderly and offensive, we expose the rule and form of "the normal" in the regulation of leisure conduct.

This paper seeks to investigate whether (or not) conceptual sense can be made of "dark leisure". In the process, a greater insight into, and fuller understanding of both the negative and positive aspects of leisure may be provided.

The structure of the remainder of the paper is as follows. Much of the literature that may contribute to the conceptualisation of "dark leisure" employs the term "deviant". To see whether conceptual sense can be made of "dark leisure", first, the relationship between the terms "deviant" and "dark" is briefly explored. The exploration concludes that in order to decide whether conceptual sense can be made of "dark leisure" we need to be clear about what leisure is. Four different ways of conceptualising leisure are then considered, and dismissed as inadequate since none pay sufficient attention to the content and quality of leisure. An alternative, Neo-Aristotelian conceptualisation of leisure is contextualised in terms of MacIntyre's (1981) conception of social practices. This is followed by an exploration of the notion of "pleasure" in terms of a critique of hedonistic utilitarianism from a Neo-Aristotelian perspective to facilitate a greater understanding of the relationship between leisure, pleasure, social practices and "dark leisure". McNamee's (1994: p. 293) claim that "the pursuit of pleasure itself does not demarcate any special class of activities except those logically thus defined" is elaborated upon. The implication in MacIntyre's (1981) thesis is that it is the character of the activities that is important. If peoples' activities are bad or base then their lives will be bad or base. If peoples' lives are bad or base, it follows that they are not living meaningful and worthwhile lives. Thus, they are not living a 'good' life within the context of MacIntyre's (1981) conception of social practices. It is concluded that the activities considered as possible candidates for conceptualising "dark leisure" cannot be conceived of as leisure. It follows that if they cannot first be conceived of as leisure they cannot then be conceived of as "dark leisure" or any sort of leisure for that matter. Thus, from the same standpoint, it is also concluded that Stebbins' (1997: p. 20) concept of "casual leisure" is not leisure. It follows that "deviant activity", a species of Stebbins' (1997: p. 17) "casual leisure", also cannot be conceived of as leisure and, consequently, cannot be conceptualised as "dark leisure" either. Thus, the exploration of the relationship between Neo-Aristotelian leisure and "dark leisure" concludes that "dark leisure" is an oxymoron.

Conceptualising "dark leisure"

Much of the literature that may contribute to the conceptualisation of "dark leisure" refers to the term "deviant". Literature from a number of disciplines including sociology, psychology and criminology can be drawn on. The leisure literature includes that from the related fields of sport, recreation, tourism and crime, and covers a range of conceptual and empirical research. For instance, Gorer (1965, quoted in Walter, 1984: p. 71) refers to the "pornography of death" to describe the body of literature and cinema that focuses on death[1]. Issues relating to "body culture"[2] include sex tourism and the exploitation of sport, leisure and tourism contexts by paedophiles (Brackenridge *et al.*, 1995, in Lawrence *et al.*, 1995). Lyng (1990: p. 882) describes his risk-taking concept of "edgework" in terms of a kind of "experiential anarchy" characterised by activities such as skydiving and hang gliding that share the common feature of being a clear danger to the participant's physical or mental well-being. Criminal or illegal behaviour and activities may contribute to the conceptualisation of "dark leisure" from a materialist perspective (Jones 1997) or from a phenemonological perspective (Katz 1988, cited in Lyng, 1993). According to Katz (1988, quoted in Zey, 1992: p. 145):

> ...a lot of juvenile forms of violent crime and an important segment of serious adult crime do not fit the sentimentality of materialism. Neither does the central thrust that guides men and women to righteous slaughters, nor the project of primordial evil that makes "senseless killings" compellingly sensible to their killers, nor the tactics and reverberations of sneaky thrills.

Similarly, in a 1996 conference presentation entitled "The significance of serial killing for leisure studies", Rojek argued that some serial killing can be conceived of as leisure. The idea that the act of killing and the preparation for the act of killing by serial killers may be conceived of in terms of leisure was expressed earlier in Holmes and De Burger's classification of serial killers, of which a type is "...the *hedonistic* whose primary motive is pleasure" (Holmes and De Burger, 1988, quoted in Bavidge, 1989: p. 16).

The relationship between what may be thought of as "dark" and the kinds of behaviour and activities that are commonly thought of as "deviant" can be explored by considering the concept of "casual leisure" developed by Stebbins (1997: p. 17) in response to his earlier conceptualisation of "serious leisure"[3]. Stebbins defines "casual leisure" as "...immediately, intrinsically rewarding, relatively short lived pleasurable activity requiring little or no special training to enjoy it" (1997: p. 18). He explains that the main difference between "serious leisure" and "casual leisure" is that all "casual leisure" is hedonic (Stebbins, 1997: p. 21):

> ...all produce a significant level of pleasure for those who participate in them. It follows that terms such as "pleasure" and "enjoyment" are the more appropriate descriptors of the rewards of casual leisure in contrast to terms such as "satisfaction" and "rewardingness" which best describe the rewards gained in serious leisure.

It may be that "dark leisure" is a species of "casual leisure". Stebbins classifies "sensory stimulation" as a type of "casual leisure", within which are the "thrills of deviant activity" (1997: p. 20). He indicates that most "deviant leisure" can be categorised as "tolerable deviance", undertaken for pleasure as "casual leisure", and generally tolerated by society. Included are a variety of "immoral" "deviant" sexual activities such as cross-dressing, homosexuality, watching pornographic films and group sex. Heavy drinking and gambling are also included along with illegal drug-use and the use of prescription drugs for pleasure (1997: p. 22).[4] Stebbins also identifies a category of "intolerable deviance" (1997: p. 22), activities and behaviour not tolerated by society, which includes incestuous relationships, vandalism, sexual attacks, and the "sneaky thrills" referred to by Katz (1988, quoted in Stebbins, 1997: p. 22) such as burglary, shoplifting and joyriding. It may be that the "deviant" activities referred to by Stebbins (1997), that are morally shallow and lack respect for persons, could just as easily be termed "dark": that is, "deviant leisure" and "dark leisure" may be one and the same thing.

Stebbins (1997: p. 22) also identifies a category of "deviant serious leisure" that consists mostly of aberrant religion, politics, and science which are characterised by their non-individualistic nature. Deviant religion includes sects and cults; deviant science includes the occult; deviant politics includes the radical political fringes. The notion that political activity is a form of leisure is supported by Rojek (1995) who believes it is wrong to see "deviant leisure" only as the unintelligent or unpremeditated infringement of rules. Rojek (1995: p. 100) argues that "the deviant necessarily challenges the moral authority and practical wisdom of the law itself"[5].

If "dark leisure" is to be conceptualised in terms of "deviance", Stebbins' (1997) classification of certain activities as either "tolerable" or "intolerable deviant casual leisure" or "deviant serious leisure" raises questions about what is meant by "deviant". Thus it is important to identify how behaviour is classified as "deviant" in the first place and on what basis "tolerable" and "intolerable" deviant behaviours are differentiated. Much of the theorising about terms such as "safe deviance" (Downes *et al.*, (1976, quoted in Bruce and Johnson, 1992: p. 204), "positive deviance" (Hughes and Coakley 1991:

p. 307), "conduct problems" (Rutter and Giller, 1984 quoted in Skogan and Wichstrom, 1996: p. 153), "conduct disorders" (LeBlanc and Frechette, 1989 quoted in Skogan and Wichstrom, 1996: p. 153) and so on, incorporates a wide variety of behaviours and perspectives. Consequently, there appears to be a wide discrepancy over the exact meaning of these terms (Rojek 1988; Figler and Whitaker 1995; and others cited by Hughes and Coakley, 1991).

The literature also suggests a relationship between the "dark" and the "deviant"; indeed, that "dark leisure" and "deviant leisure" are one and the same thing. Moreover, the notion of "pleasure" seems to be common to many of the candidates for "dark leisure" referred to here. "Deviant activity", a species of Stebbins' concept of "casual leisure" (1997: p. 20), has been described and characterised in terms of pleasure and seems to include many of the other "dark leisure" candidates referred to here. In fact, Stebbins' "deviant activity" seems to sum up the main features of the literature and to best represent all of the candidates for "dark leisure" referred to here. Therefore, It is most likely to contribute to this investigation of the conceptual sense of "dark leisure".

The range and variety of literature referred to here, and the ways in which the relevant concepts and contexts overlap and interrelate, implies that in order to see whether conceptual sense can be made of "dark leisure" we need first to be clear about what "leisure" is. The ways in which leisure is conceptualised will be briefly explored below.

Conceptualising leisure

Haywood *et al.* (1995) identified a number of different ways of conceptualising leisure that revolve around four consistently recurring themes: leisure as residual time; leisure as functional; leisure as freedom; and leisure as activity[6]. Although all of these conceptualisations have some advantages[7], they all fail, in varying degrees, to satisfactorily consider the quality and content of leisure[8]. For instance, leisure conceptualised as "free time" fails to address what we are "free" to do in our free time since residual definitions "avoid the question of values" (Parker, 1979: p. 150). This is illustrated by De Grazia (1962: p. 13) who, drawing on the Aristotelian ideal of leisure, declared "...one senses a different element, an ethical note, a hint that spare time when misused is not leisure". This implies that unobligated time should not be used for (just) any chosen purpose. Leisure conceptualised as "functional" is a utilitarian view that prioritises society over the individual, so does not rate highly any intrinsically motivated leisure that is carried out simply for its own sake (Telfer, 1987 in Evans, 1987). The relationship between leisure and freedom has been observed at least since Aristotle pronounced that "leisure is freedom from the necessity to labour at menial tasks" (*The*

Politics, *II.8*, quoted in Hemingway, 1996). But when leisure is conceptualised as "freedom", it's definition becomes a matter of the attitude of the individual to his or her activities. On this view, the "leisure attitude" is compatible with any activity, including destructive, antisocial and pathological experiences or perceptions of leisure[9] (Mullett 1988; Parry and Long 1989 in Parker, 1989). Parry and Long (1989, in Parker, 1989) also criticise leisure conceptualised as activity, asserting that the sorts of definitions offered by Kelly (1990), Coalter *et al.* (1986, cited in Parry and Long, 1989), and so on, are virtually meaning-less as, although they can doubtless be applied to most leisure activities, they do not provide a criterion by which leisure activities and non-leisure activities can be differentiated. It would seem, then, that conceptualising leisure simply in terms of activity would appear to include almost anything, even the most distasteful and evil kinds of human activities.

None of the conceptualisations briefly outlined above pay sufficient attention to the content and quality of leisure. Yet, as Barrett (1989, in Winnifrith and Barrett, 1989) suggests, even if there is no distinct activity or groups of activities that are wholly leisure activities and if there is no activity that cannot be considered a leisure activity, this does not necessarily mean that there is not a set of activities that portrays 'ideal' leisure. In other words, conceptualising leisure as activity would seem to be suitable if certain criteria can be identified to enable evil and distasteful activities to be excluded from the conceptualisation.

Throughout this brief exploration of the different conceptualisations of leisure, reference has been made to the writings of Aristotle and others who share similar views, to illustrate the inadequacies of those conceptualisations. Consequently, a Neo-Aristotelian conceptualisation of leisure will be explored below to see whether conceptual sense can be made of "dark leisure".

A Neo-Aristotelean conception of leisure

Telfer (1987, in Evans, 1987) has attempted to illuminate contemporary definitions of leisure by returning to the Aristotelian view, offering a Neo-Aristotelian account of leisure which includes enjoying contemplating truths and beauties and enjoying discovery and creation[10]. Despite the elitist and sexist disadvantages of Aristotle's leisure ideal, Telfer's (1987, in Evans, 1987) Neo-Aristotelian conception of leisure can be understood in contemporary terms when it is contextualised in terms of MacIntyre's (1981) conception of social practices. Consequently, to complete the account of the preferred conceptualisation of leisure, more needs to be said about MacIntyre's (1981) conception of social practices.

McNamee (1992: p. 18) draws attention to the shared perspective of MacIntyre's (1981) and Taylor's (1989) theses by observing that

"...commonality can be found in their insistence that morality and moral theory is incomplete if it focuses solely on the nature of our obligations". According to Taylor (1989: p. 3):

> Much contemporary moral philosophy [...] has tended to focus on what it is right to do rather than what it is good to be, on defining the content of obligation rather than the nature of the 'good' life; and it has no conceptual place left for a notion of the good as the object of our love or allegiance.

Like Taylor (1989), MacIntyre (1981) also presents a version of the 'good' life based on the Aristotelian ethical ideal of living well rather than acting right:

> What MacIntyre attempts to supply is a revised Aristotelianism with its focus on a narrative self, situated in place and time, who is possessed of a core of virtues that are acquired, displayed, and produced in a variety of shared social practices that are themselves constitutive of broader cultural traditions. (McNamee, 1995: p. 61)

MacIntyre's portrayal of the 'good' life, then, centres on a life lived in harmony with the virtues: "The exercise of the virtues is itself a crucial component of the 'good' life for man" (1981: p. 172). He describes the virtues in terms of "excellence" and proposes that a "practice" provides "the arena in which the virtues are exhibited" (1981: p. 175). A practice is defined as:

> ...any coherent and complex socially established co-operative human activity through which goods internal to that form of activity are realised in the course of trying to achieve those standards of excellence which are appropriate to, and partially definitive of, that form of activity, with the result that human powers to achieve excellence and human conceptions of the ends and goods involved are systematically extended. (MacIntyre, 1981: p. 175).

Under this conception, throwing a football is not a practice but the game of football is. Likewise, "bricklaying is not a practice but architecture is" (MacIntyre, 1981: p. 175).

One of the main terms in MacIntyre's (1981) definition of a practice is the idea of goods internal to a practice which are differentiated from external goods. He refers to the game of chess to illustrate his point. There are goods internal to the practice of chess which can only be had by playing chess or another game of that specific kind. These goods are internal as, first, we can only specify them in terms of chess or another game of that specific kind and by means of examples from such games. Second, these goods are internal as they can only be identified and recognised by the experience of participating in the practice of chess. Those who do not have the appropriate experience are incapable of being judges of internal goods. In contrast, MacIntyre (1981) claims there are goods externally and contingently attached to playing chess and other practices such as the goods of prestige, status and money. There are always other means of attaining such goods, and their attainment is never to be had only by participating in a specific kind of practice.

Thus, following Mullet (1988), although conceptualising leisure in terms of a social practice is not incompatible with leisure conceptualised as freedom, residual time, functional, or simply any kind of activity, this more comprehensive view includes a moral dimension, and this moral dimension is objective. Moreover, the notion is that there are specific standards of excellence which we can discover, and that to identify these standards is to make truth claims and not simply to state personal attitudes or express emotions. This means that while conceptualising leisure as freedom is to characterise it subjectively in terms of intrinsic reward in the shape of the experience of pleasure or enjoyment, conceptualising leisure in terms of a social practice moves the viewpoint back to inherent value (Mullett 1988).

Having outlined the notion of the 'good' life in terms of MacIntyre's (1981) conception of social practices, we can see how leisure practices are compatible with this conception and, thus, can be a resource for the living of good, worthwhile and valuable lives.

We can now turn our attention to the consideration of whether the experiences or activities considered above as possible candidates for "dark leisure" are the sorts of experiences or activities that are worth being committed to in terms of living good and valuable lives. In other words, conceptualising leisure in terms of social practices raises the question of whether all or some of these experiences or activities can actually be conceived of as leisure. One way of attempting to answer this question is to identify what Midgley (1981: p. 135) calls "common elements" and "underlying unities" from the above candidates for "dark leisure" and the conceptualisations of leisure. The notion of "pleasure" has been a primary characteristic associated both with the above candidates for "dark leisure" and the conceptualisations of leisure discussed above. Consequently, the notion of "pleasure" will be explored in the following section from a Neo-Aristotelian perspective to facilitate a greater understanding of the relationship between leisure, pleasure, social practices, and "dark leisure".

A critique of hedonistic utilitarianism from a neo-Aristotelean perspective

McNamee (1994) explains that to evaluate some thing or activity as worthwhile or valuable is to be able to provide relevant reasons when comparing that thing or activity with another. Moreover, McNamee (1994), following Taylor (1989) and MacIntyre (1981), emphasises that the notion of value is not timeless and asocial. Rather, people's ways of life are "rooted socially and historically" (McNamee 1994: p. 289). The way people participate in and/or evaluate an activity, practice or object is guided by the resources open to them. Thus, the composition of the 'good' life varies depending on the ideals, hopes and aspirations which belong to that way of life.

The debate then, is about the value of different ways of living. Rather than questioning whether there is such a thing as value, we can question whether a nominated value such as 'pleasure' is really valuable. In other words, we need to know in what ways, if any, can pleasure contribute to the 'good' life. The justification for focusing on the value of pleasure is twofold. First, throughout the history of philosophy the notion of pleasure has played a major part in conceptualising the 'good' life, from the Cyrenaics to the Epicurians to Aristotle, through to Bentham and Mill (Graham, 1990). Second, pleasure has long been associated with contemporary perspectives on leisure. For example, empirical research illustrates a strong link between leisure and pleasure through the way the value of sport and leisure activities is often described by participants in subjective hedonistic terms such as "pleasure", "fun" and "enjoyment" (Podilchak, 1991; Floyd, 1997).

McNamee (1994) highlights five weaknesses in the kind of hedonism-centred value argument in which the value of an activity is determined wholly by the activity's ability to elicit pleasurable feelings in the experiencing person. One of these weaknesses will be elaborated here to provide a fuller understanding of where pleasure sits in relation to the conceptualisation of leisure as a social practice. But, first, a brief summary of the other four.

First, McNamee draws attention to the idea that "pleasures differ in quality" (1994: p. 293) and concludes, following Mill (1962, in Warnock, 1962), that the lives people lead cannot be explained simply in terms of pleasure, and that truth, beauty, love and friendship are good whether people desire them or not. In other words, the 'good' life is not reducible to desires *simpliciter*.

The second criticism McNamee (1994) levels at the hedonistic value argument questions whether the value of leisure activities lies only in the pleasure, fun or enjoyment derived from them. He concludes, following Kenny (1963, cited in MacIntyre, 1971) and MacIntyre (1971), that there are motives for action other than pleasure. The satisfaction that participants derive from activities such as football, hockey or hill-walking — which may require effort, self-discipline and perhaps endurance of hardship before their ends can be achieved — can be a reason for action. From this we can conclude that although pleasure might be a central feature of leisure, it is not an essential feature. For now, we can say that it would seem that if activities are defined simply by the pleasure they provide they cannot be conceived of in terms of MacIntyre's (1981) social practices, so cannot be conceived of as leisure.

A third criticism made by McNamee of the hedonism-based value argument is that "...one cannot pursue pleasure in isolation. Pleasure is derived through action and activities" (1994: p. 293). This aligns with MacIntyre (1971: p. 175), who elucidates Aristotle's view that:

> ...although pleasure is a reason for acting and that to get pleasure from doing something is a criterion of success in action, we cannot identify any specific type of action in terms of its being a means to pleasure.

His fourth criticism that "means and ends cannot always be separated unproblematically" and is illustrated in Aristotle (Nicomachean Ethics X, quoted in McNamee 1994: p.294):

> One might argue that pleasures are desirable in themselves, but not when they are achieved in a certain way; as, e.g., wealth is desirable, but not at the price of treason....

Quoting MacIntyre (1971: p. 175), McNamee argues in favour of "...the Aristotelian stress upon pleasure as not separately identifiable from the enjoyed activity". The satisfactions involved in complex activities such as hill-walking, philosophy and chess, which often extend over a life-time and frequently involve dedication, self-sacrifice, and so on, illustrate that these kinds of activities cannot be conceived of as being merely indifferent paths to gaining pleasure (McNamee, 1994).

Before moving on to an elaboration and discussion of the fifth and final weakness in the hedonism-centred value argument, we must briefly consider the issue of pleasure and satisfaction in terms of desires. Goodin (1993 in Singer 1993: p. 243) explains that "preference satisfaction" utilitarians believe that, rather than simply maximising the balance of pleasure over pains what should be maximised is the satisfaction of preferences more generally:

> Insofar as a person happens to have preferences that go beyond (or even counter to) that person's hedonistic pleasures, satisfying those preferences is nonetheless a source of utility for that person.

In most cases, the satisfaction of preferences entails hedonistic pleasure, although "preference satisfaction" utilitarianism allows consideration to be given to those activities that are not easily described as having simply maximised pleasure (Goodin, 1993 in Singer, 1993). This is shown in McNamee's (1994) example of a cross-country runner in winter who may gain satisfaction simply from completing what may have been a physically and mentally arduous race: a fact that may not be easily explained in hedonistic terms. Yet, Goodin (1993, in Singer, 1993) maintains that this is an inferior theory of the 'good' as it makes the good equal to the desired, which effectively reduces everything to a question of 'consumer demand'. The "preference satisfaction" utilitarian theory is also problematic in that it does not say that people should have only certain kinds of preferences, simply that it is good for people have their preferences satisfied, whatever they may be (Goodin, 1993 in Singer, 1993).

But if preferences are left to the discretion of the individual, what of a person who preferred burglary to boxing, or murder to mountaineering? This, then, is the fifth and final criticism made by McNamee: that "the pursuit of pleasure itself does not demarcate any special class of activities except those logically thus defined" (1994: p. 293). The implications of this for seeing whether conceptual sense can be made of "dark leisure" are discussed below.

The relationship between Neo-Aristotelean leisure and "dark leisure"

Hedonists take the view that any life filled with pleasure is not only as good as any other life filled with pleasure but is also superior to a life of pain and dissatisfaction. Thus, hedonists believe that the life of a Socrates *dissatisfied* is not better than the life of a pig *satisfied* (Graham, 1990). They avoid the notion of 'higher' and 'lower' pleasures by simply rejecting the idea that there are any differences in the worth or value of various kinds of pleasure (Graham 1990). It would follow that if pleasure itself were the only thing that mattered, we would be unable to justify a preference for (to value) the satisfaction pleasure that a mountaineer takes in successfully climbing a mountain over the sadistic pleasure a murderer takes in the sufferings of the person he has murdered. Hedonists, however, would argue that they are not recommending murder as a way of living an ideal life. Rather, they would simply say that if someone enjoyed murdering in precisely the way that a person enjoys mountaineering, then the murderer's life would be as enjoyable as the moutaineer's.

Nevertheless, it seems clear that there is an important difference between mountaineering and murder that must be considered. Consequently, to discredit hedonistic utilitarianism as a philosophy of value, a more substantial argument is found in MacIntyre's (1981) view of leisure as social practices.

One aspect of Mill's utilitarian thesis to which Taylor (1989) draws attention is that respect for persons entails respecting an individual's personality, which in turn involves respecting the individual's moral autonomy. But, as Taylor (1989: p. 12) indicates, Mill's utilitarianism entails:

> ...the demand that we give people the freedom to develop their personality in their own way, however repugnant to ourselves and even to our moral sense...

Mill (1962, quoted in Warnock, 1962: p. 197) argues that in cases of pure personal preference, no one person can decide what is best for another person:

> If a person possesses any tolerable amount of common sense and experience, his own mode of laying out his existence is the best, not because it is the best in itself, but because it is his own mode.

Thus, Mill (1962, quoted in Warnock, 1962: p. 189) presents a strong case for the freedom of individuals to live their lives as they see fit:

> A person whose desires and impulses are his own — are the expression of his own nature, as it has been developed and modified by his own culture — is said to have character. One whose desires and impulses are not his own, has no character, no more than a steam-engine has a character.

The problem, pointed out by Bond (1996), is that some kinds of behaviour are not merely the expression of personal preferences but may also negatively affect the person who is behaving in that particular way and other people and the community as a whole. Our behaviour, whether positive or negative, has an impact on our human nature, that is, on our individual thriving or flourishing. Consideration of the effects of our choices and consequent behaviour brings to the fore serious matters that affect everyone, including moral issues such as trust, honesty, cruelty, harm, injustice, exploitation, and so on. Thus the choices of a person who prefers to live the life of a serial murderer would not be justified because of the injurious effect on other people, on society in general, and on the serial murderer as a human being (Bond, 1996). This relates to an important point raised by McNamee (1994: p. 293) who states that:

...any particular and substantive account of the value of leisure practices will be related conceptually to an account of persons that it is thought desirable for one to become.

In other words, although we cannot deny a murderer's claim to have derived pleasure from murdering, we can argue that the practice of murder cannot be valued as a social practice simply for that reason, and we can argue that these are not the kinds of people it is desirable to become.

It might be argued that some of the candidate activities for "dark leisure" such as drug taking, shoplifting, gambling, or even the thoroughly evil activities of the serial murderer can, in some circumstances, display an "excellence" of a sort. If this were the case, they might seem to share some of the characteristics of a social practice and, consequently, might be thought of in terms of a social practice. MacIntyre (1981: p. 177) says that:

A practice involves standards of excellence and obedience to rules as well as the achievement of goods. To enter into a practice is to accept the authority of those standards and the inadequacy of my own performance as judged by them. It is to subject my own attitudes, choices, preferences and tastes to the standards which currently and partially define the practice. Practices of course ...have a history: games, sciences and arts all have histories. Thus the standards are not themselves immune from criticism, but none the less we cannot be initiated into a practice without accepting the authority of the best standards realised so far.

If we look closely we can see that, in certain contexts, shoplifting appears to share the characteristics of a social practice. To illustrate the point, consider Charles Dickens' "Fagin", the leader of a band of young boy pickpockets. The new boys learn from the established boys the "standards of excellence" of picking pockets that is, the skills and attributes required to succeed as pickpockets. The required attributes of Fagin's pickpockets are illustrated by Lyng (1993, in Bell and Bell, 1993: p. 125), who describes how those who practice illegal "edgework" value the opportunity for performance in terms of using the "survival" and "craft" skills that distinguish criminal activities such as safe cracking, running cons and so on. Thus, today's shoplifters may be perceived to be the descendants of Fagin's pickpockets, sharing the "history" of the established "standards of excellence" needed to be a successful shoplifter.

But this concept of shoplifting as a social practice can be dismissed when we think of it in terms of MacIntyre's claim that a practice is a "socially established co-operative human activity" (1981: p. 175) since it is exploitive and disrespectful of other members of society, and does not contribute to our happiness, thriving, flourishing or well-being.

This reasoning could also be applied to other potential 'social practices' such as serial killing. Serial killing motivated by pleasure, involves, according to Rojek (1996), the serial killer "...imagining killing, planning killing, reading about killing, watching videos of killing and fantasising about the consequences of killing others". This preparation could be thought of in terms of the killer trying to achieve the "standards of excellence" which "currently and partially define the practice" (MacIntyre, 1981: p. 177) through the development of skills, intensive planning and strategy formulation to enable the killings to be carried out successfully. Moreover, the killer's reading might include the biographies of serial killers throughout history, which reflects MacIntyre's (1981: p. 177) notion that practices "have histories".

Nevertheless, like that of a shoplifter, the life of a serial killer is not illustrative of the virtues that contribute to the 'good' life. To be a virtue, the quality or qualities exhibited must contribute to the well-being of either the person who possesses it, or the community, or both (Bond 1996). To be a vice the quality or qualities exhibited must be detrimental to the well-being of either the person who possesses it, or the community, or both. In other words, the potential vice must create unhappiness, misery and ill-being either personally or in the community as a whole. Clearly, our understanding of the qualities or characteristics that a serial killer exhibits such as cruelty, depravity, brutality, viciousness and so on, are vices rather than virtues. It follows that these do not contribute to the thriving, flourishing, happiness or well-being of the serial killer, the serial killer's victims, the victims families and consequently society as a whole.

Drug taking might also be conceived of in terms of a social practice. Becker's (1963, quoted in Dorn and South, 1989: p. 172) observations and interviews of drug-users describe their being "initiated" into drug-use by other drug-users, "learning" to enjoy the effects, and being part of a "social network" that places a premium on secrecy so that drug supplies are guaranteed. Willis (1978, quoted in Dorn and South, 1989: p. 174) also reports how it is more than the use of drugs in itself which is significant to "the hippie culture"; "it is the whole set of *practices* and discourses around the subject that preoccupies", such as the appreciation of the mysticism and spiritualism of the East. Further, the development and use of skills is believed by Lyng's (1990) "edgeworkers", referred to above, to be the most valuable part of their experiences. This is illustrated by Thompson (1971, quoted in Lyng, 1990: p. 871) who describes the way highly developed "skills", such as recognising how much of a particular drug can be ingested or what blend of drugs are safe, are required to be an successful substance abuser. Again, the reasons why drug taking cannot be conceived of in terms of MacIntyre's (1981) social practices are the same reasons why shoplifting and serial murder are also excluded. The activities of shoplifters, serial killers and drug users are not the kinds of activities that are conducive to the development and expression of justice, courage and honesty, the three most important virtues identified by MacIntyre (1981: p. 178):

> ...we have to accept as necessary components of any practice with internal goods and standards of excellence the virtues of justice, courage and honesty. For not to accept these...bars us from achieving the standards of excellence or the goods internal to the practice that it renders the practice pointless except as a device for achieving external goods.

MacIntyre (1981) has responded to the suggestion that torture and sado-masochistic sexual activities might be examples of practices by making clear the place of practices in a larger moral context. Although he is not convinced that there are evil practices *per se*, he acknowledges that the range of practices constituting the arts, the sciences and particular kinds of athletic games, may, on occasion, be sources of evil. For example, an athlete's desire to be the best may lead to his or her corruption through cheating. Thus, MacIntyre (1981: p. 189) explains that the place of the virtues must be situated in the larger arena of human life:

> ...unless there is a *telos* which transcends the limited goods of practices by constituting the good of a whole human life, the good of a human life conceived as a unity, it will *both* be the case that a certain subversive arbitrariness will invade the moral life *and* that we shall be unable to specify the context of certain virtues adequately. These two considerations are reinforced by a third: that there is at least one virtue recognised by the tradition which cannot be specified at all except with reference to the wholeness of a human life — the virtue of integrity or constancy.

According to MacIntyre's (1981) thesis, it is the character of the activities that is important. As we have already seen, a good life cannot be characterised exclusively in terms of pleasure as the 'good' life, in part, is contingent on the activity. From this we can conclude that if peoples' activities are bad or base then their lives will be bad or base. If peoples' lives are bad or base, it follows, that they are not living meaningful and worthwhile lives. Thus, they are not living the 'good' life in the context of MacIntyre's (1981) conception of social practices. Consequently, from this we can conclude that, first, the activities referred to above as possible candidates for conceptualising "dark leisure", if conceived of as being objectively bad or base as opposed to being objectively valuable or worthwhile, cannot be conceived of as leisure. Second, it follows, that if they cannot first be conceived of as leisure they cannot then be conceived of as "dark leisure", or any sort of leisure for that matter.

Thus, we can further conclude that, from a MacIntyrean perspective, Stebbins' (1997: p. 17) concept of "casual leisure" is not leisure. Stebbins (1997: p. 18) stated:

> ...casual leisure can be defined as immediately, intrinsically reward- ing, relatively short lived pleasurable activity requiring little or no special training to enjoy it.

The types of "casual leisure" Stebbins (1997: p. 18) refers to include "play, relaxation, passive entertainment, active entertainment, sociable conversation and sensory stimulation" which are defined solely in hedonistic terms, by the pleasure rather than any satisfaction they provide. The nature of these activities, under Stebbins' (1997) conception, means that none are social practices as none are "complex socially established human activity" (MacIntyre, 1981: p. 175) that have their own particular "standards of excel- lence" (MacIntyre, 1981: p. 177) which have evolved historically as a conse- quence of the achievements of preceding practitioners. In explaining why Stebbins' (1997) concept of "casual leisure" is not leisure, it follows that, all the "sensory stimulation" types of activities Stebbins (1997: p. 22) refers to, which are also characterised in terms of their hedonistic or pleasure giving qualities, and which include "deviant activity" such as vandalism, shoplifting, heavy drinking, gambling, drug taking and so on, are not leisure and, conse- quently, also cannot be conceptualised as "dark leisure", or any sort of leisure.

Conclusion

It has been the central purpose of this paper to see whether conceptual sense can be made of the notion of "dark leisure". The exploration of the relationship between neo-Aristotelian leisure and "dark leisure" in the latter part of the paper has identified that, in effect, "dark leisure" is an oxymoron. The activities referred to as possible candidates for conceptualising "dark leisure" are bad or base, so they cannot be conceptualised as "leisure", and, as they are not leisure they cannot be conceptualised as "dark leisure". Two further conclusions can be drawn.

First, those activities that have been described in terms of "deviant leisure" appear to be the same as the candidates for "dark leisure". Although it has been concluded that neither of these concepts can be conceived of in terms of leisure within the context of MacIntyre's (1981) conception of social practices, this conclusion may be useful in contributing to future conceptualisations, theoretical explorations and empirical investigations in the field of leisure studies and related fields of study.

Second, although, as we have seen, it does not make sense to describe any of the candidates for "dark leisure" as "dark leisure", it would seem that, due to the nature and characteristics of these experiences and activities, such as the way they appear to be generally motivated by pleasure, or often seem to be described in terms of pleasure, it would be more appropriate to conceptualise them as "deviant pleasure" or "dark pleasure". This may also be a useful contribution to future leisure studies related conceptualisations, theoretical explorations and empirical investigations.

Notes

1   Similarly, Rojek (1993: p. 136) refers to "fatal attractions" to depict the "black spots" that describe the world wide leisure or tourist appeal of the grave sites, suicide sites, assassination points, and locations where celebrities or large groups of people have died suddenly and violently.

2   The term 'body culture' has been borrowed from a section heading in Brackenridge (1993).

3   Stebbins (1997, p.17) defines "serious leisure" thus: "Serious leisure is the systematic pursuit of an amateur, a hobbyist, or a volunteer activity sufficiently substantial and interesting for the participant to find a career there in the acquisition and expression of a combination of its special skills, knowledge, and experience". For a detailed account of "serious leisure" including its three types: amateurism; hobbyist pursuits, and career volunteering, see Stebbins (1982).

4   For example, although Benjamin (1979, cited in Rojek, 1995) concentrates on the playful and oppositional consciousness aspects of the effects of hashish, he acknowledges that the pleasure experienced is not just a physical reaction to a chemical, but also involves stepping outside social conventions and playing with norms.

5   For example, organised mass trespass acts such as the Kinder Scout trespass in the early 1980s illustrate that such deviant behaviour is frequently political in the way it opposes and questions laws on property distribution, access rights and leisure space management (Donnelly ,1986 cited in Rojek, 1995).

6   One of the main problems in the ongoing discussion about what "leisure" is, is the lack of consistency in the definitional subject. Long (1982, cited in Parry and Long, 1989) has noticed that the meaning of leisure can differ

not only from person to person but for the same person at different times. Parry and Long (1989, in Parker 1989) suggest that the majority of writers on the concept of leisure are really writing about something else such as the impact or functions of leisure, or the determinants of leisure, or the theoretical philosophy of leisure.

7   Space constraints of this paper prohibit a fuller exploration of these conceptualisations of leisure. On leisure as residual time see Kelly (1990); leisure as functional see Haywood *et al.* (1995); leisure as freedom see Csikszentmihalyi (1975, cited in Hemingway. 1996) and Neulinger (1981, cited in Hemingway, 1996); leisure as activities see Kelly (1990).

8   It is acknowledged, first, that there are a number of less common conceptualisations of leisure not considered here due to space constraints; and, second, that this brief review is value-laden.

9   For example, drug abuse may initially be experienced purely for enjoyment, but may eventually result in addiction which will be physically and psychologically harmful to the individual, his/her partner, family and friends, and with an overall negative impact on society (for example, in increased demands on national resources to treat drug addicts).

References

Barrett, C. (1989) 'The concept of leisure: Idea and ideal', in T. Winnifrith and C. Barrett (eds) *The philosophy of leisure*. Basingstoke: MacMillan Press, pp. 9–19.

Becker, H. S. (1963) *Outsiders: Studies in the sociology of deviance*. London: Collier MacMillan Ltd., cited in N. Dorn and N. South op. cit., pp. 171–190.

Bell, N. J. and Bell, R. W. (eds) (1993) *Adolescent Risk Taking*. London: Sage Publications Ltd.

Benjamin, W. (1979) 'One way street', cited in C. Rojek (1995) op. cit., pp. 79–103.

Bond, E. J. (1996) *Ethics and human well–being: An introduction to moral philosophy*. Oxford: Blackwell Publishers.

Brackenridge, C. (ed) (1993) *Body matters: Leisure images and lifestyles*. LSA Publication No. 47. Eastbourne: Leisure Studies Association.

Brackenridge, C., Summers, D. and Woodward, D. (1995) 'Educating for child protection in sport', in L. Lawrence, E. Murdoch and S. Parker (eds) *Professional and development issues in leisure, sport and education* (LSA Publication No. 56). Eastbourne: Leisure Studies Association, pp. 167–190.

Bruce, A. C. and Johnson, J. E. V (1992) 'Toward an explanation of betting as a leisure pursuit'. *Leisure Studies* Vol. 11, No. 3: pp. 201-218.

Coalter, F., Long, J. and Duffield, B. S. (1986) *Rationale for public sector investment in leisure*. London: Sports Council/ESRC, cited in J. Parry and J. Long (1989) op. cit., pp 1-15.

Csikszentmihalyi, M. (1975) 'Beyond boredom and anxiety: The experience of play in work and games', cited in J. L. Hemingway (1996) op. cit., pp. 27–43.

De Grazia, S. (1962) *Of time, work and leisure*. New York: K Kraus Reprint Co, pp. 3–33.

Donnelly, P. (1986) 'The paradox of the parks: Politics of recreational land use before and after the mass trespasses', cited in C. Rojek (1995) op. cit., pp. 79–103.

Dorn, N. and South, N. (1989) 'Drugs and leisure, prohibition and pleasure: From subculture to the drugalogue', in C. Rojek (ed) (1989) op. cit. pp. 171–190.

Downes, D. M., Davies, B. T., David, M. E. and Stone, P. (1976) 'Gambling, work and leisure: A study across three areas', quoted in A. C. Bruce and J. E. V. Johnson op. cit., pp. 201–218.

Driver, B. L., Brown, P. J. and Peterson, G. L. (eds) (1991) *Benefits of leisure*. Pennsylvania: Venture Publishing, Inc.

Figler, S. K. and Whitaker, G. (1995) *Sport and play in American life: A textbook in the sociology of sport* (3rd ed). London: Brown and Benchmark Publishers.

Floyd, M. F. (1997) 'Pleasure, arousal and dominance: Exploring affective determinants of recreation satisfaction', *Leisure Sciences* Vol. 19, No. 2: pp. 83–96.

Goodin, R. E. (1993) 'Utility and the good', in P. Singer (ed) op. cit., pp. 241–248.

Gorer, G. (1965) 'Death, grief and mourning in contemporary Britain', quoted in J.A. Walter op. cit., pp. 67–76.

Graham, G. (1990) *Living the good life: An introduction to philosophy*. New York: Paragon House.

Haywood, L. J., Kew, F. C., Bramham, P., Spink, J., Henry, I. and Capenerhurst, J. (1995) *Understanding leisure* (2nd ed). Cheltenham: Stanley Thornes (Publishers).

Hemingway, J. L. (1996) 'Emancipating leisure: The recovery of freedom in leisure', *Journal of Leisure Research* Vol. 28, No. 1: pp. 27-43.

Holmes, R. M. and De Burger, J. (1988) 'Serial murder', quoted in M. Bavidge (1989) *Mad or bad?*. Bristol: Bristol Classical Press, pp. 15–34.

Hughes, R. and Coakley, J. (1991) 'Positive deviance among athletes: The implications of overconformity to the sport ethic', *Sociology of Sport Journal* Vol. 8, No. 4: pp. 307–325.

Jones, R. L. (1997) 'A deviant sports career: Toward a sociology of unlicensed boxing', *Journal of Sport and Social Issues* Vol. 21, No. 1: pp. 37–52.

Katz, J. (1988) 'Seductions and repulsions of crime', in M. Zey (ed) (1992) *Decision making alternatives to rational choice models*. London: Sage Publications, pp. 140–157.

——— (1988) 'Seductions of crime: Moral and sensual attractions in doing evil', cited in S. Lyng (1993) op. cit., pp. 107–130.

——— (1988) 'Seductions of crime: Moral and sensual attractions in doing evil' quoted in R. A. Stebbins (1997) op. cit., pp. 17-25.

Kelly, J. R. (1990) *Leisure* (2nd ed). New Jersey: Prentice Hall.

Kenny, A. (1963) 'Action, emotion and will', cited in A. MacIntyre (1971) op. cit., pp. 173–190.

LeBlanc, M. and Frechette, M. (1989) 'Male criminal activity from childhood through youth', quoted in K. Skogen and L. Wichstrom op. cit., pp. 151–169.

Long, J. (1982) 'Leisure viewed from before retirement', cited in J. Parry and J. Long op. cit., pp. 1-15.

Lyng, S. (1990) 'Edgework: A social psychological analysis of voluntary risk taking', *American Journal of Sociology* Vol. 95, No. 4: pp. 851–86.

Lyng, S. (1993) 'Dysfunctional risk taking: Criminal behaviour as edgework', in N. J. Bell and R. W. Bell (eds) (1993) op. cit., pp. 107–130.

MacIntyre, A. (1971) *Against the self–images of the age: Essays on ideology and philosophy*. London: Gerald Duckworth and Co Ltd.

MacIntyre, A. (1981) *After virtue: A study in moral theory*. London: Duckworth.

McNamee, M. (1992) 'Physical education and the development of personhood', *Physical Education Review*, Vol. 15, No. 1: pp. 13-28.

McNamee, M. (1994) 'Valuing leisure practices: Toward a theoretical framework', *Leisure Studies* Vol. 13, No. 4: pp. 288–309.

McNamee, M. (1995) 'Sporting practices, institutions, and virtues: A critique and a restatement', *Journal of the Philosophy of Sport* Vol. XXII: pp. 61–82.

Midgley, M. (1981) *Heart and mind: The varieties of moral experience*. Brighton: The Harvester Press Ltd.

Mill, J. S. (1962) 'Bentham', 'On liberty' and 'Utilitarianism', in M. Warnock (ed) (1962) *Utilitarianism* (5th ed). London: Collins Clear-Type Press, pp. 78–321.

Mullett, S. (1988) 'Leisure and consumption: Incompatible concepts', *Leisure Studies* Vol. 7, No. 3: pp. 241– 253.

Neulinger, J. (1981) 'The psychology of leisure', cited in J. L. Hemingway (1996) op. cit., pp. 27–43.

Parker, S. (1979) *The sociology of leisure*. London: George Allen and Unwin, pp. 146–152.

Parry, J. and Long, J. (1989) 'Immaculate concepts', in S. Parker (ed) (1989) *Work, leisure and lifestyles* (LSA Publication No. 33). Eastbourne: Leisure Studies Association, pp. 1–15.

Podilchak, W. (1991) 'Distinctions of fun, enjoyment and leisure', *Leisure Studies* Vol. 10, No. 2: pp. 133–148.

Rojek, C. (1988) 'The convoy of pollution', *Leisure Studies* Vol. 7, No. 1: pp. 21–31.

———— (ed) 1989) *Leisure for Leisure*. Basingstoke: The MacMillan Press Ltd.

———— (1993) *Ways of escape: Modern transformations in leisure and travel.* Basingstoke: The MacMillan Press Ltd.

———— (1995) *Decentring leisure: Rethinking leisure theory.* London: Sage Publications.

———— (1996) 'The significance of serial killing for leisure studies', unpublished paper presented at LSA/VVS 1996 conference, "Accelerating leisure? Leisure, time and space in a transitory society", Wageningen, The Netherlands (12–14 September).

Rutter, M. and Giller, H. (1984) 'Juvenile delinquency, trends and perspectives', quoted in K. Skogen and L. Wichstrom op. cit., pp. 151–169.

Simpson, S. and Yoshioka, C. (1992) 'Aristotelian view of leisure: An outdoor recreation perspective', *Leisure Studies* Vol. 11, No. 3: pp. 219-231.

Singer, P. (ed) (1993) *A Companion to Ethics* (2nd ed). Oxford: Blackwell Publishers Ltd.

Skogen, K. and Wichstrom, L. (1996) 'Delinquency in the wilderness: Patterns of outdoor recreation activities and conduct problems in the general adolescent population', *Leisure Studies* Vol. 15, No. 3: pp. 151-169.

Stebbins, R. A. (1982) 'Serious leisure: A conceptual statement', *Pacific Sociological Review* Vol. 25, No. 2: pp. 251–272.

Stebbins, R. A. (1997) 'Casual leisure: A conceptual statement', *Leisure Studies* Vol. 16, No. 1: pp. 17–25.

Taylor, C. (1989) *Sources of the self: The making of the modern identity.* Cambridge: Cambridge University Press.

Telfer, E. (1987) 'Leisure', in J. D. G. Evans (ed) *Moral philosophy and contemporary problems.* Cambridge: Cambridge University Press, pp. 151–164.

Thompson, H. S. (1971) *Fear and loathing in Las Vegas: A savage journey to the heart of the American dream*, quoted in S. Lyng (1990) op. cit., pp. 851– 86.

Walter, J. A. (1984) 'Death as recreation: Armchair mountaineering', *Leisure Studies*, Vol. 3, No. 1: pp. 67-76.

Willis, P. (1978) 'Profane culture', quoted in N. Dorn and N. South op. cit., pp. 171-190.

Yoshioka, C. and Simpson, S. (1989) 'Aristotelian view of leisure in Athens, Sparta and Rome', in S. Simpson, and C. Yoshioka op. cit., pp. 219–231.

Young, J. (1973) 'The hippie solution: An essay in the politics of leisure', in I. Taylor and L. Taylor (eds) *Politics and deviance: Papers from the national deviancy conference*. Middlesex: Penguin Books Ltd, pp. 182–208.

10   Space constraints prohibit a fuller exploration of Telfer's (1987, in Evans 1987) critique of Aristotle's conception of leisure in the *Nicomachean Ethics*.

Sport — A Moral Laboratory?

Graham McFee

The Chelsea School, University of Brighton (UK)

Introduction

Part of the motivation of the Olympic Games — in the rhetoric of Pierre de Coubertin at least — turned on the *moral* possibilities of sport: that participation in sport was (potentially) morally educative. For example, Article VIII of the Congress of 1894 justifies the Olympic Games "from the athletic, moral and international standpoint" (MacAloon, 1981: p. 167)[1]; and De Coubertin writes that:

> [w]ise and peaceful internationalism ... will penetrate the new stadium and preserve within it the cult of disinterestedness and honour which will enable athletics to help in the tasks of moral education and social peace.... (MacAloon 1981: pp. 188–189)

This idea of sport as morally educative had, of course, a developed history, to which De Coubertin appealed, in the athleticist rhetoric of the English public schools — with two fundamental theses emphasising the [supposed] moral benefits of participation in sport. As expressed by Peter McIntosh (1979: p. 27):

> [t]he first was that competitive sport ... had an ethical basis, and the second was that training in moral behaviour on the playing field was transferable to the world beyond.

If correct, such a position has the *potential* to justify a quite widespread concern with sport, for it claims to identify a valued characteristic intrinsic to sport. I am drawn to such a *general* idea of sport as having some such morally educative potential — indeed, I do not see how *else* some general (intrinsic) value might be ascribed to sport.

But is such moral justification for sport needed? Doesn't its place (its 'social role') as a leisure activity provide all the justification that is required? For me, this is no justification at all, because no intrinsic justification is provided. So that if one wants to justify *sport*, that justification must rely on features of sport as such — hence on intrinsic features — rather than on features which, while explaining concern (say, "I do it for the money"), fail to explain that concern in terms of sport's features: features *extrinsic* to sport could be in place for something entirely without merit — as one might regard soap-operas as entirely without merit and yet not deny their importance viewed as commodities. Moreover, those who regard sport as "our most sophisticated and sensitive cultural lens" (Beckles, 1995: p. 1) use sport to investigate society, using the cultural form to interrogate the culture — as this "lens" metaphor makes plain. Although both legitimate and rewarding, this is not the only interest that one might have in, say, cricket (Beckles's example), or in sport more generally.

This discussion identifies, as it were, a sport-shaped hole in those social theories which take sport as, say, opiate of the masses, prison of measured time, force in the civilising process, and so on. And, of course, the pressure for some such *intrinsic* justification is intensified if one regards sport as having a place in (formal) education: there, *some* justification, more powerful than one couched in terms of enjoyment, and with an explicit connection to the educative, is required if curriculum time is to be found for sporting activities.

Yet the first athleticist thesis — that competitive sport had an ethical basis — seems just *false*: sport neither necessarily promotes ethical performance on the field nor necessarily teaches ethical principles. Even those formalists[2] who take merely playing sport according to the rules to be ethically approvable behaviour should admit that the rules must be actualised in practice. Yet this is problematic. For the behaviour must *depend on* the rules, not simply conform to them. And, as Wittgenstein (1953: pp. 84–86) recognises, no rule can uniquely circumscribe the behaviour it requires or prohibits: rather, its application to behaviour involves an exercise of judgement, of a kind a referee or umpire might make. And this indicates the need for making practical sense of these ('formal') rules. Thus, for any activity, appeal to rules *alone* cannot be sufficient (a point to which I will return). But even for such formalists there should remain a gap between sporting activity and the moral (McFee, 2000: pp. 173–174), such that merely participating in sport might or might not actualise the rules in a morally-relevant way. But the claim here need not (indeed — if I am right — *cannot*) be that sport *always* has this impact — rather, that it *might* in certain cases. Even *that* connection of sport to the moral sphere is sufficient to warrant taking sport seriously.

But how might this educational potential for sport be *argued* for? In reply, I will be presenting just a research *agenda* of mine — motivating both the general agenda and its specific premises. If this presentation resulted in you conceiving of the issue this way, we might then (collaboratively) work towards testing the conclusions by reviewing in detail each premise, and its contribution to those conclusions.

As Ronald Dworkin (1978: pp. 22–28; 71–80) urges, *principles* (in contrast to *rules*) provide a *learned* background essential for appropriate participation[3]. Since central moral *principles* concern *fairness* (and therefore *justice*), if the potential value of sport is moral value, considering sport here is indeed considering a sense of justice as inculcated via leisure activities — hence, sport as a contribution to *just leisure*[4].

Explanations and qualifications

It is worth entering three notes of caution and a fourth in explanation.

First, my reference to *the moral* must be understood as to the *sphere* of morality, rather than simply to what is (morally) good. Second, morality has a complex relation to questions of human harm — better, to explaining some of the ways humans can *be* harmed. Here, I simply put that issue to one side, accepting without demur Konrad Lorenz's view that human sports aim "to ascertain which ... [team] ... is the stronger, *without hurting the weaker*" (Lorenz, 1966: p. 94). For this locates *our* issue — although we might still want to highlight the degree of ear-biting and cheek-breaking in the 'sporting' world that is thereby put aside!

Third, we must recognise that potentials are not always achieved: although one cannot assert it in Switzerland without fear of legal redress (Jennings, 1996: pp. 301–304), some other IOC members are scoundrels, self-serving and corrupt. We should not conclude that the Olympic Ideal therefore does not exist — although we might wonder about its realisability! Here, it is the *execution* of the project that is flawed, not the project itself. So the view to be explored here accepts an *educational* potential to sport (and especially a *morally* educative potential), even if that is neither *inevitable*, in ways De Coubertin seems to have thought, nor to be understood as generalising in quite the way sometimes hoped (or idealised).

A fourth element concerns our *starting* point in connecting sport to the moral sphere. The rhetoric of sport is replete with metaphors employed in general ethical discussion — our examples: the idea of 'fair play' and of 'a level playing field'. These reflect ethical concerns *within* sport. And De Coubertin's amateurism (whatever its faults in theory or practice) was fuelled by concerns with sport done 'for its own sake', and with fairness: as we might say, with behaving fairly (appropriately, justly) towards others ... here, in the sporting context.

Yet what exactly do these two metaphors — 'fair play' and 'level playing field' — offer to *sports*-practice: what precisely do they suggest or proscribe? While we may have some sense inside the sporting context, it may be hard to extend. Also, what does some *root*-metaphor tell us about moral situations more generally — what would it be to require fair play or a level playing field in one's business dealings, say, or one's interactions with others?

Still, our initial concerns are with the sporting case. So let us briefly consider each of these examples:

(a) **'Fair Play'**: notice: not fairness, which might have to do with the starting point of the contest [and is picked up in the other metaphor] but with the manner of the contest, having implications for how to interpret the rules as they relate to the manner of playing. For example, if there is no rule specifically against taking a knife into the rugby scrum, but there are rules about what it *is* permissible to take onto the field, then other questions are raised. Here, a principle on which to base, say, refereeing decisions is more helpful than list of what is permitted, since it offers help with as-yet unconfronted cases.

(b) **'Level Playing Field'**: we roughly understand the root metaphor, and the reason for it: that neither side should be unfairly advantaged initially — this is also the basis for, say, the practice of changing ends at half-time: that in-built advantage be equalised.

So, as suggested, the primary concern of each is with considerations of justice: with getting one's just deserts (on the day!).

These two metaphors are (among) the things ethics gets from sport: I shall suggest that *a* value in sport resides precisely here — for not only are the metaphors/slogans available in sporting contexts, but sport also provides concrete instantiations of relevant principles. Moreover, this possibility offers some detail to *an* account of sport's value.

The argument

At last, to the argument itself. In summary, and presented hypothetically, the argument is this:

1. *if* sport is valuable, of its nature or intrinsically;

2. *if* such value has some connection to the moral (as it must, for Olympism);

3. *if* moral judgements are essentially *particular*;

4. *if* sport can present the particularisation of (moral?) cases;

5. *and if* such cases concretise moral metaphors, such as 'fair play', 'level playing field';

6. *then*, sport might function as a moral laboratory.

In explaining *how* sport might function in the moral sphere, I offer both *reason* to think that it does and a *basis* for investigation.

Now, any argument may contested only either (a) by contesting the premises or (b) by disputing that the conclusion follows from those premises. So those who find this conclusion uncongenial, or even those who think it wrong, must show what is amiss with the argument that leads to that conclusion.

As to the logic of the argument — that the conclusion follows from those premises — it is easy to see that the conclusion *does* depend on those premises and, even if the argument is not formally valid, it should be accepted as compelling. Making the formulation impeccable would make it both a lot longer and considerably more complex. But surely this argument is sufficiently transparent at present, as we can see if we indeed make the assumptions articulated by those premises.

From the identification, in the first premise, of a *value* for sport, we recognise that value as moral (second premise) and then characterise moral value as particular (third premise). Once these premises are granted, it follows that sport *has* a moral value of a particularised kind (like other moral value). Now premises four and five contribute the idea that this (particularised) value might be exemplified in sporting situations, and hence might be learned from them. And this suggests how sport might function as a site of moral exploration, investigation and education. So granting the truth of the premises *does* (at first blush) guarantee the conclusion's truth; or, at least, give us reason to adopt it.

We must now turn to the question of *whether* the truth of the premises should indeed be granted. And here I shall urge simply that we have reason to adopt each. Indeed, part of my sense of this as a research *agenda* is precisely that the truth of each premise requires investigation. If the conditional importance of the argument is granted, such investigation becomes justified.

However, before saying something in explanation — and in justification — of each premise in turn, notice that finding my *argument* flawed is not *equivalent* to finding my conclusion flawed: that other arguments might yet be offered. But, first, in that situation one has no *reason* to accept my conclusion — as one would have if the argument were sound; and, second, I would not be considering *this* argument if another were obvious.

Let us, therefore, consider each premise, reminding ourselves what it contributes to the argument, and asking if it seems plausible.

The first two premises: sport as morally valuable

The first premise picks out a condition to be met if sport is to be accorded an importance which I, and others, think attaches to it. If this premise were denied, some other starting point for the value of sport must be offered: but if, as I assume, such a justification must be an *intrinsic* one, it will come to this one. For value attaching to the inter-personal is typically moral. And that is what the second premise asserts, in taking the value at issue to be a *moral* value. Now, although the truth of these premises is not *demonstrated*, I hope to have done enough to make them more plausible than their respective denials.

Premise three: moral judgement as essentially particular

My point here is served if it is granted that we learn moral concepts in particular cases: learn what lying is, and what is wrong with it, by considering cases of lying, in the 'real world' or in fictions; and that even if we are sometimes presented with general abstract 'rules' ("thou shalt not kill"), we must make sense of them in concrete contexts, applying them to the situations in which we find ourselves.

And this can be difficult. A young soldier who thinks that, say, this general rule against killing might be rendered inapplicable by, for instance, his duty to his country in a just war, or an order of his commanding officer, might revise that conclusion, faced with a real, live enemy soldier. Equally, he might not! Clearly, one would have liked (and hoped) to have resolved such a question before one was in front of the enemy's bayonet. Yet how might moral judgements be learned with less risks?

Notice, one cannot *simply* appeal to one's rule ("thou shalt not kill"): for what does that rule amount to in *this* situation? Knowing the rule alone does not look promising here: for that is just a *formalisation*, to be applied (where possible) in the new situations faced. Is killing still as *absolutely* prohibited in this new context? Or was the prohibition never *that* absolute? The rule alone cannot decide. Equally, further rules will not help — on pain of the regress where an interpretive rule is needed for each new rule mentioned, and then one for that rule, and so on. And this was part of our earlier rejection of *formalism*.

Yet how does one *learn* moral concepts, learn to *use* them and to *understand* them? The insight of particularism is that, in learning morality, one does not learn a set of principles (only?), much less a set of rules — rather, one learns to make moral judgements; and one learns that first in specific contexts (Dancy, 1993 pp. 56–57). Since any such learning must take place in *some* particular situation, one might *hope* for 'learning-situations' *not* ones of maximum risk to life, limb, sanity or world peace.

Clearly, this particularist conception of moral judgement is both a specific thesis in philosophy and highly contentious. Still, the cases here give us reason to adopt it. What might seem to speak against it are two misconceptions: first, the view of morality as a system of *rules* — we have highlighted the mistakes here, namely that the application of rules cannot itself be a matter of rules. So something *other than* rules is required. Second, the assumption of a tension between particularism and moral principles; but particularism is only opposed to *substantive* moral principles, not to moral principles *as such*. For such 'substantive moral principles' are of precisely the kind claimed to apply clearly in one situation because applying in another. Our discussion of "thou shalt not kill" highlighted the difficulties here. So, on the contrary, for particularists:

> ... the moral relevance of a property in a new case cannot be predicted
> from its relevance elsewhere. (Dancy, 1993: p. 57)

Here "predicted" is the key term: for, of course, we will agree — once the plan of action is decided upon — that this case *instantiates* the principle. It is just that we could not know this 'before the fact'.

Thus far, then, we have suggested the particularised character of sporting value. Suppose such a conception is granted. But, then, how is that value to be learned, or explored?

Premises four and five: particularisation through cases exemplifing sporting situations

Premises four and five together sketch our solution. Crucial here is the central moral role of *justice*. Ronald Dworkin (1985: p. 219) rightly calls:

> ... the practice of worrying about what justice really is... the single
> most important social practice we have (my order)

And that is just what is going on here. To begin with premise five, the metaphors of *fair play*, *level playing field* give only the abstract form of, say, the complaint against unfairness, or the requirement for equal consideration: sporting situations can make these considerations concrete (in line with the particularism of premise three).

Sporting contests always admit the possibility of someone not participating fairly or of participation from a position of unfair initial disadvantage — this seems built-into the possibility of competitive activity.

So a framework for any practice worthy of the name "sport" may support these two metaphors ("fair play; "level playing field"). Two features suggest that the contextualisations here are indeed *moral*: the first, already mentioned, is the prevalence of the sporting metaphors in moral contexts. For the second, reflect on the (typical) experience of learning sporting principles. This usually happens in *appropriate* teaching of the sporting activity: what one learns is not — and could not be — just a formulation of the principle (a principle-formulation) but how to *behave* in accordance with the principle: for instance, how to manifest 'fair play' (which is, of course, no guarantee that one will then actually play fairly). In effect, then, principles are taught when rules are properly taught — where the term "properly" makes just that point! In teaching the rules of a game (for example, cricket), a teacher sensitive to the principles might inculcate those principles too: indeed, those of us who were well-taught can remember this process. So, if we cannot *say* how to teach these principles, we do at least *know*. Thus the model is of abstract principles learned from (and in) concrete instances in sport, then applied to concrete moral situations[5]. Taken together, these warrant my commitment to the moral possibilities of sport.

The argument's conclusion: the moral laboratory

Recall the insight of particularism: that, in learning morality, one learns — not a set of rules, not even a set of principles (only?) — but, rather, to make moral judgements; and one learns that first in specific contexts.

Sport, then, has the *possibility* of providing us with just such concrete cases where we can behave fairly (or justly) — examples of fair play — and also cases where inappropriate initial advantage can be taken (cases where there *isn't* a level playing field): hence, sport offers people a chance to operate with these concepts, and to act on them; to use them in discussion and to have others offer them. It also offers opportunities to confront others *not* acting on them — and, even, to fail to act on them oneself. In this way, one can explore the contours of morally-relevant possibilities. And this is what I mean in speaking of sport as a *moral laboratory*.

Is the term 'laboratory' justified by this? One might think not. Yet experiments in laboratories are characterised by their 'controlling' for certain possibilities: by not confronting all the vagaries of the real world at once — hence as offering a clearer (and simpler) 'version' of real situations. And that is what the 'moral laboratory' of sport offers, for sport has — typically — at least two main advantages as a learning site over encountering moral problems in one's life more generally. Both relate to the 'essential nature' of sport. First, sport typically has a set of *codified* rules: in this way, the rules (and the manner both of implementing and of changing them) are more straightforward than (other?) moral rules — which is not to say, of course, that their implementation is straightforward: judgement is still required. Second, the consequences of *failing* to behave in line with the rules (etc.) are typically much less severe: no-one ends up dead or maimed, for example — even if this does happen *sometimes*. So sport offers the possibility of learning judgement with less (than usual) consequences, less risked.

Suppose these ideas are accepted; do they achieve what is required? The original De Coubertin position, drawn from athleticism, urged *both* the moral character of sport *and* the transferability of that morality to the rest of one's life. Our particularist account of morality might accord *a* place within sporting situations for (the possibility of) moral choice — not the kind of *essential* moral education De Coubertin believed in, but more plausible for that. So we have a limited defence of this thesis.

Yet its very particularism might seem to undermine the usefulness of such a conclusion: for what I learn in the 'moral laboratory' is crucially *sport-morality*, rather than something which automatically generalises. Yet Olympism's justification lay in the possibility of a quite *general* good — a good not circumscribed by sport. But, as we shall see, our particularism is not a kind of 'no-transfer' thesis. For, if what one learns in learning moral judgement is "how to go on" (Wittgenstein, 1953 §151), one is *automatically* learning notions which might, in principle, have application elsewhere; and, since every later application will typically be *different* (from a particularist perspective), learning the concepts at all amounts to the first steps in learning to apply them *outside* of familiar cases.

Thinking about the moral laboratory

An over-riding concern of the 'moral laboratory' is with fairness: rules in sport are sometimes changed to facilitate just performance ("fair play"). For example, the introduction of the idea of a professional foul into soccer: that is, a foul which would be penalised sufficiently to equalise the situation. And this is regularly offered as an explanation of proposed rule-changes.

Two points about this thesis concerning rule-changes are important here: first, this is a silly *method*, given the need for judgement in the application of *all* rules (that is, the impossibility of *sealing off* all possible [mis-]interpretations). So one cannot expect any rule-change to necessarily succeed in imposing fairness, no matter how well drafted. For, however carefully one builds-in details of this situation only, other 'readings' of it — and hence other ways of treating it — are always possible (Travis, 1996 pp. 454–459): indeed, this is a quite general thesis from the philosophy of language. And a revealing example of the contextual nature of such 'rules' might be found there. It might be thought that, when rules are not clear, this is simply due to 'borderline cases'. But what are sometimes treated as exemplary of 'borderline cases' can, instead, be cases where (once characterised appropriately) a clear answer is available. As Charles Travis (1985) suggests, we might be puzzled as to how to react to the suggestion that there was an oil tanker in the harbour, faced with a hovercraft containing barrels of oil. As Travis notes, our conclusion might take one of three forms:

(a) **that it was true** — that this is the company's new kind of tanker;

(b) **that it was false** — that this was no tanker;

(c) **that it was a borderline case**.

And, in the particular case, our comment might be the appropriate, or true, one.

Travis' point (surely correct) is that — while we may not know, at a particular moment, which of these three worlds we find ourselves in — once we do know, the truth (or otherwise) of the claim we made about the tankers is perfectly determinate between, roughly, these three cases: it will be one or the other. But we can only come to this clarity once we have particularised the matter.

So the first point to learn was that the hope for rules which in-and-of themselves 'improve' fairness in a particular sport is vain — if we cannot find such exceptionless rules elsewhere, we should not expect them for sport. Yet the second point is to recognise that, nevertheless, this does represent one rationale! The proposed rule-change would indeed be justified to the extent that it really enhanced fairness or fairplay. And, to that degree, this aspiration is consonant with, and exemplifies, the moral character of sport. That it fails in *practice* might just be taken to reinforce that point.

We began from the interpenetration of moral notions with our lives — the moral metaphors from sport recognise that these notions (also?) have a role in sport. But those ideas are either *not* metaphorical or are *less* metaphorical in the sporting context, where there really can be fair playing and the levelness of actual playing fields. Seeing how these ideas interact with the rules and principles (and spirit) of sport can show us how such notions might *apply* — and hence, perhaps, how they might be applied more generally. This is to acknowledge a generality of application *very different* from simply generalising: it is the generalisability of the particularist. So the 'moral laboratory' is only teaching morality in sport (if it is) but that might have the possibility to achieve more: that is, to teach one to be a better human — perhaps, in learning to take *fragments* of one's life seriously, one learns to take life seriously.

This parallel also makes plain a limitation of the moral laboratory, a problem for the practice, not the theory. For, just as someone might be a master of pure mathematics but unable to 'manage' elementary applied maths (say, unable to quickly check one's change after buying a round of drinks), so one might be a master of the moral concepts in the sporting context but unable to apply them outside the 'laboratory'. There is no theoretical safeguard here, no guarantee that generalisability won't be thwarted (*pace* de Coubertin) — although eternal vigilance might work against this being a regular occurrence; and valuing sport partly as a moral laboratory might make such vigilance easier to organise!

As moral laboratory, sport is not a site for *trying out* morality: rather, it concerns learning to play within rules ... to circumscribe one's conduct within explicit rules ... later, such 'rules' will not (typically) be (so) explicit. So having learned *principles* will be more important.

Now, its possibilities as a moral laboratory are *intrinsic* to sport — they derive from its being rule-governed, involving human interactions where both fairness and harm are possible, and where the risk is not too great (perhaps there are other characteristics too). But this possibility is not *unique* to sport — although I cannot (now) think of plausible candidates.

So this argument, if accepted, would save a *great deal* of what de Coubertin *hoped for* from sport: the moral possibilities of sport would be *intrinsic* to it.

Problem: the moral nature of sport?

But is sport as I have said it is? For if it is not, this project is misconceived.

Certainly, not all uncontentious sport *conforms* to this description — a fact not *that* important, if most sport did. But it also seems inappropriate to be 'counting heads' here, to determine what *most* sports do (in theory and in practice).

Certainly, not all sport *operates* by emphasising fairness etc. (the rules of basketball [as interpreted] *require* players to foul). A horrible possibility here is the morally *harmful* side of sport. For if the connection is just to moral *issues*, then (first) there is no guarantee that contact with sport will be *positively* educative in respect of morality *and* (second) it is not clear that sport is *always* committed to the educative matters; or, better, that *all* sport is.

It is difficult to move on from here in the abstract: some concrete cases are needed. Yet sport operates for many purposes, and at many levels of performance and spectatorship. Which should be selected? As I began from De Coubertin (and in line with some of my interests), I shall draw my examples from high-level performance: namely, from Olympic sport. But my thought is that the *substance* of these points could be re-structured for other cases. (For example, with playground activities where considerations of fairplay had *no* place, one can readily imagine disputes about the sport-status of the activity.)

One way forward from *these* recognitions, then — especially for Olympism — would be the road of exclusion. Only some sports are appropriate to the moral laboratory, which is not to deny the interest of others, but just to deny them *this* interest. Take this to supply *appropriate* sports [for Olympism] as a basis for including/excluding 'candidate' Olympic events, given the need to reduce the size of the Games.

Let us briefly consider some candidates, to show *some* of the relevant considerations:

• **boxing** — the essential violence of the sport, the essential damage to others, precludes it from sensible consideration for the moral laboratory. Whatever the redeeming social values of, say, fighting for the Holy Family[6], there is little of *moral* worth to be found in boxing itself, even in its amateur incarnation (that is, before we turn to the place of biting chunks from the opponent's ear). And if I were wrong, advocates of boxing would show that it has *indeed* a place in the moral laboratory — that is, conduct the argument in my terms, so that (at worst) I am just wrong about the empirical details.

• **synchronised swimming** — this activity does not conduce to inappropriate moral values (as one might urge for boxing) so much as have no bearing on morality one way or another. Again, if this were clear, its place could then be argued against — if a retort emphasises its competitive nature, our counter-blast should stress the difficulty of integrating such competitiveness into essentially aesthetic activities. (And then we should also look hard at gymnastic vaulting, for instance.)

• **basketball** — basketball was initially a non-contact sport[7]: under one of its original thirteen rules[8], "... shouldering, holding, pushing, tripping or striking an opponent was not allowed". Equally, these rules are now interpreted so as to require, of players, *foul play* (rule-breaking in precisely this aspect)[9]. So that there is certainly a conflict here between the spirit of one rule and the interpretation of others.

The issue for basketball is *not* just that of players seeing 'what they can get away with' — what the referee will not notice, for example; or will not blow up. So the situation differs from that in some other sports.

Specific penalties for rule-breaking *within* the rules of the game do not exclude the player from the game permanently, do not result in automatic advantage to the other side in terms of the score (although giving a high probability of the other side scoring). An initial rationale for such rules was to equalise a situation where a player makes *accidental* contact with another (say, through over-enthusiasm), and where this would advantage his team. Moreover, the fixing of some permitted *number* of such infringements (and the associated penalties) is explained by the thought that accidents and over-enthusiasm do not strike in the same place ... well, an infinite amount of times ...: more than a few looks deliberate.

But, *more important* for us, the proscribed behaviours are *now* seen as what a player *ought* to do in certain circumstances — further, the idea of 'drawing the foul' means that this is 'part of the game' not only for those who perform this behaviour, but equally for their opponents.

Therefore, is this activity genuinely rule-breaking? Is the word "foul" here is really taken seriously any more? (In light-hearted moments, I imagine the 'powers that be' spelling the word F-O-W-L.) For this activity is brought *within* the rules of basketball — the distinction between the spirit and the letter of the rules (or between principles and rules) seems to break down. It has been argued that cheats are not playing the game at all, because they are not abiding by its constitutive rules (Leaman, 1995). Here, though, rules of the game *relate* to this way of behaving.

While showing nothing in-and-of themselves, these points sketch good reason to suppose that participation in such a sport (basketball is not alone here) could not possibly be morally educative through the inculcating of moral principles.

Here we see some practical possibilities of our investigations. With no place in the moral laboratory, such activities need have none in the Olympics (I am suggesting).

These three cases illustrate one aspect of pursuing the idea of a 'moral laboratory' where it leads, as well as a (potential) normativity to such an idea, one which might be applied elsewhere — say, in schools or in leisure centres — although I have not suggested how! And, of course, we should now turn to *other* cases, as well as to the interrogation of the premises of the argument that generates such conclusions.

Conclusion

As I said earlier, I regard this whole argument as a *research agenda* I am sharing with you. My suggestion, then, is that — in offering concrete realisations — sport can function as a *moral laboratory* for the (particular) engagement with moral concerns. In this way, it has the *potential* for a kind of 'moral educative-ness' not so far removed from De Coubertin's dream.

[Of course, this is (at best) only *one* aspect of sport: I am *not* urging that it is the most important.]

Nothing here sustains De Coubertin's *optimism* about sport: the 'moral laboratory' may teach *immorality*; or some people learn nothing from it — there is no *guarantee* of learning; and also no guarantee, even for those who have picked up the moral dimension *of sport*, that there will be any 'transfer' to the rest of their behaviour. These are reasons for pessimism about the Olympic Ideal. But they also indicate *potentials* or *possibilities* of sport, ways in which sport might help us to transcend our petty concerns with self etc.; and thus might serve the grand purposes De Coubertin envisaged.

Notes

1   Quotations from De Coubertin taken from MacAloon, 1981, since he
    translates them all, and also since his references are not always complete.

2   D'Agostino (1995: pp. 48–49) invented the term, although he is taken
    beyond simple formalism by his reference to an 'ethos' as "... that set of
    unofficial, implicit conventions which determine how the rules of that
    game are to be applied in concrete circumstances". For discussion, see
    Morgan (1995). Interestingly, then, the objection to arch-formalists [such
    as Meier (1995)] is not that their account of rules leaves out non-rule-
    based conditions on games/sport, but that they misunderstand the nature
    of rules, whether constitutive, regulative or whatever.

3   One might argue (as does Haugeland, 1998: p. 289, note 13) that there
    are really *no* chess pieces away from the game — that, once in the box,
    they are just bits of elaborately carved wood (say). Hence, calling them
    by the expression "chess pieces" was a kind of *alienans*, like "counterfeit
    money" — which is not money at all. Whatever one makes of the chess
    case, it *cannot* be straightforwardly true (*mutis mutandis*) for sports-
    persons: take them away from the game and they revert to being *human
    beings* (with human rights) — at least, if they do not 'revert' to being *stars*!

4   Although I see all of this debate as within Leisure Studies (if not only there),
    some of the theses are in philosophy in general (and therefore readily
    discussed there), some more specific to sport — and all concern the *poten-
    tial* of sport, not what will *inevitably* result from our engagement with it.

5   A third feature concerns the role of *narratives* — especially *particular*
    narratives — in acquiring moral concepts. For, as others have urged (see
    Whannell, 1992: pp. 140–147), just these narrative structures are used
    in explaining sport — with the suggestion of *uncovering* the narrative
    structure of (at least) *some* sport.

6   See Sugden (1996), where this is the title of chapter three. My point here
    could be exemplified by seeing how — having described boxing's political
    economy in general terms, and engaged it careful ethnographies — the
    last chapter (Chapter Six) is a discussion of boxing and society, concluding
    with an analysis of boxing in relation to inequality and poverty: as we are
    told, "The boxing subculture grows when poverty stands in the shadow
    of affluence" (p. 195). This is, of course, a comment — arguably, a
    profound comment — on what boxing can 'tell us' about the global social
    order: boxing is here our "sensitive cultural lens" (Beckles, 1995: p. 1
    [quoted earlier]).

7   As summarised by Mumford and Wordsworth, 1974 p. 19: "There will be no contact between opponents".

8   As recorded in Ebert and Cheatum, 1977 p. 4: this was to instantiate the principle "no tackling or other rough conduct" (p. 4). A more modern commentator expressly discusses this idea in terms, not of the prohibition against contact, but of the personal foul: see Wilkes (1994): "A *personal foul* results when contact is made with an opponent while the ball is alive" (p. 96). "In general, the personal foul is charged to any player who causes bodily contact ... [with an opponent]" (p. 97).

9   As Wilkes (1994 p. 96) notes: "Though basket ball is sometimes referred to as a noncontact sport, it is far from that — aggressive play with bodily contact is the rule rather than the exception".

References

Beckles, H. McD. (1995) 'Introduction', in Beckles, H. McD. and Stoddart, B (eds.) *Liberation cricket: West Indies cricket culture*. Manchester: Manchester University Press, pp. 1–4.

D'Agostino, F. (1995) 'The ethos of games', in W. J. Morgan and K. V. Meier (eds.) *Philosophic inquiry in sport* (2nd edition). Champaign, IL: Human Kinetics, pp. 42–49.

Dancy, J. (1993) *Moral reasons*. Oxford: Blackwell.

Dworkin, R. (1977) *Taking rights seriously*. Cambridge, MA: Harvard University Press.

——— (1985) *A matter of principle*. Cambridge, MA: Harvard University Press.

Ebert, F. H. and Cheatum, B. A. (1977) *Basketball* (2nd edition). Philadelphia, PA: W. B. Saunders Co.

Haugeland, J. (1998) *Having thought*. Cambridge, MA: Harvard University Press.

Jennings, A. (1996) *The **new** lords of the rings*. London: Simon & Schuster.

Leaman, O. (1995) 'Cheating and fair play in sport', in W. J. and K. V. Meier (eds), *Philosophic inquiry in sport* (2nd edition). Champaign, IL.: Human Kinetic Publishers, pp. 193-7.

Lorenz, K. (1966) *On aggression*. London: Methuen.

MacAloon, J. (1981) *This great symbol: Pierre de Coubertin and the origins of the modern Olympic games* Chicago: University of Chicago Press.

McFee, G. (1998) 'Are there philosophical issues with respect to sport?', in McNamee, M. and Parry, S. J. (eds.) *Ethics and sport*. London: Routledge: pp. 3–18.

——— (2000) 'Spoiling: an indirect reflection of sport's moral imperative?', in Tannsjo, T. and Tamburrini, C. (eds.) *Values in sport*. London: Routledge: pp. 172–182.

McIntosh, P. (1979) *Fair play*. London: Heinemann.

Meier, K. (1995) 'Triad trickery: playing with games and sports', in W. J. Morgan and K. V. Meier (eds.) *Philosophic inquiry in sport* (2nd edition). Champaign, IL: Human Kinetics, pp. 23–41.

Morgan, W. J. (1995) 'The logical incompatibility thesis and rules: a reconsideration of formalism as an account of games', in W. J. Morgan and K. V. Meier (eds.) *Philosophic inquiry in sport* (2nd edition). Champaign, IL: Human Kinetics, pp. 50–63.

Mumford, K. and Wordsworth, M. A. (1974) *A beginner's guide to basketball*. London: Pelham Books.

Sugden, J. (1996) *Boxing and society: An international analysis*. Manchester: Manchester University Press.

Travis, C. (1985) 'On what is strictly speaking true', *Canadian Journal of Philosophy*, Vol. 15: pp. 187–229.

——— (1996) 'Meaning's role in truth', *Mind*, Vol. 105: pp. 451–466.

Whannel, G. (1992) *Fields in vision*. London: Routledge.

Wilkes, G. (1994) *Basketball* (sixth edition). Madison, WI: Brown & Benchmark.

Wittgenstein, L. (1953) *Philosophical investigations*. (trans. G. E. M. Anscombe) Oxford: Blackwell.

Part III

PROFESSIONALISM

Applying the Principles of "Green Games": An Investigation into the Green Practices of Event Organisers

Graham Berridge

London School of Tourism, Hospitality and Leisure,
Thames Valley University, London (UK)

Introduction

This paper discusses the use of sustainable practices by organisers of mountain bike events in the United Kingdom (UK). The research was conducted between February 1999 and June 1999. The aim of this study was to examine the extent to which Chernushenko's (1994) concept of a green games ethic for sports events was a feature of event organisation. This paper summarises Chernushenko's 12 principles for sustainable sport and sets these in the context of wider social initiatives on sustainability, such as Agenda 21, and then applies these, through the means of a questionnaire, to the specific context of mountain bike events.

Chernushenko's 12 principles

In 1994 a concept for a sustainable green games ethic for sports events was developed (Chernushenko, 1994). This ethic, for looking at sport and sporting events, reiterated the ability of sport to involve mass participation, to inspire and motivate people, but it also identified that sport:

> when pursued without the limitations of a guiding ethic, (it) can cause severe and even irreparable harm — to people's health and well being and to the health and well being of the planet. (Chernushenko, 1994: pp. pxii)

The main thrusts of Chernushenko's argument were that a) organisational practice (of sports events) contributed to global and environmental concerns

Table 1   Summary of Chernushenko's 12 principles of sustainable sport

Conservation —	preserving natural resources — e.g. forests, habitat. Sport tends to take this for granted, but does not have a strong 'code' to protect such environments.
Stewardship —	individuals and organisations recognising their duty to manage and safe-keep resources for posterity
Partnership —	organisers and sponsors, host communities, working together from the earliest stages to limit waste/impact on environment
Leadership —	organisations acting to show good practice/saolutions for others to emulate
Quality —	moving away from 'higher, faster and stronger' ethic, which induces unnatural, synthetic and dangerous developments
Responsibility —	adopting appropriate attitude to participation; retaining ethical and moral stance, denouncing cheating
Democratization —	consulting with stakeholders over decisions
Investing in the future —	leaving a positive legacy for the host community via finance, facilities, community spirit etc.
Equity —	seeking to include rather than exclude particular social groups
Diversity —	ensuring different conditions exist through different facilities rather than monoculture conditions and facilities
Active living —	recognising activity and participation rather than high performance and sophisticated equipment

through energy consumption, air pollution, waste disposal, habitat loss, soil erosion and so forth and b) ecological degradation made it difficult (and may make it impossible) for some sports to be pursued. To support his ideas, Chernushenko uncovered the wanton wastefulness associated with sports events and called for a green games ethic whereby organisers would embody a combination of environmental stewardship, economic efficiency and social responsibility. He catalogued how a number of sports events were damaging to the environment and that such practice was wide in range across sporting disciplines. This viewpoint of sports event organisation was explored in further detail down through international, regional and local events to illustrate that sporting events were being organised in a manner that exacerbated waste and which was potentially and explicitly harmful to the environment, participants and spectators.

Chernushenko attempted to offer some direction for the adoption of green practices as he explored the economic and political influences on sport and the costs of sport to athletes, society and the environment. The outcome of his study was to produce a way forward for sports organisers to embrace a green ethic and to adopt sustainable practices. These practices he called the 12 principles of sustainable sport and are summarised in Table 1. Some are relatively straightforward to adopt, such as the use of recycled paper whilst others, the idea of green sponsorship, require a more fundamental shift in attitude. It is these principles that this research is concerned with investigating by collecting data from mountain bike event organisers to assess how effective they are in currently adopting green practices.

Wider social context

Such observations of the use of resources were not, of course, a new issue or a new discovery especially where the focus is not only on effective land-use but also on effective organisational process. However for sport, this kind of analysis was relatively new, although it must be observed that the introduction of a planning guide for sport (Sports Council, 1993) did attempt to instil some sense of environmental awareness into planning for facilities if not into their actual organisation. In not recognising the need for greater organisational ethics it could be argued that we are consequently undermining a central element of many sporting activities, which is that, they are inextricably linked to ideas of health, well being, pursuit of purpose and morality. Indeed many of these ideals form the basis of our definitions of sport and leisure generally (Torkildsen, 1999; Kelly, 1982; Neulinger, 1974; Kaplan, 1975; Roberts, 1970) and leisure activities are seen as an ingredient that makes our quality of life much improved (Argyle, 1996). The Government's Sport For All policy is also part of a drive where the benefits of sport and recreation are being used to deal with social exclusion and promote health. Furthermore, in developing a code of practice on conservation, access and recreation, the Department of the Environment, Transport and the Regions (DETR) states that the:

> main considerations should, therefore, be to: use sporting and recreational activities as a way of increasing awareness of, and appreciation for, the environment and to increase support for its protection; provide and design facilities and activities which follow the principles of sustainable development. (DETR, 1999: p 5.1)

Therefore, in offering such provision it is logical that we should be careful to assist in, and not destroy, the betterment of the environment we are using to provide such activities. Sport has been recognised as a central activity in the formation of leisure and leisure experiences (Rossman, 1989) and if the organisation of it begins to harm this environment it can, from a sustainable viewpoint, be seen as neither an improvement nor perhaps an essential.

It is because some of the underlying premises of sport are reflected through this image of health and well being that the practices of the organisers of sporting events is an issue of interest and in particular the extent to which a guiding ethic on the use of resources is present. Interest in this also reflects wider society concerns with how we manage the environment in general. While concerns for environmental practice in sport are not obviously apparent, concerns for environmental practice in society are. To the public at large the focus of such concerns stems from the 1992 UN Conference, the commonly referred to, Earth Summit. Agenda 21 was the main document to come out of the conference, and although it is not legally binding, it provides a blue print for securing a sustainable future and a compelling practical and moral force for not only governments but also local democracies (Lipman *et al.*, 1995). Written by representatives of governments responsible for its implementation:

> Agenda 21 places a strong emphasis on people and their communities and an organisational approach, which stresses the needs of the poorest. Furthermore the conference recommended that each country should incorporate Agenda 21 at local level and coined the phrase "think globally, act locally". (Harris, 1997: p. 5)

Barber (1996) explains that this summit also helped concretise the definition of sustainable development that is universally acceptable and which is "development that meets the needs of the present without compromising the ability of future generations to meet their own need" (Barber, 1996: p. 1). Whilst applying his argument to the role of sustainable leisure in cities, Barber also rationalises the place of leisure activities in society as a belief that "opportunities for recreation are essential to sustaining all that is best in society as well as improving the environment in which we live" (1996: p3.). In other words leisure activities should contribute meaningfully to our way of life and should act to enrich our social environment.

This view of the place of leisure is emphasised by the DETR (1997: p. 1) which states:

> The key sustainable development objectives are to maintain the quality of the environment in which leisure takes place, and which is an essential part of the UK's attractiveness to tourists, for future generations to enjoy; thus contributing to the quality of life of those taking part in leisure activities, and maximising the economic contribution of tourism, while protecting natural resources.

Whilst the inclusion of sustainable indicators for sport and leisure is welcome, the adoption of Agenda 21 missions are more commonly associated with tourism based developments (Cater and Lowman, 1994; Lipman *et al.*, 1995; Harris, 1997). There are therefore wider social interests in sustainability and, particularly, the impact of tourism (Travis, 1982; Brockleman and Dearden, 1992). Having a sustainable component as a significant feature of tourism has developed with the emergence of the concept of eco-tourism (Boo, 1990; Wight, 1993; Western, 1993) which, with the impetus of Agenda 21, has led in turn to the emergence of voluntary codes of practice as a method for promoting environmentally sound development and management (Williams, 1993). Codes of practice in tourism have been led, for example, through the United Nations Environment Programme and have been transferred into practice via organisations such as the World Travel and Tourism Council and the World Tourism Council. Sport is, by comparison, some way behind in a practice that is even for tourism, admittedly, still in its infancy. Associations like the Canadian Olympic Committee, Pan-American Games and the Sydney 2000 Organising Committee have issued documents on how sustainable practice will feature in their events and are currently acting as regional and global messengers. However the Atlanta 1996 Organising Committee had a well publicised green programme but which in practice suffered by, for example, high pollution, travel conditions and competition environments. What remains unclear is whether ethical codes of practice are intrinsically present in the organisation of sports, not just at high profile international events but at regional and local ones as well.

If sport event organisation is going to adopt a consistent green ethic how will it emerge? In some cases certain sports appear to already have a guiding ethic, whether intrinsically or one that has been thrust upon them, but usually as a result of the sports' need to address environmental issues at various stages of its evolution. Activities such as mountaineering, rambling, fell running and canoeing might well fit into this bracket but so too do newer sports where voluntary codes of conduct have been established. This is especially the case where the sport uses natural outdoor resources and is exposed to the potential of recreation conflict with other users and landowners. Writing about jet-skiing, Anderson and Johnson (1998: p. 76) observe that:

> Management of potential impacts in the UK has focused on the establishment of relevant byelaws, together with voluntary codes of practice for specific sports and non-statutory management plans for defined geographical areas, within the coastal zone ... jet skiers are perceived by many as a problem.

Mountain biking in particular falls into this bracket as it has experienced a number of conflict issues since its introduction into the UK in the mid 1980's. As the above authors comment the growth of mountain biking and snowboarding is similar in occurrence to jet-skiing which is part of the "growth and challenge of a new 'lycra' activity along side more well established activities" (p: 80).

Mountain bike context

Mountain Bike events were selected to test Chernushenko's principles for a number of reasons, some of which are cited above. In the management of mountain bike events there exists a spread of organisation types with a high proportion reflecting Parker's (1999) notion of volunteering, others having moved from voluntary into commercialism (Tomlinson, 1979) with a few being purely commercial. Like most sports whose infrastructure is made up of hundreds of volunteers (Watt, 1998) so too is mountain bike event organisation with the majority linked to mountain bike or cycle clubs who promote the sport and events without any direct personal financial gain. Whilst only a very few organisers exhibit commercial traits, most of these being linked to cycle retailers, there are a several organisers who are quasi voluntary in the sense that some financial gain is made but extensive use is made of volunteers and money donated to charitable causes. This profile would allow for a spread of opinions on the underlying principles of running a mountain bike event.

In addition, the development of the sport of mountain biking has reflected and raised green issues in a number of ways: access to the countryside; environmental impact concerns; promotion of activity as having green credentials; location of events; nature of land use. Mountain bike events take place outdoors at countryside locations using natural terrain as the location for challenge. The creation of courses for organised competition requires some inevitable shaping of land for the layout of a course and this may involve some terrain damage as a result. The impact of 500 plus riders travelling over a course, some up to 4 or 5 times, also causes erosion of the land. Recreational riding and the use of trails also causes an impact and has been the issue of recreational conflict in the countryside in areas such as the Malvern Hills, Forest of Dean, Cannock Chase, Exmoor and the Lake District. These issues have been debated and reflected in practice through many of the countryside land owning, managing and access control agencies such as the Forestry Commission, Countryside Commission, National Parks Authority, Countryside Landowners Association as well as the Ramblers and the Horse Society. In some cases cycling has led to the banning of events and restrictions imposed on riding in specific areas (Berridge, 1996). As a sport there exists an established governing body, the British Cycling Federation, and an international authority, the Union Cycliste International (UCI) and as such there is a hierarchy responsible for racing sanction, management and development. The importance of a governing body is noted by Watt (98) who states that "they act as the representative voice of a specific sport at all levels, the demands on the organisation are substantial" (Watt, 1998. p 59). As a disseminator of initiatives, developments, and government policy, the governing body has a crucial role to play in the direction a sport may take and its involvement and influence is highly significant. The organisation of mountain bike events, then, reflects a number of issues that have a direct relevance to wider concerns over how we use resources and the impact this has on the environment.

Methodology

The first stage of the research consisted of adapting Chernushenko's 12 principles so that they were specifically relevant to the nature of mountain bike events. This resulted in a twenty-item questionnaire with the vast majority having option check/button boxes relating to specific green issues reflected in organising mountain bike events. Organisers of local, regional and national mountain bike events were then contacted. Two methods were used to collect data. A traditional paper questionnaire form was available and there was also an on line questionnaire made available which was accessed via a "mountain bike events survey" website. The website was specifically set up for the survey and posted via Freeserve a popular internet service provider. This site was then meta-linked to internet portal search engines Yahoo!, AltaVista, and Lycos. A link was also established through an existing website, CycleLondon. Using this approach served a number of purposes. It allowed remote access to the survey from event organisers who did not form part of a direct mailshot. It also gave those organisers contacted via a land mailshot the option of completing either a paper survey or an online one. Furthermore organisations that were listed with email could be contacted directly as part of a internet mailshot. The last method was also aimed at overseas (typically USA and

Australia) organisations, although the responses gained from that part of the mailshot do not form part of this particular paper. Organisers were selected from events diaries in specialist magazines, direct promotional material and web site addresses and all were promoting competitive events. Additional email addresses were obtained from the public domain website CyberCyclery.com which lists cycling organisations and clubs and a brief summary of their activities/events. These were contacted and asked to complete either a hard copy or on-line copy of the survey. The total number of UK responses accounted for over 50 separate mountain bike events with the majority of these classified as regional or local based.

Results and observations

The results were categorised according to which one of the 12 principles the answers related. The heading from table 1 of quality has been used to assess the overall extent to which the events could be said to be incorporating green practice within a qualitative framework rather than a quantitative one and was based on the overall results from the survey. This is an assessment of whether or not mountain bike events generally are effective in practice for the principle of quality using a simple range: very poor — poor — mixed — good — very good. Using the overall assessment principle of quality the results show that for 7 out of the 11 headings, event practice was rated as good. This would suggest that mountain bike events are not pre-occupied with the "higher faster stronger" motto of the Olympic Games as the sole driving force behind their events but are in fact incorporating values that Lenk has called "smaller, more beautiful, more intimate, more participatory, more humane" (Chernushenko, 94: p 81).

This feature of organisation is also reflected in the results for the responsibility principle, which, asked organisers if they actively promoted no cheating/no bad behaviour. 65% actively did in their literature and public address announcements with reminders of the rules of participation and race etiquette being rigorously employed, especially at the race sign-on area. This reflects what is known as the self-sufficiency rule in mountain bike events. This rule, which is the formal and moral core of mountain bike racing and has been a feature of mountain bike racing since its first inception, states that solely the rider must repair any mechanical failures during the race. This means that any rider getting a puncture, for example, has to carry with them the appropriate tools to fix the puncture (new inner tube, tyre levers, air pump). If they do not then their race is effectively over since any rider seeking outside assistance from spectators or team support is disqualified. On occasions riders at national and international level have tried to bend this rule and have been instantly disqualified. Similarly prestigious teams with high profile sponsors have sought to have the rule replaced so that team support can be on hand to assist any rider who has a mechanical failure. This would mean, in effect, that a rider could replace their whole bike if the original one was damaged, a rule that is a feature of cyclo-cross. Such a situation as in cyclo-cross clearly tends to favour well-financed teams or individuals who can have a whole array of support equipment and helpers to overcome a mechanical failure. The retention of the self-sufficiency rule maintains the equal chance aspect of the sport and in doing so also retains an element of quality of purpose instead of quantity of finance and support.

A further issue of responsibility is that of ethical behaviour. Mountain bike racing has an established race etiquette that is used in cases of overtaking and general trail behaviour and this forms part of officially sanctioned rules of racing. It espouses fairly good etiquette such as lapped riders should give way to leading riders and riders overtaking should inform the rider in front which side they will pass on. Equally, it states that boisterous abuse of slower riders and physically aggressive rider contact is not permitted, neither is abuse of officials. Transgression of this principle, if discovered and reported to the organiser, can result in disqualification. One organiser running a weekly set of races made the practice of publicly humiliating any rider found to transgress such rules by calling their name out at the start line of the next race and in some cases banning them for one race. In another instance an organiser of a national status event disqualified a rider of international renown and ranking for verbally abusing a course marshal. Enforcement such as this serves to remind riders of the need to practice race etiquette and supports the notion of a strong ethical element to organisational practice and a desire to ensure that intimidation of newer and slower riders is not acceptable. It should be noted however that such public actions of disqualification are very rare and in most instances their exists an internal ethical practice on the part of riders.

These are further supported by the principle of active-living. Organisers were asked to grade the extent to which they promoted any strong social attitudes for participants and were asked to rate this between 0–5 with 5 being a high feature. Overall support for active living type features was rated 3.95 out of 5 which means a high proportion of organisers focused on promotion of healthy lifestyles, respect for the environment, personal challenge, camaraderie and being there participating. By contrast, the status symbol features of the event reflected in the outlook of ultra competition, fashion and trend setting was rated only 2.25. This suggests that the underlying values of behaviour and attitude of riders is not one of win-at-all-costs but is much more reflective of taking part for personal achievement rather than public glory.

A similar theme is also evident in the responses to the principle relating to equity and access, which asked organisers if they encouraged a wide range of social groups to participate. Whilst none promoted or gave unwaged concessions all events had an entry fee structure related to age and ability category with, in some cases, seven different pricing options. 70% had reduced entry fees for age groups under 16; 100% stated they did not tolerate sexist commentary or behaviour; 100% held specific races for novices and women; whilst 55% also ran under 12's races which were on a shorter version of the main course. Spot prizes were handed out at 57% of events, a prize given on a whim to any rider deemed worthy of merit. This can be for colour of shirt/bike, name, style etc. and seeks to award random participants not only those who are successful in competition. Overall the results for this section highlights that organisers do attempt to make their events accessible to all, up to a certain point. Whilst all events had age and ability categories for both male and female riders, there were significant differences in how this was implemented, often reflected in the status of the event. Although not specifically the result of the data collected here it is common practice at mountain bike events to have age range categories from under 12's up to over 55's and ability categories within those.

Answers to the question of using and recycling materials for the event gave an indication of the eco-efficiency principle. This was well supported with 85% recycling materials in one form or another suggesting an awareness of the need not to unnecessarily waste resources in endlessly creating from scratch. However racing materials such as race numbers 57% and number ties 42% are not so well supported indicating that the major area of recycle usage is in paper materials i.e. publicity, entry forms and more physical course marking i.e. stakes. This view of eco-efficiency is also supported by organisers of regional events for example a group in the south of England co-operated to reuse central event supplies such as podiums, directional course marking and banners. The Governing body also assists in this process by supplying similar centrally based materials that any organiser can use. This is a practice that most regional status series events would be likely to adopt.

One issue that has plagued mountain biking both competitively and recreationally is that of land erosion and terrain damage where the perception by other land users is that mountain bikers cause extensive erosion and damage compared to other users (Berridge 96) although evidence and research on this topic is minimal. The idea behind the principle of stewardship is that organisers act effectively to prevent long term or permanent damage. Asked whether or not they caused damage to terrain in building a course 100% of organisers admitted that putting on the event did result in damage to terrain. This can be further qualified with 85% noting that this was occasional and only 15% saying damage was frequent. Their response to such damage provides a key to organiser attitudes with 70% indicating they made some effort to repair this damage, and of those 42% cited rebuilding of a specific area, 28% tree planting and 30% general repair work. This indicates that effective stewardship is a concern although the evidence is inconclusive that practice on preservation of the terrain is wholeheartedly applied.

Preservation for the future is also reflected through the principles investing in the future and democratisation. For the former, organisers were asked if they made any kind of return, financial or otherwise, to the area where the event took place and responses showed a strong awareness of the impact on the host community with all making at least one worthy return to the immediate area and 84% making more than one. Donations to charity (56%) was the most preferred method, but other options included controlling access to the site (42%), with 58% involved in any clean-up of the area surrounding the race site. Linked to this is the idea of democratisation, which offers some insight into how an events future may be shaped. In response to the question of consultation with stakeholders, 85% directly consulted stakeholders of one type or another and of these over 50% consulted with more than one group. 42% directly consulted riders, 15% spectators, 30% other event organisers, 85% local landowners, 15% the local community, 42% with volunteers and 12% with other agencies, (mainly service support). Asked if they considered riders' needs specifically only 54% said they did. Of these, 44% provided drinks stations, 28% advice on sun exposure and 42% attempted to avoid river crossings (land layout permitting). All events, as is common practice, varied the start times of racing. So whilst stakeholders were generally consulted this was mostly a reference to the landowner not the host community and there were clear gaps in approach to dealing with and looking after riders. The issue of land used for races being off-limits to recreational riding is a factor and, historically, some landowners in the UK have discontinued events because riders have attempted to access a site post-event. A clear and active working relationship with the immediate area, both landowners and community is crucial to this as also is the support of those who participate and service an event. In this respect, organisers demonstrated a number of ways of achieving this such as donations to local youth groups or ambulance services, which undoubtedly reflected the local context.

As stated above, riders were directly consulted and, whilst not part of the data collected, it is likely that this consultation had more to do with the actual course design rather than race operations. This last point can be linked to the principle of diversity, which was addressed through the question of changing course design. 85% of events consistently made efforts to re-design race course layouts on sites that were used more than once, averting criticism of adopting a monoculture towards race conditions and courses and of providing a sterile racing environment.

Concerning overall conservation principles there were some inconsistencies in organisers' practice, both between different events and within the same event. Much of this can perhaps be put down to the poor documented aspects of practice amongst organisers since only 14% stated they had a written policy on general conservation. What is also clear is that reference points for good practice were almost invisible as codes of practice for organisers were primarily concerned with how to put the event on. The governing body for the sport, the BCF, had extremely limited input on green practice other than very general guidelines. It is interesting to note here that due to political circumstances the access network of mountain biking is no longer a part of the Governing body but resides in a separate more recreationally based organisation the Cycle Touring Club. The access network is a regionally organised, voluntary run grouping and represents mountain biking on the issues of land access with landowners and managing agencies. Its separation may explain why written policy is so sparse and why there is emphasis, by the BCF, on race organisation but not equally on land conservation and green practice. The anomalies in this principle between policy and practice are further indicated in the leadership principle. Although clearly strong in some areas, leadership was weak in others. Here organisers were asked if they made riders aware of good environmental practice and some, who had highly effective green features elsewhere, failed to consistently make riders aware of how they could adopt green practices. Only 57% said they made riders aware by advising them not to discard air canisters or inner tubes and 14% advised on using environment friendly lube. This could be seen as a contradiction since support for self-sufficiency is a race rule but advice on safe disposal is not strongly applied.

The last principle to be considered is that of partnerships and in this respect organisers at this level were not willing to compromise potential sponsorship. Asked if they vetted or refused sponsors on ethical grounds, of the 85% who had sponsors, none vetted a sponsor on green principles (again evidence of the failure of a written policy) and none had ever rejected a sponsor on ethical grounds. Some did make the point, however, that they did not chase sponsorship in certain areas (tobacco and alcohol) although this only accounted for 20% of responses. Notably, and this information was given informally but there is no reason to doubt its authenticity, the Governing body itself had rejected sponsorship offers in the past with products it felt were not appropriate, which suggests it is taking the lead in some areas if not others.

Conclusion

In summary, mountain bike organisers appear to have a commendable approach to green event organising albeit with self-preservation evident. It is clear though that there are aspects of practice that need developing and, crucially, further guidance since poor environmental management of a racing site could lead to any further events being banned on that site. Their efforts warrant further praise due to the poor leadership offered by the governing body. In effect the leadership on sustainable practice comes from within the sport itself, consisting of riders, the organisers and their regional groupings. The reasons behind this are primarily to do with the conditions in which mountain biking has emerged, whereby in order to be accepted as a viable user of the countryside by managing agencies (on a par particularly with ramblers and horse riders), it has had to show due respect for the land through its practice in organised events and application through recreational riding. In the majority of cases surveyed here it appears to be doing this but despite some regional exceptions this is being done mostly in isolation rather than as part of a co-ordinated national strategy. Mountain bike event organisers are practising the principles of sustainable events, up to a point, and are doing so primarily through their own good faith and need to preserve future usage of any areas they use. What is missing is a much clearer organisational structure to make green practice consistent at all events and this is where the governing body has a role to play in adopting these principles in a more formulated policy so as to assist in disseminating information more effectively than it is currently doing, a process which Chernushenko would strongly advocate.

References

Anderson, J and Johnson, D (1998) 'As charmless as chain-saws?: Managing jet ski use in the UK', in U. Merkel, G. Lines, G. and I. McDonald (eds) *The production and consumption of sport cultures: Leisure culture and commerce* (LSA publication 62). Eastbourne: Leisure Studies Association, pp. 75–86.

Argyle, M. (1996) *The social psychology of leisure*. London: Penguin

Barber, A. (1996) Sustainable leisure in the international city. Paper presented to WLRA 4th World Congress. Cardiff.

Berridge, G. (1996) Mountain bike access to the countryside. Paper presented to LSA/VVS Conference, Wageningen.

Brockleman, W. Y. and Dearden, P. (1992) 'The role of nature trekking in conservation: A case study in Thailand', *Environmental Conservation* Vol. 17, No. 2: pp. 141–148.

Boo, E. (1990) *Ecotourism: The potentials and pitfalls*. Volume 1 and 2. Washington DL: World Wildlife Fund.

Cater and Lowman. (1994) *Ecotourism: A sustainable option?*. London: Wiley.

Chernushenko, D. (1994) *Greening our games: Running sports events and facilities that won't cost the earth*. Ottawa: Centurion Publishing.

Code of practice on conservation, access and recreation consultation draft. chapter 5. recreation. (1999 May 6). London. Department of the Environment and Transport and the Regions. Retrieved June 10, 1999 from the World Wide Web: http://environment.detr.gov.uk/consult/copcar/chap5.htm.

Harris, D. (1997) Sustainable tourism: Examples of best practice for the London Borough of Hounslow. Consultant publication.

Indicators of sustainable development for the UK: leisure and tourism indicator family. (1997, December 11) London. Department of the Environment and Transport and the Regions. Retrieved June 10, 1999 from the World Wide Web: http://environment.detr.gov.uk/epsim/indics/isdc. htm.

Kaplan, M (1975) *Leisure theory and policy*. New York: Wiley.

Kelly, J. (1982) *Leisure*. New Jersey: Prentice Hall.

Lipman, Savignac and Strong. (1995) *Agenda 21 for the travel and tourism industry: Towards environmentally sustainable development*. London: WTTC/WTO.

Neulinger, J. (1974) *The psychology of leisure*. Springfield IL: Charles, C Thomas.

Parker, S. R. (1999) 'Volunteering: Altruism, markets, causes and leisure', *World Leisure and Recreation* Vol. 39, No. 3: pp. 4–5.

Roberts, K. (1970) *Leisure*. London: Longman.

Rossman, J. R. (1989) *Recreation programming: Designing leisure experiences*. Champaign Il. Sagamore Publishing.

The Sports Council (1993) *Planning and provision for sport factfile*. London. Sports Council.

Travis, A. S. (1982) 'Managing the environmental and cultural impacts of tourism and leisure development', *Tourism Management* Vol. 3, No. 4: pp. 256–262.

Tomlinson, A. (1979) *Leisure and the role of voluntary clubs and voluntary groups*. London: Sports Council/SSRC.

Torkildsen, G. (1999) *Leisure and recreation management* (4th ed). London. E and FN Spon .

Watt, D. C. (1998) *Sports management and administration*. London: E and FN Spon.

Wight, P. (1993) 'Ecotourism: Ethics or eco-sell?', *Journal of Travel Research*, Vol. 31, No. 3: pp. 39.

Williams, PW (1993) 'Environmental business practice: Ethical codes of conduct for tourism', *Hospitality Trends* Vol. 7, No. 1: pp. 8–11.

Western, D. (1993) 'Defining ecotourism', in K. Lindberg and D. E. Hawkins (eds) *Ecotourism: A guide for planners and managers*. North Bennington: The Ecotourism Society, pp. 7–11.

The Professionalisation of Museum Volunteers: An Ethical Dilemma

Margaret Graham

Moffat Centre for Travel and Tourism Business Development, Glasgow Caledonian University (UK)

Introduction

This paper draws from a multi-method study of volunteering in a Scottish urban museum service and considers emergent professional characteristics among volunteers and the ethical dilemmas that develop as a result. Research methods include data drawn from elite interviews with stakeholders involved in volunteer policy and supervision. An exploratory study of volunteer profiles and experiences was drawn from data acquired from a questionnaire survey, focus groups and participant observation as volunteer. Following essential background, this paper will focus on the pros and cons associated with volunteer professional characteristics and traits. The results will be presented under various headings that reflect different aspects of the professionalising process of contemporary volunteering in the context of this particular museum setting.

Background

In the midst of a raft of fundamental change, museum professionals have to follow new directions to accommodate innovatory recreational roles if they are to survive. Commentators argue that the values museums cling to originate in the project of modernity. This in many ways hinder them from reassessing their purpose to meet the real needs, rather than the perceived, idealised needs of contemporary society (Graham and Foley, 1998; MacDonald, 1996; Davies, 1994). Lima de Faria (1995) argues that as well as creating more exciting interactive exhibits museums need to provide specialists trained in communication skills if they are to attract and hold the interest of a more diversified public. Further problems emerge as museums are having to reassess their civic purpose as they move away from financial dependence

185

and become more accountable towards their potential market role as part of their local leisure and tourism economy (Ambrose, 1994; Graham and Foley, 1998). Hence a serious deficit in professional skill means that museums are relying more on cost-effective flexible employment opportunities. This has generated immense implications concerning their professional credentials and heightens their dependence on a more diverse and knowledgeable pool of volunteer support.

Increasingly volunteers are being trained and utilised as the interface between visitor and exhibit at many levels, from the research process, through to the interpretation, conservation and delivery of the museum collection as cultural product (Conway, 1996 and Graham, 1996). However, as more is expected from volunteers there is more pressure to maximise their effective utility (Graham *et al.*, 1999). Raising standards of performance through good practice management and training has been addressed as a positive step forward by leading museum agencies such as the Museums Association and the Culture and Heritage National Training Organisation (the former Museum Training Institute retitled to encompass its much wider role as Government training agency for culture and heritage). However, the complexities involved in formalising control over and developing the skills of museum volunteers are two-fold. Firstly, museums generally lack appropriate people management skills. Secondly, there are ethical issues to be addressed regarding on the one hand the potential of professionalising volunteers in museum skills and on the other hand the potential of managing unpaid workers.

Up until the mid 1980s museum voluntarism involved a limited supply of volunteers willing to support the work of paid staff. The stereotypical profile of voluntarism tended to be enshrouded in pejorative, gendered, stereotypes. Attitudes towards volunteers assumed them to be middle aged, middle class, women with limited ability. Although there has been a complete turnaround, with demand for museum voluntary positions exceeding supply, some categories of volunteer are becoming more sought after and marketable than others. Indeed American commentators such as Tedrick, Davis and Coutant, (1986) use the term volunteerism to describe a new professional profile being attached to volunteers. They argue that volunteering in recreation and the arts is more likely to be undertaken by highly educated people who expect their voluntary work to be 'meaningful and purposeful'. Although their existing skills and their potential to develop them further are a central focus of the effective management recommendations made by the authors, they suggest a rise in cost benefits will add to their value credentials.

This section on background will help guide the analysis of this paper which will examine how social change impacts on the activities of volunteers in terms of a professionalisation process.

Professional Accountability in Museums

In this particular urban museum service, some museums are more conventionally orientated than others. They have maintained their historic scholarly attachments that has legitimised their professional role as purveyors of truth and fact. For example, respondents representing some of the more orthodox university and public sector sites preferred using more experienced archaeology student placements for important museum projects such as tasks that involved identifying and cataloguing archaeological objects. In contrast, the ideals of postmodernity can be associated more with sites represented by all sectors that interpret conflicting and abstract aspects of popular culture and contemporary art, while encouraging active visitor involvement. They can be described as new age organisations that question the logic and rationality of modernity and target a more unconventional visitor base. For this purpose a large pool of community volunteers were used by the public sector to create a diverse oral history archive of the life experiences of local citizens. Visitor satisfaction is particularly important when dealing with the unconventional. Student volunteers were used to survey visitor responses to new displays following a major refurbishment in one public sector site. Furthermore, technology has a significant role to play in some postmodern museums. For example, as well as containing postmodern images incorporating virtual computer technology, a public sector site of contemporary art used skilled 'network volunteers' to provide assistance and instruction for visitors who wished to gain access and learn about the internet. Here the interplay between postmodernity and modernity merge.

Change and resource hardship within the museum sector, linked to much broader socio-economic developments, has pushed forward more commercially driven priorities to join traditional public service duties. Subsequently, for the public sector, chronic restructuring involving a radical reduction in permanent professional specialists has not only reduced staff morale but put pressure on established staff to broaden their existing skills base. The increasing dependence on computer technology is typical. Most of the museum professionals who spontaneously emphasised their regular use of computer based skills appeared to be younger members of staff. The only museum professional who could provide an accurate and immediate record of the number of active volunteers she hosted referred to her computer data base record for the information. However, established staff reported that computer technology was having an increasing role in their work which added to the number of existing tasks. For example, when asked to what extent she has had to learn new skills concerning new technology one public sector professional replied:

What technology? We don't have internal e-mail. I haven't had a computer that I could use at work until 6 months ago. Now I use it all the time.

When asked if volunteers were involved in using computer based technology the same respondent referred to her increased dependence on skilled student volunteers for one major data base project:

A very large data collection system is just being created ... It is a big problem I inherited. It isn't for unskilled volunteers ... I tend to go for ... students in their third or fourth year. We have got through about 2,000 objects by now. I would never have been able to do that on my own.

In this way computer skills and traditional skills associated with museums combine to create new tasks and projects for volunteers who have skills associated with higher education and new technology.

The raised status of academic disciplines such as business management have been central to change in museums in the city and have added to professional disillusionment. Managerialism brings into play a sort of power role reversal as the problems with conventional museum professionalism become more apparent. Most of the volunteers in the independent museum are involved directly in museum management as trustee board members. Issues related to management skills were repeatedly reported by them. They included changes concerning: the documentation demands now being made by potential funders; identified changes in management style at the museum; a stronger business sense among trustees and increasing pressure to manage volunteers more like paid staff.

It can be argued that the development of a new museum professionalism acts as a control mechanism that dilutes concentration on orthodox museum goals and objectives. However, problems of communication between those concerned with management and those concerned with the collection have been a particular problem in the public sector. For example, one public sector respondent reported that her line manager gave low priority to her specialism and failed to understand what her outputs were about. She referred to her inability to complete one major project because of staff shortages:

My line manager said to me, "What you need to do is some time management ...". I think I do set myself really good time management. I couldn't do it because there are things that come up that have to be dealt with straight away and they need me to do them.

Conflict between management priorities and traditional museum priorities create uncertainties about what tasks museum professionals should prioritise and what new skills need to be accessed. To varying degrees this was linked to a strong element of confusion and resistance when new priorities tended to clash with more orthodox tasks. This problem was evident in all sectors but was specifically and repeatedly highlighted by public sector museum professionals. The impact of change in museum social purpose to include its new found economic role created uncertainties about the direction museums were beginning to follow. One museum respondent explained that communication within management and between management and museum professionals was poor, with the result that the museum profession were uncertain about what was expected from them. Another public sector respondent reported her concerns and suggested feelings of low morale:

> I really do fear for the future of museums ... You have to retain something because otherwise it's just a visitor attraction ... and the unique aspect that made it so specially original would be very much diluted. It's a ... downward spiral because you can't output if you're not ... settled inside ... in your own work.

However, museum volunteers in this urban research environment have been active in a variety of museum tasks ranging from routine to core tasks both orthodox and innovative. Volunteers therefore have a key role to play in the future progress of museums and have been particularly involved in keeping museums alive to the contemporary needs of society. However, one museum professional warned:

> If you show you are totally reliant on volunteers as I am ... our bosses will think, "we do not need anybody with any specialist knowledge" ... I will stand up for my specialism from all corners.

She explained that she could not delegate highly skilled work, even to the more experienced university placements as their level of expertise was inadequate for all the tasks that came under her responsibility.

The second issue instigating a professional dilemma in all organisations concerned the reported variable degrees of resource depletion, particularly funding and staffing. However, for many organisations coping with change has involved restructuring programmes that introduce more flexible employment opportunities to encourage a much broader pool of skills to be accessed. These include contract, freelance and volunteer workers. The curator and volunteers of the independent museum reported that continued funding difficulties are set to increase their dependence on volunteers. However, the crisis within the museum profession in the public sector was particularly intense. Throughout this project the multiple site public sector museum service suffered the chronic erosion of paid professional staff. One museum professional from the public sector reported how this impacted on museum work:

> Among the proposed job losses in one department alone only one conservation post will remain from an existing four, all held by people under 50 years old. All have different conservation specialisms such as in metal, furniture, textiles or taxidermy. Already there is a serious shortage of this type of specialist staff. As a result new acquisitions are not receiving the care and protection they require and many are not yet catalogued ... Our ... project manual is crying with hysteria.

Another public sector respondent reported that the supply of volunteers tended to reflect the supply of permanent staff whose work they supported. As the museum sector increasingly becomes reliant on a wider spectrum of conventional and more unconventional skills and tasks there appeared to be limits to which museums were able to contract out work to paid freelancers. This respondent added that permanent staff were more dedicated than contract staff by being personally involved in unpaid work themselves:

> In the past, as a goodwill gesture, professional staff ... have been prepared to work unpaid overtime to meet deadlines ... Up until now this has served to mask the problems of staff shortages. It is unlikely that freelance professionals will display this level of commitment ...

The public sector were particularly sensitive about volunteers doing work that would normally be carried out by paid staff. Indeed, one public sector museum professional stated that volunteer recruitment had been frozen as there were fewer museum professionals to supervise their work. This coincided with a reported slump in the number of active volunteers at approximately this time. However, almost one year on and following specific marketing for new volunteer recruits, museum professionals and volunteer guide organiser respondents reported an increase in the number of volunteers being recruited. At this time it was noted that some redundant museum professionals had been reinstated on temporary contract.

Cost / benefit analysis of volunteers

Placing a value on voluntary work was problematic. One academic respondent argued that monetary calculations need to include the down time incurred by paid supervision. He argued that higher levels of skill and competence among new volunteer recruits would reduce the costs attached to their supervision. A retired museum professional from the public sector reported that the ability for museums to be more selective meant that there are less problems associated with volunteer support:

> It's all down to money ... Volunteers of all categories ... provide a significant proportion of cheap labour. ... Students, particularly those with specialist skills are very important to the museum. They bring in skills that can be channelled to good use.

This respondent estimated the monetary value of unpaid work already undertaken by volunteers in the public sector alone ran into "hundreds of thousands of pounds sterling". Costs incurred hosting volunteers in museums were reported to be negligible due to different forms of selective recruitment. In most museum sites this minimised the amount of down time paid staff allowed for volunteer supervision. Training costs were also reported as meagre with training being delivered primarily inhouse by museum professionals or trained volunteer organisers who had been trained externally through a division of Scottish Enterprise.

In order to measure the monetary value of museum volunteering in this urban example, as a starting point, the total number of hours worked by questionnaire respondents was calculated. After eliminating non-responses to the question on annual hours, the remaining 58 volunteers contributed 11,588.5 annual hours of work to museums in this city. This averages out at almost 200 annual hours per volunteer. The 40 respondents from the public sector alone contributed 8,237 hours of work, making an average contribution of almost 206 annual hours per public sector volunteer. Working hours reported ranged from 20 annual hours to 1,040 annual hours. Eliminating non-responses, the 11 remaining university respondents contributed 2,133.5 annual hours to their respective museums, averaging out at almost 194 annual hours per volunteer. Working hours reported ranged from 15 annual hours to 675 annual hours. Eliminating non-responses, the remaining 7 independent museum volunteers contributed 1,218 annual hours of work to the museum. This averages out at 174 annual hours per head. Working hours reported ranged from 24 annual hours to 500 annual hours.

Placing a monetary value on museum volunteering is particularly difficult due to the range of skills involved. The Volunteer Development Agency (renamed the National Centre for Volunteering at the close of this investigation) measure voluntary work using average earnings in Great Britain. However, average part-time earnings for men and women over the age of 16 in Scotland was deemed more appropriate as most museum work is carried out on a part-time basis. For the year 1998, part-time hourly earnings for women averaged

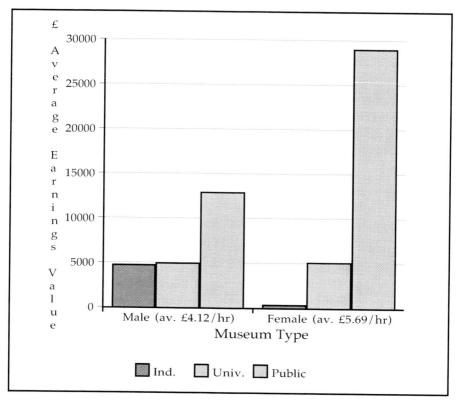

Figure 1   Value of voluntary Work By Gender and Sector

at £5.69, with men recording average part-time earnings of £4.12 (EOC 1999). Interestingly the part-time hourly rate for women in Scotland is the only example in the UK where women's earnings exceed that of men. This is attributed to the fact that most men who work part-time in Scotland are younger than their female counterparts. Indeed, average part-time earnings in Great Britain as a whole in 1998 were £5.58 per hour for women and £5.65 per hour for men. Using 1998 part-time hourly earnings for Scotland, Figure 1 shows a breakdown of total annual unrealised earnings by gender and sector.

Figure 1 also shows the value of voluntary work by gender. The total value for the independent museum is £5,131.20; £10,216.66 for the university museum; and £41,958.83 for the public sector museum. Taking into account that there were 5 non-responses, the gross value of voluntary work provided by the 58 respondents who reported their annual hours is £57,306.69. This averages out at £988 of unrealised earnings per annum for each volunteer.

Although the number of volunteers used in the survey consists of a minority of the total number of volunteers active in museums in this city, it provides some idea of the diversity concerning average annual hours contributed by individual volunteers.

Museum / volunteer as professional partnership

This section considers to what extent the relationship between museum paid staff and their volunteers can be defined in terms of professionalism. To varying degrees all museum interview respondents provided evidence that their relationship with their volunteers can be justly interpreted as a professional partnership. Museum professionals revealed that their volunteers provided a wide range of professional expertise that not only helped fill gaps left through staff shortage but helped the museum cope with functional change. Indeed in some cases volunteers provided skills and knowledge beyond that of professional staff.

Indeed, museums in this Scottish city are looking more optimistically at volunteering as a means of realising both orthodox and new objectives. More volunteers are involved in core functions as a support mechanism to help museums cope with staff shortage. Since staff redundancies, one public sector professional reported that she could not do her job without the use of volunteers, particularly undergraduate placements. She explained that most student volunteers worked on three week placements while those who chose to follow museum careers stayed for longer. No specific projects were created for them as they carried out projects that she herself would be working on. She claimed working with placements increased the number of tasks completed in a fraction of the time.

Another public sector professional reported the importance of rapport building between museum volunteers and the museum professionals whose work they supported. This respondent explained that a successful partnership like this may result in longer term voluntary commitment.

Respondents from the university and public sectors agreed that a good working relationship depended on volunteers having the correct level of ability and expertise. A public sector professional explained that professionals can draw from the knowledge of student volunteers to help them keep pace with developments in their area of expertise:

> The good thing about using people who are still in training ... specifically in this case 3rd or 4th year university students who are starting to be ... useful in their field for different reasons. They ... are working with people who are teaching them what is happening now. I was a student 20 years ago. Obviously ... I am not at the forefront

of various areas. I am at the forefront of my own field ... I don't have the time to keep up ... in other fields ... so it is possible to use people who are still in training ... for the benefit of the museum.

Secondly, she argued that she benefited on a more personal level:

I prefer someone that I can get on with, obviously ... Just someone else you can talk with about something ... in your specific field ... They understand what you mean, when there isn't anybody else in the organisation that you can do that to.

A university respondent reported that although student placements had the correct skills, a more meaningful relationship had developed with some older longer term volunteers.

Some volunteers have been volunteering for years and years. They are retired professional people. We have a retired female school teacher and a man from ... industry with a special interest in a specific field of archaeology ... He has advanced towards becoming our research specialist in his area of specialisation and is recognised as such by our own specialists who can learn from his knowledge and experience.

Interviews with museum professionals who worked with volunteers suggested that they were unsure what volunteers thought about them and the tasks they were delegated. However, as volunteers become more knowledgeable and expert in their specific field of specialism their relationship with paid colleagues could suffer. A university professional reported that one highly regarded male volunteer tended to undermine her authority by being demanding and patronising.

On the positive side all questionnaire respondents reported that they had a good relationship with museum paid staff. However, there was a very high non-response rate to the question in the volunteer questionnaire, asking participants if they felt their work was appreciated. During discussions with volunteers some mentioned that they were unsure how much their work was appreciated. One volunteer from the independent sector wanted less responsibility and one volunteer from a university museum felt that he was exploited by the museum.

Museum voluntarism: amateur model

This section will consider, firstly to what extent museum volunteers demonstrate amateur, non-professional characteristics and secondly, the role routine work has concerning volunteer work experience.

Generally, the analysis of qualitative data argued age as an unreliable indicator of volunteer professionalism. In line with the unpredictable nature of postmodern society, experiences and attitudes towards volunteers tended to vary from organisation to organisation and from individual to individual. For example, the volunteer liaison person for the public sector argued that some people are not suited to volunteer because they lack appropriate skill and attitude. Although her experience with volunteers tended to be favourable some of her colleagues had preconceived ideas about the older category of volunteer. She added: "People laugh ... but I would not underestimate them at all". She explained the experience of a colleague:

> ... she cannot stand volunteers. She has been working with one for
> 3 years and both get on very well. I am sure she is unaware that she
> is working with a volunteer.

A university respondent also had difficulty with traditional types of volunteer claiming that they were 'disastrous as attendants' for various reasons linked to lack of necessary skill. However, she believed it was inappropriate to suggest that older volunteers were unprofessional as she tended to channel their tasks in other directions that did not involve contact with visitors. For example, she explained that some of the older volunteers who remained were asked to go to the library to help research reference literature for special events.

A volunteer guide organiser from the public sector reported that the independent museum friends association, who provided museum volunteers in the city, was becoming less tolerant of unprofessional volunteer types. She explained:

> The type of volunteer that comes in with no ability usually doesn't
> stay. We have had some really horrible ones over the years ... not only
> no use ... but most unpleasant people.

This friends association's main focus is directed towards a tour guide service in four public sector organisations. Although the service was generally successful, one public sector respondent recognised a serious unprofessional characteristic among his vsolunteer guides who tended to be unreliable. This problem, however, was rectified following a new phase of volunteer recruitment which included two new volunteer chairs and one new volunteer organiser. Both Chairmen have a special interest in the collection and pulled in similar volunteer types with specific skills of use to the museum.

A university respondent reported that different categories of volunteer demonstrated different problems. In her experience very young school placements and unemployed categories of volunteer were particularly unsuitable and tended to have little interest and limited ability.

Most respondents reported examples when individual volunteers proved to demonstrate amateur characteristics that were not typical under their volunteering group. One respondent was particularly concerned about an increase in international students with poor language skills being accepted on post graduate museum studies courses. This argument was backed up by a student from Taiwan whose placement project involved communicating with the public concerning their perceptions of museum exhibits. She claimed that visitors seemed reluctant to speak to her with the result that she failed to meet her project deadline within the allocated time.

A university respondent explained that undergraduate students, presented problems that could be interpreted as unprofessional, as some appeared to show "little enthusiasm". A respondent from the public sector who drew from the same pool of student volunteers explained that routine tasks were delegated to less able placements. However she explained that routine tasks were an important and interesting part of museum work. She referred to her delegation of a documentation project to volunteers involving one hundred years of museum correspondence and which contained some "particularly interesting reading".

Another university respondent reported that although her museum demanded a high level of specialist skill, she did not categorise volunteers who carried out routine museum work as amateur. She referred to one retired female volunteer who enjoyed routine work because it allowed her time to "switch off".

Although this section has looked below the surface of museum voluntarism's amateur label and its association with routine work the next section explores volunteers' professional credentials more closely.

Museums volunteerism: professional model

Undoubtedly the most innovative category of museum volunteer who presented the strongest professional characteristics were members of the independent museum friends association's Volunteer Guide Service. It can be argued that this group of volunteers are both controlled and empowered through training. Training incorporates input from museum professionals and instructors in guide training undertaken by local enterprise agencies. For example, museum professionals instruct Volunteer Guides about the collection while Scottish Enterprise agencies provide tourism training instruction. Some of the volunteers themselves are trained as instructors who in turn train new recruits. In order to maintain standards of performance volunteer trainers undertake a regular critical assessment of the guide service and carry out programmes of retraining. In this way Volunteer Guides are used as the interface between the collection and the visiting public. Although training programmes ensure an element of collective discipline they are flexible enough to encourage a degree of individuality when Volunteer Guides have the opportunity to introduce an element of novelty. For example, a volunteer friends administrator reported that one volunteer guide who dressed in full highland dress was particularly popular with foreign tourists.

Individuality is demonstrated in a variety of ways. Some guides are particularly skilled at communicating with the public. This was noted during covert participant observation on a guided tour of a public sector site. The volunteer guide, a retired school teacher, incorporated elements of specialist knowledge mixed with anecdotal interpretation. The success of the tour, which lasted almost two hours can be measured by the obvious pleasure demonstrated by the large following of visitors he attracted on his way. A curator from the public sector reported that volunteer guides could arrange tours in advance to suit groups with a special interest.

One museum professional reported that the independent museum friends association themselves acted as gatekeepers to discourage unsuitable members from volunteering. A volunteer guide organiser explained that volunteer recruitment is now more selective and tends to look for specific skills linked to the subject matter of the museum. She explained that the association's organisers and guide trainers were selected because of their leadership and communication skills linked to their skills used in past employment.

A museum professional reported that volunteer guides were now demonstrating a high level of professional awareness which she associated with both their voluntary work and interaction with professional staff. This is a crucial point suggesting a hidden assumption about the meanings attached to professional personality traits and skills. She explained that the association's most valued volunteers were either the partners of professional people or were professional people themselves. She also identified more male volunteers from the highest echelons of public service professions, like retired teachers, medics, lawyers and a chief of police.

There appeared to be more than an assumed link between people in top public service professions and a high degree of knowledge about the museum collections they helped supported. More importantly, the museum professionals who supervised them reported that there was more effort made by the museum profession to encourage, communicate with and in some cases confide in this group of volunteers. However, when one public sector museum professional was asked if there were any volunteers retired from business management positions, she explained that they were inappropriate as they would "tend to want to take over".

Expectations regarding volunteer professionalism appears to be rising as more skills are expected from them. The data revealed that knowledge and skills may be acquired from the following five sources.

(i)   Hobbies and leisure interests

Knowledge and skill acquired from leisure pursuits such as hobbies, has been identified as a significant source of volunteer skill. Indeed a hierarchy of volunteer professionalism has been identified in all museum types. A respondent from one of the university sites reported having a retired industrialist working with museum experts. This elderly volunteer had exceptional knowledge related to his own personal archaeological collection. The museum used this volunteer as an expert in this specialist field. In the longer term, the museum were optimistic that the volunteer would bequest his collection to the museum.

A Friends administrator in the public sector added weight to this argument. She said she noticed an increase in the number of male volunteers who were all retired medics with a keen interest in fine arts. Generally, the emergence of professional criteria in recruitment was evident. This was confirmed by a gallery guide during participant observation at a conservation talk and Annual General Meeting of guides. She stated that unlike most established volunteer guides, potential recruits are expected to have more than a passing interest in art history. She noticed that the museum professionals were becoming less inclined to spend time training volunteer guides beyond the bare minimum. Staff shortages and an increased demand for voluntary positions meant that museum staff could be more selective in the volunteer recruitment process by choosing volunteers who had more appropriate knowledge with less need for training and supervision.

(ii)   Education

This second category concerns student volunteers on placement. This group can be identified as the new generation of museum professionals and are a significant source of accessing conventional and to a lesser extent less conventional skills. This accounts for the advancement and diversification of student volunteering being accessed by museums in this city.

One placement co-ordinator from the public sector identified a hierarchy of professional expertise among students:

> I have been very interested in placements and how you encourage the next generation of museums ... Manchester, Leicester and St. Andrews are dedicated museums courses ... and have a proven track record in the quality of their students ... and we don't hesitate to welcome them ... Our oriental art specialist has placement schemes

> from Edinburgh ... who are of a very high standard. There is no course
> so specialised in oriental art. We also have international conservation
> placements who are on post- graduate work. They are very useful ...
> some ... we would love to employ. The marketing section have a range
> of French students who have been incredible. We also have placements
> from focused HND design, technical design and conservation ... from
> Glasgow Art School or the College of Building and Printing Our design
> department... take on ... only quality students as they are hard pressed.

She explained that the public sector museums service could not provide a
standard arts management placement experience. Although students had
to be focused in one area like publicity, marketing or retailing, the quality of
their work was essential:

> Although my problems come with broad based courses, ... we actually
> have had fabulous placements ... of ... extremely high quality students
> ... for about 4 years running.

One public sector museum respondent explained her preference for younger
volunteers with computer skills acquired from school or university. She
explained that her network volunteers tended to be younger but difficult to
retain because of their commitment to their studies. Her museum was target-
ing volunteers with information technology skills for weekend work to instruct
museum visitors on how to access the internet in their computer network
gallery. Another respondent recruited volunteers from local job centres who
were involved on a Museum Information Technology (MITech) project.

(iii)   Present or past paid employment or domestic work

This third category of volunteer professionalism is linked to present or past
employment. The public sector use the skills of a retired antique dealer and
a retired expert in fabric conservation. Both volunteers have such a high level
of expertise in their particular field that museum professionals can learn from
them. A similar situation concerns volunteers with outdated skills such as
in mechanical maintenance. These skills have been particularly important
for the independent museum and one public sector organisation. Volunteers
have been used for oral history accounts relaying their employment experience
or have been more practically utilised in the workshop. Skilled routine work
has been identified with women's traditional work roles, both in paid
employment and unpaid domestic work and includes administrative and
sewing skills. This type of 'routine work' has been essential for supporting
paid functions in the public sector. A fabric conservation expert explained
that these skills have been crucial in helping her complete major cataloguing
and sewing projects.

(iv)   Life experiences

The fourth source of skill concerns knowledge gained through life cycle socialisation. This category has been particularly important for oral history interpretations concerning the history of community life. This type of knowledge has been utilised to a high degree by museums in both public and independent organisations. The curator of the independent museum reported that the wealth of local knowledge provided by volunteers assisted with the quality of service delivery.

(v)   Hidden aptitudes and gifts

This final category refers particularly to some younger volunteers. They were identified as having particular attributes that set them apart from their counterparts. Exceptional commitment to projects, a particular gift in handling fragile porcelains and a passion for the task in hand were all mentioned by museum professionals.

There is no doubt that volunteers in museums in this urban example demonstrate a high level of professional characteristics that were compatible with those of the professionals who supervised them. However, traits and skills tended to lean towards those of orthodox museum professionals. More importantly there appeared to be an awareness of the need to develop the professional credentials of volunteers further, particularly through training. In the case of the Volunteer Guide Service and job centre volunteers, training was influenced less by the museum profession than with most other volunteer types.

The professionalisation of museum volunteers

The professionalisation of museum volunteers is tied up in policies concerning raising their standards of performance through training. The professional characteristics of the Volunteer Guide Service has already been interpreted in this way. As standards of performance rise alongside increased demand for volunteering positions, more skill and knowledge can be expected from new recruits. However, the museum sector has been open to criticism for its failure to exploit training to its full potential.

An Edinburgh academic specialising in arts management has been actively involved in various European museum training programmes. He argued that training could help rid volunteering of its poor image:

> Volunteering is ... seen by and large, certainly at director and curatorial level as a human resource management issue rather than ... a human resource development issue. The status of volunteering ... has to be raised. ... In countries like Canada ... volunteering is

> providing a valuable contribution, but it is also a part of a contract
> where there is an expectation that the volunteer will be supported
> and trained ... nurtured and encouraged.

Apart from placements, no volunteers reported that they were involved in museum specific open learning training programmes organised by the Museums Training Institute (MTI) as part of a pilot scheme.

One university respondent reported that work concerning training specifically for volunteers was developing. She explained that there were limitations involving volunteers in training as many were too short term. Another university respondent from a different university museum reported that he had two new retired university lecturers who were interested in formulating a training programme for volunteers geared towards accreditation.

It can be argued that resistance from the museum sector to incorporate unconventional skills has a knock on effect on the task activities of volunteers. For example, a significant number of volunteers in museums in this city are involved in visitor contact. The public sector's Volunteer Guide Service incorporates training in skills learned from local enterprise agencies combined with knowledge acquired from museum professionals. A tourism training manager from an area enterprise agency reported that two significant problems stifled the potential of training museum volunteers. First, she claimed that museums at a national and local level were resistant to any radical change that would threaten their core purpose:

> Their priorities were number one to the collection and then most
> definitely to education and then possibly to the tourist. They were
> quite resistant to the work that we do and they firmly believed that
> tourism was not what they were about.

She argued that although museums in this particular city had been receptive in trying to create a cultural change no organisation was willing to make the commitment: The broader museum purpose incorporating the needs and expectations of tourists tended to be given low level priority.

Secondly, she reported that volunteers may demonstrate similar values to those of the professionals they support and resist training. She explained the experience her colleague had when trying to introduce tourism training in other heritage organisations who relied on volunteers:

> She nearly had anarchy on her hands trying to arrange a tourism
> induction programme which staff thought tried to change the system.
> This suggested more controls on them which they thought would get
> in the way of what they were there to do.

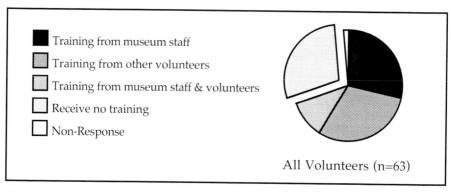

Figure 2   Record of Training — All Volunteers

Interviews with museum professionals indicated that most training was undertaken by museum staff and other trained volunteers. No museum reported a specific training budget for volunteers. Generally, the public sector and university museums trained volunteers for specific long to short term projects. For example, the first phase of an oral history project in the public sector involved a multi-media training partnership between a Government-led employment training initiative and museum staff. The most formal training programme was undertaken by the Volunteer Guide Service and included ongoing performance monitoring. No respondent reported a formal long term training schedule specifically for their museum volunteers. Most training tended to be on the job, with more emphasis being placed on recruiting volunteers who required minimal training.

Figure 2 graphically displays the extent of volunteer participation in training according to questionnaire responses. Figure 2 also shows that 70% of questionnaire respondents have received some form of training; 29% of this group claimed they were trained solely by museum staff; 30% by other volunteers; and 11% claimed both museum staff and other volunteers were involved in their training. This was broken-down to show training records by museum type.

Figure 3 shows that the majority (87.5%) of public sector volunteer respondents reported they had received training. Only a minority (12.5%)) of volunteers claimed they had received no training. Most training (51.4%) was provided by other volunteers with, (28.6%) being delivered by museum staff and (20%) being delivered jointly by volunteers and museum professionals. One long term volunteer who received training from volunteers in guiding skills commented that over the years he had noticed that the quality of training had improved greatly. He also mentioned that volunteers also brought in more expertise than previously. This volunteer was active as a

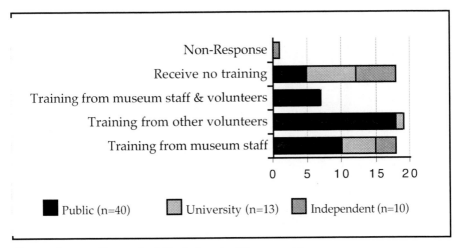

Figure 3   Record of Training by Museum Type

guide as well as in museum conservation work. Another volunteer guide claimed that she received training from museum staff and also undertook private study to improve her knowledge and expertise. This guide delivered talks and slide presentations from the museums collection on specialised areas of art history. Most people who received training from volunteers and museum staff were involved in guiding as well as other museum tasks. For example, one respondent was trained in guiding skills by volunteers as well as interview techniques by members of staff involved in an oral history project. One of the minority (12.5%) of public sector volunteers who received no training suggested that he would expect his levels of satisfaction to increase if he were given training.

The majority (53.8%) of university respondents claimed they received no training. Of the remaining 46.2% that received training only 1 volunteer reported she received training from other volunteers. This unemployed French volunteer, aged between 19 and 25 was involved in a museum documentation project. Another volunteer who received 'limited training' from museum staff suggested that the questionnaire should have asked more specifically for volunteers' academic qualifications. His Master of Arts degree in Classics and Archaeology was very relevant in providing the expertise needed to carry out his task of cataloguing the museum's Roman collection. A volunteer who reported he had no training was a retired lecturer at the university who was re-employed part-time in paid work and part-time as a volunteer.

Figure 3 shows that the majority (60%) of volunteer respondents from the independent museum received no training. Taking into account the 10%

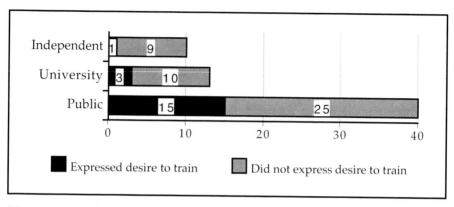

Figure 4   Attitudes Towards Training By Museum Type

non-response rate, the remaining 30% of volunteers reported they received training from museum staff. Most of the volunteers who received no training failed to provide specific details about what their voluntary work entailed. One volunteer who received training from museum staff held a senior position on the management board and also volunteered regularly in the museum. He commented that there was an increased interest in training among volunteers.

Only a minority (30.2%) of volunteers expressed a desire to be involved in further training. Taking into account that questionnaire respondents were weighted in favour of female volunteers, there appeared to be no gender correlation associated with the desire to train. 42.1% of respondents who desired more training were male while 57.9% were female. 18.2% of the 69.8% that did not express a desire to train further were already in training. Figure 4 shows the breakdown of responses by museum type.

On the surface, **Figure 4** shows that the majority of volunteers in all museum types did not express the desire for further training. However, the following analysis suggests that this does not mean a lack of interest among volunteers to develop their existing skills: 37.5% of volunteer respondents in the public sector desired further training. However, of the 62.5% that did not desire further training, 44% responded that they wanted to develop their existing skills. 65% of volunteer respondents from the public sector, therefore, can be interpreted as wishing to develop their skills either through training or by other means. This leaves only a minority, 35% of volunteers who did not express a wish to be involved in any form of skills development.

Figure 4 shows that 23.1% of volunteer respondents in the university sector desired further training. However, of the 76.9% that did not desire further training, 60% responded that they wanted to develop their existing skills. Therefore a total of 69.2% of volunteer respondents from the university sector can be interpreted as wishing to develop their skills either through training or by other means. This leaves only a minority, 30.8% of volunteers who did not express a wish to be involved in any form of skills development.

Regardless of the comments made by a senior management board member of the independent museum about an increased desire to train, (see comments after figure 3), Figure 4 shows that only 10% of respondents from the independent museum requested the desire for further training. Of the 90% of volunteers who expressed no desire for further training only 11.1% responded that they wanted to develop their existing skills. Unlike the other museum sectors, only a minority (20%) of independent museum respondents can be interpreted as wishing to develop their skills either through training or by other means. This leaves the majority (80%) of independent museum volunteer respondents who did not express a wish to be involved in some form of skills development. One long term volunteer from this group of volunteers argued that: "Volunteers are being treated more like paid staff."

This would suggest that some volunteers may think skills development is not in keeping with voluntary work.

With the exception of the independent museum example, there is no doubt that a significant amount of volunteering in museums in this city is under-taken to provide work experience to improve skills. However, there appeared to be no take-up of recently announced accredited courses for volunteers, although one volunteer, involved in a specialised aspect of fabric conservation, reported undertaking a City and Guilds qualification at her own expense. This will ultimately benefit the quality of any fabric conservation work she provides to the museum.

Volunteer skills flexibility

Museum tasks have become fragmented and confused as orthodox museum core goals become scrutinised by managerial staff seeking more effective 'best practice' work routines. Indeed, the idea of the postmodern museum involves interpretation and consumption that are oppositional to the logic and rational purpose of the traditional museum function. For example, in order that museums may earn the appreciation of a wider audience they need to reconsider the way they communicate to their audience. Volunteers in this urban example have demonstrated their potential to communicate more appropriately with visitors than some museum professionals whose language may be too museum specific. The post-Fordism imperative is useful in demonstrating how voluntary work can be organised to accommodate the unpredictable nature of postmodern consumption. Volunteerism allows immense numeric and functional flexibility, particularly with the recent development of the

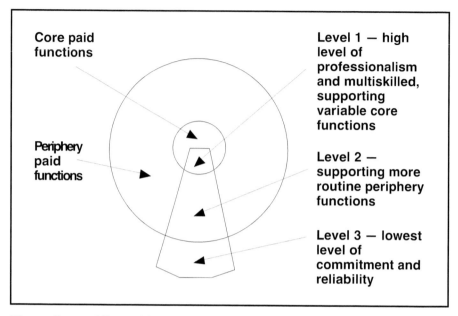

Figure 5   Hierarchical Model of Volunteering Support

Volunteer Guide Service and the increasing multi-skill dimension becoming attached to voluntary work, as demonstrated in Figure 5.

Figure 5, the hierarchical Model of Volunteering Support, demonstrates a core periphery model drawn from the ideas of Atkinson and Gregory (1986). This shows three levels of voluntary support. Contained within Level 1 support is the volunteer guide service that involves volunteers in a development programme of training, supported by regional enterprise and development agencies. This group function on a day to day basis with minimal support from museum professionals. Volunteers are trained in tour guide skills, providing a service for variable markets — from the specialist with a particular interest to the casual visitor. This service has become a core function of museums in the city, particularly in public sector museums. Level 1 support demands more commitment from volunteers than functions on the periphery. The majority of short-term university placements come under this category. Many volunteers active in this category provide a significant amount of skills flexibility. They can be pulled in to be involved in various tasks utilising museum specific skills, such as interpretation and conservation. Level 1 support has the potential to be a major growth area of voluntary support. However, some volunteers in this category have considerable control over their work and may have expertise beyond that of the museum experts. In this way museum professionals learn from their volunteers. However, this can have an adverse effect on the relationship between volunteers and paid staff. For example, it has been argued that the more active museum volunteers become in core functions, the more they threaten their relationship with paid functions.

Level 2 support although peripheral, involves volunteers freeing museum professionals from time consuming routine tasks. As with level 1 support a high level of volunteer commitment is required. Volunteers tend to be more involved in some form of administration and clerical work, although poorer university and college placements have been categorised under this level. This category also includes administrative functions carried out by volunteers on behalf of the independent museum friends association, which are peripheral to museum functions.

Level 3 support, however, may involve volunteers with variable levels of skill. Due to their informal relationship with the museum volunteers would tend to be involved in activities beyond the periphery. This includes short term voluntary work like school placements, where the purpose of the voluntary work is to observe and participate in a one week of museum work experience. More supervision would be required, for example, school placements often shadow members of professional staff. This category includes other volunteers who are unable to commit themselves to the museum on a regular bases. They provide a pool of volunteers who can be pulled in to help when available and when required. Some volunteers with health problems were identified operating under this category. This level of volunteer support provides a higher degree of flexibility on both sides.

Figure 5, the Hierarchical Model of Volunteering Support is designed to act as a guideline only. However, it is worth considering the financial value of volunteerism in terms of museum tasks completed and, alternatively, the professional benefits gained by the volunteers themselves.

Conclusion

This paper connects changes in the role and function of museums with new museum tasks, inadequate numbers of paid staff and raised expectations from volunteering. The professionalisation process of volunteering has involved a meshing of trait identities between museum professionals and volunteers such as higher education students and retired public service professionals with compatible, skills, values and interests. The link between volunteer professionalism, skill and training is also important. This is particularly evident among elite volunteers with exceptional expertise as well as services delivered exclusively by volunteers. The expectations of volunteers, however, have also to be served, not only to maintain loyalty and raise morale, but to ensure their needs are met as well as those of the museum. In this way appropriate management practices that empower and engage volunteers can be applied to customise their needs and those of museums, so that good practice policy can be developed, effectively delivered and readily accepted.

No longer can the stereotypical image of voluntarism be applied to contemporary museum volunteerism. The relationship between paid and unpaid staff has developed considerably, not least in the area of skills development. In the first instance, it is important to consider the profile of contemporary museum volunteers, in the context of professionalism. Increasingly, there is a cross-over between the work of paid employees and the volunteers who support them. Perhaps the most problematical issue concerns the threat posed by volunteers on paid staff, be it imagined or real. This is an area requiring further research. However, the less professional volunteers present themselves, the more supervision they require. More importantly, as more reliance is placed on volunteers the more pressure there is to manage them more effectively. In the final analysis, as the professional characteristics of volunteers develop further, the cost benefits to be gained will undoubtedly raise the status as well as the value benefits of volunteering, pulling in a broader spectrum of skill and volunteering opportunity.

References

Ambrose, T. (1994) 'Comment', *Scottish Museums News* Vol. 10, No. 2 (Autumn): p. 1. Edinburgh: Scottish Museums Council.

Conway, L. (1996) 'The context: Heritage perspectives on volunteering', in *AIM: Focus 3, Managing Volunteers for Visitor Care* (April), p. 4. London: Association of Independent Museums.

Davies, S. (1994) 'A sense of purpose: Rethinking museum values' in G. Kavanagh (ed) *Museum provision and professionalism*. London: Routledge, pp. 33–40.

EOC (1999) *Facts about women and men in Scotland*. Glasgow: Equal Opportunities Commission.

Graham, M. (1996) 'Cultural tourism: The role of philanthropy in museum interpretation', *Leisure Studies Association Newsletter* No. 44 (July): pp. 22–25.

Graham, M. and Foley, M. (1998) 'Volunteering in an urban museums service', in N. Ravenscroft, D. Philips and M. Bennett (eds) *Tourism and visitor attractions* (LSA Publication No. 61). Eastbourne: Leisure Studies Publications, pp. 21–38.

Graham, M., Foley M., Litteljohn, D. and Hughes, B. (1999) 'Job design and work organisation', in A. Leask and I. Yeoman (eds), *Heritage visitor attractions: An operational management perspective*. London: Cassell Plc, Chapter 7.

Lima de Faria, M. (1995) 'How much education and how much recreation are we prepared to deliver?', *Museology Review* Vol. 1, No. 2: pp. 13–32.

MacDonald, S. (1996) 'Introduction', in S. Macdonald and G. Fyfe (eds) *Theorizing museums*. Oxford: Blackwell Publishers, pp. 1–18.

Tedrick, T., Davis, W. W. and Coutant, G. J. (1984) 'Effective management of a volunteer corps', *Parks and Recreation* (February): pp. 55–70.

An Examination of Coaches' Responsibilities for Premature Athletic Disengagement of Elite Greek Gymnasts

Konstantinos Koukouris

Department of PE and Exercise Science
Aristotelean University of Thessalonikli (Greece)

Introduction

There is a problem in Greece and all over the world that many advanced gymnasts drop out from the sport. The reasons for this are unclear. Yet it is widely believed that gymnastics is an excellent sport for the cultivation of a range of virtues such as courage, discipline, self-respect, self-control, and solidarity amongst team-mates (Kaimakamis, 1997) Coaches, in particular, believe that young athletes benefit a great deal from their training in a number of ways: self-discipline for life in general , self-respect, respect for others, friendship, joy, opportunities to travel, participation in competitions, financial support and first-hand experience of perfect professional role models of athletes (Duncan, 1997: p. 162)

As Brown (1993) recommended, the role of a coach as a socializing agent in the process of withdrawal should be examined in future research. Although the phenomenon of drop-out or premature retirement has recently attracted some attention from researchers at an international level, research on disengagement from gymnastics is still very limited.

More particularly Cote et al. (1995) constructed a model that illustrates the sport-specific expertise of gymnastic coaches. Coaches emphasize the importance of many other facets apart from competitions and training factors that contribute to the personal development of athletes. He outlines (i) the structure of the sport, (ii) the personal characteristics of the coach, (iii) the personal characteristics of the athlete and (iv) other social reasons. The most successful gymnasts expect psychological incentives and emotional support from their coaches (Massimo, 1987) To the contrary, however, less successful gymnasts expect only technical support from their coaches.

Elite gymnasts train every day for at least three hours under the supervision of a coaches who is usually in charge of up to seven children. In no other sport is there such an intimate relationship between a coach and his athlete (Kaimakamis, 1992) When one considers the young age profiles of elite gymnasts, the long training hours and the closeness of interpersonal relationships, we can see how coaches are capable of exerting a tremendous influence on their gymnasts. Coaches are in a uniquely powerful position to transmit their values. A question arises, however, as to whether coaches should be permitted to develop such overwhelming power over their athletes? Moreover, we can ask whether young and inexperienced coaches, for instance, understand fully the extent of their responsibilities? As it stands, the life of elite athletes is strictly controlled by more powerful others. The hours they train, their traveling arrangements, their diet and the hours they sleep are regulated by coaches and federation administrators (Werthner and Orlick, 1986)

Coaches are therefore crucial socializing agents for these elite sports-children. According to Patsantaras (1994; 1996) ethical values such as respect for the rules and opponents have lost ground in relation to the pursuit of the athlete's personal interests. In citing the importance of such positive values Patsantaras overlooked the use of violence by coaches against their athletes. As Boumann and Tzorbatzoudis (1995: p. 23) point out, the development of the personality of these children should not be based on the number of wins or losses they have. Moreover, as Dervisis and Tzorbatzoudis (1995: p. 10) mention, the educators (in our case, coaches) are responsible for satisfying not only the physical and intellectual demands of the students (athletes) but also their social demands in helping towards the smooth adjustment of the athletes to society.

What are the reasons why elite Greek gymnasts drop out of gymnastics, and to what degree are their coaches responsible? The coaches' responsibility for elite gymnasts' disengagement from gymnastics is examined in this study.

Methodology

The sample studied examined the experience of 19 top former Greek gymnasts who were either from Thessaloniki or had gone there to train. The training conditions of gymnasts in the two largest Greek cities, Athens and Thessaloniki, and those from the provinces are very different. Most of the former gymnasts were P.E. students. The sport of gymnastics was selected because it is (swimming notwithstanding), unique in relation to the early age at which performers retire. The selection of the athletes interviewed was based on the general recognition of their high level by their teammates and coaches, through whom access to the gymnasts was effected.

Because of the in-depth interviewing, the exploratory nature of the analysis and the limited number of top gymnasts in Thessaloniki (about 35–40) at the time of the research, the sample was regarded as representative of elite Greek gymnasts.

One of the aims of the analysis was the creation of categories for reasons given by former athletes as to why they had given up their sport. The cognitive mapping method was used. In other parts of the research the categorization of data into sentence-forms (Jones, 1985) and the constant comparative method (Glaser and Strauss, 1967; Cote *et al.*, 1995) were employed. The concentration of units of meanings which accrue from "properties" and, in the final analysis, "categories" were used in the largest part of the study.

Selection of data

The structured interviews were based around open questions and allowed the former athletes to use their specialized knowledge. All the interviews were recorded at the researchers institution. There was an initial introduction given about the aim of the research. Later the interviews focused on the social and sport background of the interviewees. At the end of each interview there were some questions asked which clarified whether the athletes had discussed all the reasons that they regarded as important for the phenomenon of dropping out from their sport. Each interview lasted between one to three hours. The researcher attempted to fully understand the world of the subject without interrupting his/her train of thoughts (Puig and Morrell, 1996)

Discussion

A large number of the former athletes interviewed talked about the tough attitude of their coaches. Some coaches actually used corporal punishment in order to discipline their athletes. Some coaches functioned within a totally authoritarian regime. To achieve maximum performance from their athletes, they launched psychological warfare against them. Training was transformed from being tough to brutal. Instead of joy there is terror. As Cote and Salmela (1996) mention, coaches in gymnastics become tough with themselves and do not accept any excuses or compromises in training. Many coaches put their athletes' health at risk with the sort of training methods that they use (Krane *et al.*, 1997) Some of these practices are well known to the Gymnastic Coaches' Association. As the members of the coaches' administrative council admit "the brutality of some of the coaches has damaged the good name of gymnastics" (Administrative Council of the Panhellenic Association of Coaches in Gymnastics, 1997: p. 6)

The following discussion is thematized according to the data.

Psychological warfare

The following excerpts from interviews illustrate those points: "We were afraid of him (the coach) from the moment that we started training until the end, we couldn't talk, we couldn't laugh, only work". Corporal punishment is used as a last resort, whereas an autocratic tone of voice is used frequently. As Dervisis and Tzorbatzoudis (1994 p. 61) point out, teachers should the teacher should talk from the bottom of his/her heart: "His voice was high-pitched. He didn't beat us much, we weren't full of bruises every day but the psychological warfare was more than enough" (T).

Under the principles and values of coaches, training could be transformed into a form of hard labour. The preparation and development of elite gymnastics is marked by a gradual shift from traditional joyful training to professionalized joyless training. For Rigauer (1969) there is a clear connection between labour and training. Since both behaviour systems enhance prestige and achievement, we should expect a similar behaviour and conscience in both fields.

As Cote, Salmela and Russel (1995) found, coaches influence gymnasts very little during the actual competition. On the contrary, coaches' work during the preparatory period is most influential. Coaches spend between 20 to 60 hours per week, with their athletes. Their leadership style consists of giving support to the athletes, assigning of responsibilities, teaching and giving positive feedback. Male coaches of female gymnasts pointed out the importance of keeping a distance from their female gymnasts yet an important part of their role is to help female gymnasts to overcome the anxiety which gets with training and competing.

According to Dervisis and Tzorbatzoudis (1994), the teacher-centred model is the most prevalent teaching model in Greek schools. The teacher is the centre of attention, disciplines the students, 'emits' knowledge, and finally he becomes like a God-like figure. As a result of this old-fashioned and authoritarian teaching model, a student might attain good standards but is unlikely to develop a free and creative personality.

All the above mentioned points were illustrated and amplified by the interviewees::

"Gradually things got very serious and we had to train harder. From that point onwards things went rough. I wanted to quit. During the last three years I used to cry every day before the training sessions". (T)

"The coach used to chase us around all day. He shouted at us every day. You would start training but you would have no idea how you would spend the day." (T)

Club coaches in gymnastics are promoted into federal coaches after their athletes had been very successful. To achieve success there is frequent exploitation of the athletes. But there are contradicting views: "A seven-year-old child trains four hours per. This is exploitation. This child will acquire many problems". On the other hand there were contradictory views:

> "I don't think that they exploit the children until the time that they need the children. Nor do they force them to quit." (K)

The psychological warfare waged upon them is one of the chief reasons why gymnasts quit the sport. Gymnasts demand equal opportunities for all in order to reach the top. When training conditions are unequal this is regarded unfair. Yet there was clear evidence of such inequity:

> "We weren't allowed to train in the best gym-centre. We used to go there secretly but the head coach of the national team, the coaches and the caretakers used to kick us out of the gym. This was unfair because we belonged to the pre-national team and we were destined to join the national team. Equal training conditions for pre-national and national team members should have been a prerequisite so that we could cover the ground and become equals with the national team members." (S)

Gymnasts would expect their coaches to help them with both their physical and emotional needs. The indifference of some coaches towards the gymnasts' needs is regarded as unacceptable and a potential cause of premature disengagement.

> "When your coach doesn't help you with anything at all you lose your spirit. You realize that you have reached a saturation point, Why should I stay here any longer? Why should I lose my spirit?" (S)

The picture was not, however, unequivocal. On the other hand, there are coaches who are interested in their athletes as human beings and take care of the former athletes' job career. This did not mean that they ignored their own interests:

> "I believe that coaches helped us as much as they could. As you know only medals awarded during the last three years of High School count as a bonus. Coaches used to visit former athletes in their houses in order to persuade them to compete again, win a medal and register with the P.E. Department. I don't think that coaches wanted you to quit." (K)

Coaches' punishment of gymnasts

The punishment inflicted upon the athletes by the coaches included suspension from training, intimidating phone-calls and complaints to the parents, derogatory comments, checking the athletes' rooms in hotels, deliberate double training, locking the gymnasts into the changing room, hurling heavy items at the athlete, putting them on a very strict diet, physical assault, and intrusion into the athlete's private property.

According to Brackenridge (1997) the absolute power of a coach over the athletes aiming for the top, as well as over the parents and the administrators, resembles the priest's authority who is supposed to derive this right from God and whose absolute knowledge is never questioned. As Donelly (1997 p. 393) highlights:

"Parents and coaches use a variety of disciplinarian penalties, ranging from not showing any affection towards the child to physical assault, in order to achieve maximum performance of the children-athletes under their charge".

But as Dreikurs and Soltz (1979 p. 235) point out, fear is a restraining force for learning, "fear undermines courage". In contrast to what coaches would expect, the use of punishment does not achieve the expected results. "The use of punishment makes the child more resistant and challenged" (ibid.) . The forms of punishment were varied. They too the form of (a) dietary controls "He prohibited us from eating a piece of bread as a form of punishment. For three consecutive evenings we ate only an orange" (T); (b) intrusions of privacy: "During the preparation period he used to intrude into our rooms. He used to open our suitcases with our clothes in them and whenever he found chocolates, chewing gums etc. he would create havoc" (T); (c) double training: "He used to enforce double training as a punishment. For example when the first training session was over he used to say "relax for an hour but afterwards you will start another four-hour session" (T).

The intimidation could take more serious forms. If anyone dared to revolt against this regime reprisals could take the form of expulsion or the intimidation of the performer by phoning parents to exert further control. In a limited number of cases, coaches might lose their self-control and seriously threaten the physical integrity of athletes by throwing various items at the performers:

"My coach used to throw chairs and keys at me! I once remember, he threw his keys at me but I ducked and managed to avoid being hit.

Sometimes you can't correct your movement and the coach gets angry. He would throw a chair or keys at you, or slap you. It is strange but all the athletes improved their performance after being beaten. It was one of his tactics , it didn't happen everyday." (D)

Other performers said that they had suffered similar treatment:

"One day he locked us in the changing room and we got beaten up. To be locked in a room you get all mixed up." (T)

"When I started training I used to be beaten every day! Our coach used to cut down thick branches from the trees and beat us. I couldn't perform well on exercise and he chased me all over the gym centre in order to beat me. But he couldn't get hold of me. I was so scared of him that I ran faster than ever. Eventually another coach got hold of me and I was beaten black and blue. Too much beating." (A)

As a result of this brutal behaviour the gymnast quit the sport because she became overwrought.

For another female gymnast who was brought up in two countries, Greece and Romania, being beaten was a habit. In Romania the state used to give everything to their aspiring champions but it expected the athlete to take full advantage of the services offered, there was no choice. Beating was institutionalized. In Greece, beating is also widespread. As one performer said:

"I was beaten a lot during my athletic career. Romania offers you everything but you've got to do it. They push you to do it. Sternness and beating." (D)

When the athlete moved to Greece with her parents she experienced a similar situation.

"He slapped me on the face so hard that I've never experienced anything like it. But you can't say anything, what can you say? You are a 15 year old child. I was used to being beaten from Romania. I tolerated all that." (D)

Thoroughly initiated into such an abusive regime it is alarming (though not surprising) that in contrast to previous athletes, she did not give up gymnastics because of being beaten.

The enforcement of "law and order" from some coaches leaves no room for faults or negligence. According to Adler (p. 492) anger might be part of the inferiority complex, just like tears or apologies. The inferiority complex appears when a person is not properly equipped to solve a problem and admit his inability.

> "Shouting at an athlete might be needed sometimes but never without reason. But I was slapped on my face twice without any reason at all. He asked me why I had thrown the keys of the changing room to my team-mate. He was very angry "Do you think there is anarchy here?" He slapped me with great force. I laughed. He slapped me again." (G)

The behaviour of some coaches, however, is very violent:

> "Some coaches assault you physically. They would wear heavy boots and kick you on your shin or they would get hold of your hair and pull you up. Things have improved a little now." (Z)

> "My old coach got hold of a female gymnast by the pigtail and put her on the parallel bars. He has a piece of wood in his hand permanently and chases the female gymnasts with it." (I)

> "Just because my team-mate used to answer back, he used to direct his anger against me and beat me... I was full of stress. I used to be afraid of competing on the beam because I wasn't that good but he used to tell me" if you don't want to compete I will smash your head in' just before the competition. This created a lot of stress. In the end I broke my leg and I told him "I don' want to train with you, I want to change coach." (A)

Other athletes believe that instead of violence, coaches should discuss any behaviour problems with their athletes and if nothing is solved then they should contact their parents. A few former athletes justify the use of violence by coaches:

> "If you are not afraid of your coach you can't go very far. I believe that in Greece there must be strict discipline and fear. There must be a distance between the coach and the athlete." (D)

Little control over their lives

Others believe that there are some striking similarities between training in gymnastics and military training. According to Farris (1975) a sergeant achieves a radical transformation: he moulds his group of soldiers, his soldiers obey the institutionalized authorities and are actuated by the dominant values. Some of the characteristics of military training are the following: 1) extreme isolation from the rest of society and lack of any private life; 2) emphasis on aggressiveness and manliness; 3) planning of training so that the trainee is under physical and emotional stress.

The same characteristics seem to appear in the gymnastic training of the interviewees. They became isolated from the rest of society simply in virtue of the vast amount of time they spent in exhausting training and recovering from it. The key concept of training was an aggressive desire for victory. Training is designed to be even tougher than the competition itself so that gymnasts will be able to cope with the mental and physical stress of competition. A former female athlete mentioned some of these points:

> "Coaches don't teach you how to think and how to protect yourself.
> They treat you like a soldier. They don't let you take the initiative." (K)

Faris (1975) describes the ideal sergeant as a veteran of war, as an authoritarian figure with paternalistic tendencies, changing roles according to circumstances, conventional inside the barracks, more approachable outside and finally changing roles with the passage of time. In a similar manner, the ideal coach is usually a top former athlete, a strict but paternalistic figure, more conventional within the gym and finally when the athlete improves and manages to reach the top, the coach alters their behaviour accordingly.

It is worth noting that two thirds (64%) of Canadian Olympic athletes thought that they had very little control over their lives during their athletic careers. Many other athletes (18%) reported that they had personal control of their lives but in fact it was a wrong sense of personal control. Coaches and administrators had the real power (Werthner and Orlick, 1986) Many Canadian athletes ended their careers feeling bitter and dissatisfied because of their coaches. Dacyshyn (1999) reported that Canadian female gymnasts lacked power and control over their lives and competition regimes. It was coaches who dictated what was to be done in training, even in their lives outside the gym-centre. It is clear that the gymnasts in this study reported feelings that corroborated such data.

Athletes' resistance to coaches

In relation to these damning data some key questions arise: "What are the athletes' rights? Should they submit to or resist authority?"; and "How can athletes be protected from the arbitrariness of coaches and administrators?" At present, in Greece, the relationship between coaches and their athletes is very often as described below. One could say that external rather than internal discipline is cultivated during sports training, human rights are restricted, athletes cannot easily react in a tough situation. Freedom of speech is restricted, obedience instead of initiative is fostered. In such a social environment every effort to stand up for one's rights is regarded as a "revolutionary" action. The "revolutionaries" might be confronted with criticism in the beginning, ending in expulsion from the club as a final measure. According to Adler's personal psychology, a teacher (coach) should aim towards the enlightened upbringing of children so that they can live each day as mature and well-rounded human beings. It is important to bear in mind that the likelihood of athletic progress is unthinkable if gymnasts seek litigious redress against coaches and sport-administrators because federations are private associations these matters are seen as private business (Panagiotopoulos, 1993) As Coakley (1986, p. 81) points out, although coaches treat athletes like employees, the official recognition of athletes as employees would create serious problems for the authorities.

How do gymnasts react against their punishment? Do they resist physical assault or not? As a former gymnast said, the expression of any personal viewpoints were regarded as disobedience. The patterns of response are heterogeneous:

> "I have regrets because very often I could have reacted and said "you are restricting my freedom". Of course, you couldn't say anything at the time. You accepted everything, you couldn't answer back. You accepted your coach swearing at you but you didn't have the right to speak because if you answered back you were going against the coach himself." (T)

Compare the above with another athlete who answered back.

> "Once I was beaten by my coach but she didn't dare do it again. I was a woman. She hit me because I didn't perform an exercise. But I was courageous and I answered back. "What are you doing?" I asked her. (G)

Yet for another top athlete there should be sternness, even a light beating when the coach has "good" intentions to push the athlete:

> "I never reacted because of being beaten. I personally believe that being beaten is not bad as long as it is not done with bad intentions. To be slapped on the face is not bad because you wake up. I know it from personal experience, you are frightened and you perform better." (D)

Recommendations

The data, though contextually-specific to a certain degree, yields some clear policy recommendations that extend beyond the sport and national barriers of the data. In addition, to the support of the data presented here, the recommendations is integrated here with portions of the received literature.

The following suggestions could be made for improving the relations between coach and athlete:

(i)   Gymnasts should be allocated to different training groups according to their abilities (Cote and Salmela, 1996);

(ii)   Gymnasts should be asked with whom they want to train. Their opinion should be taken into consideration (Cote and Salmela, 1996; Krane *et al.*, 1997);

(iii)   Coaches, administrators and parents should be informed about alternative training methods. Coaches, and generally all adults, should emphasize the importance of effort, personal improvement, positive relations with their team-mates and not competition or public appraisal (Krane *et al.*, 1997);

(iv)   Coaches and administrators must ensure that gymnasts have many social, cultural and educational experiences and that their perception of self-worth should not be exclusively dependent on achievement within their sport (Dacyshyn, 1999);

(v)   There should be written legal rules about the control of behaviour of athletes. Coaches or administrators should be allowed to decide themselves who has committed a breach of discipline (Kidd and Eberts, 1982);

(vi)   Coaches should be ethically educated. The use of physical violence by coaches should stop (Koukouris, 1994) It must be made clear to the strict disciplinarians that most athletes are adults and that they have every right to control their athletic activity in cooperation with coaches and administrators (Kidd and Eberts, 1982);

(vii)   Cooperation between coaches should be improved. Gymnasts should not change coaches as soon as they join the National Team. The reasons for coaches being discharged should be made explicit and not remain obscure (Koukouris, 1994);

(viii) Putting an athlete under pressure to take a significant decision without adequate information is a violation of human rights. Athletes should be trained to demand their rights (Kidd and Eberts, 1982; Wertner and

Orlick, 1986) Human rights abuses should be dealt with collectively and not individually (Wertner and Orlick, 1986);

(ix)   Coaches should be trained to learn how to facilitate the disengagement process (Wertner and Orlick, 1986);

(x)   The coach should identify some positive aspects of his athlete and declare them publicly. Doganis (1999) suggests that coaches should make known the athletes' qualities to his colleagues;

(xi)   Coaches should use positive feedback and cooperative methods during their teaching and they should consult the gymnast during decision-making (Krane *et al.*, 1997; and Williams, 1991)

Concluding remarks

The methodologies used in earlier quantitative pieces of research carried out on the disengagement from sport (e.g. Brown, 1983) were found to have had weaknesses. In this present research it is argued that disengagement from sport can best be examined from the phenomenological perspective presented here (see Figure 1).

In this study it was clear that coaches were in fact all too frequently responsible for elite gymnasts giving up their sport for the following reasons. First, there were many athletes interviewed who emphasize the sternness and authoritarian approach of their coaches. Many Greek coaches do not hesitate to use physical violence against their athletes in order to "educate" and "discipline" their athletes. Many athletes interviewed emphasized the strict authoritarian approach used by their coaches as a deciding factor in their giving up the sport. A further reason given was the fact that some coaches launch a form of psychological warfare against their own athletes.

Some limitations must be observed here. Coaches' views of the disengagement process were not examined in this study. In future studies they should be asked directly to define why particular gymnasts dropped out from sport and their views should be compared with those of the gymnasts. The conclusions of this study are only applicable to this sport Walker (1982) I kept to the limits imposed by the sample selection. However, there was an overrepresentation of female gymnasts in the sample.

From the data presented above, however, it is clear that it is the coaches' behaviour and not other commonly cited factors such as parental influence, poor administration, personal injuries that is more influential in the gymnasts deciding to cut short their athletic career. Disengagement from sport can result from the desire of some coaches to satisfy their own interest and egotism (Koukouris, 1991; 1994)

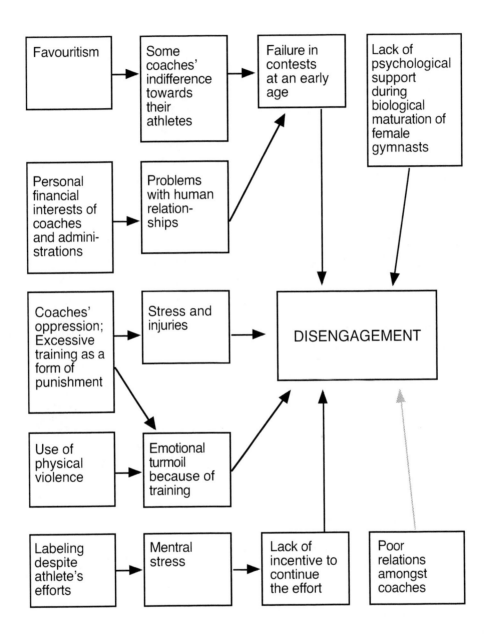

Figure 1   **How coaches are responsible for top gymnasts discontinuing gymnastics — Cognitive map**

The present law in Greece gives preferential registration in P.E. Departments to gold medallists and has the effect, indirectly, of granting tremendous power to coaches, because winning a gold medal very often depends on a coach's decision to select an athlete for the National Team. Beyond the concepts win–defeat "the most important thing is what the athletes benefit from when they leave the gym" (Bailie, 1997: p. 30)

Coaches' views of the disengagement process were examined indirectly. In future studies they should be asked directly to define why particular gymnasts dropped out from sport, and their views should be compared with those of the gymnasts. The present study involved both male and female gymnasts. However, future researches should focus more on female gymnasts because this is where most problems appeared in this study.

References

Adler, A. *(nd) Modern thought. Introduction to psychology.* Introductory and selective writings of Adler. Thessaloniki: Centre for the Study of Adler.

Bailie, T. (1997) 'Take a stance against negativity!', *International Gymnast* Vol. 39, No. 8–9, pp. 30–31

Baumann, S. and Tzormbatzoudis, H. (1995) *Psychology in Sport.* Maiandros, Thessaloniki, Greece.

Brackenridge, C. (1997) '"He owned me basically"…Women's experience of sexual abuse in sport', *International Review for the Sociology of Sport* Vol. 32, No. 2: pp. 115–130.

Brown, B. (1983) 'Factors influencing the process of withdrawal by female adolescents from the role of competitive age group swimmer'. Unpublished doctoral dissertation. University of Waterloo, Waterloo, ON, Canada.

Blinde, E. and Greendorfer, S. (1985) 'A reconceptualization of the process of leaving the role of competitive athlete', *International Review of Sport Sociology*, No. 20: pp. 87–93.

Coakley, J. (1986) *Sport in society. Issues and controversies* (3rd edition) Saint Louis: Mosby Co.

Cote J., Salmela, J. and Russel, S. (1995) 'The knowledge of high performance gymnastic coaches: Competition and training considerations', *The Sport Psychologist* No. 9: pp. 76–95.

Cote J., Salmela, J., Trudel, P. and Russel, S. (1995) 'The coaching model: a grounded assessment of expert gymnastic coaches' knowledge', *Journal of Sport & Exercise Psychology*, Vol. 17, No 1: pp. 1–17.

Cote J., Salmela, J. (1996) The organizational tasks of high performance gymnastic coaches. *The sport psychologist*, 10, 261–277.

Dervisis, S. and Tzorbatzoudis, H. (1994) *Theoretical and methodological approaches of teaching–learning in Physical Education.*

Doganis, George (1999) "*Self-fullfilling prophesy in the relation between coach and athlete*". Speech during a seminar "The role of sport psychology on youth sport", Thessaloniki Greece.

Donnelly, P. (1997) 'Child labour, sport labour: Applying child labour laws to sport', *International Review for the Sociology of Sport* Vol. 32, No. 4: pp. 389–406.

Dacyshyn, A. (1999) 'The sport and retirement experiences of elite female gymnasts', in J. Coakley and P. Donelly (eds) *Inside Sports*. London: Routledge, pp. 214–222.

Duncan, J. (1997) 'Focus group interviews with elite young athletes, coaches and parents', in J Kremer, K. Trew and S. Ogle (eds) *Young people's involvement in sport*. London: Routledge.

Faris, J. (1975) 'The impact of basic combat training. The role of the drill sergeant in the all-volunteer army', *Armed Forces and Society*, Vol. 2, No. 1: pp. 115–127.

Glaser, B. and Strauss, A. (1967) *The discovery of grounded theory: Strategies for qualitative research*. Aldine de Gruyter, New York, USA.

Jones, S. (1985) 'The analysis of depth interviewing', in R. Walker (ed) *Applied Qualitative Research* (pp. Aldershot: Gower, pp. 56–70)

Kaimakamis, V. (1992) *Gymnastics at school*. Thessaloniki: Maiandros Editions.

Kaimakamis, V. (1997) 'The use and contribution of school artistic gymnastics', *Journal of Artistic Gymnastics*, Vol. 3 (March) [in Greek]

Kidd, B. and Eberts, M. (1982) *Athletes' rights in Canada*. Toronto: Ministry of Tourism and Recreation.

Koukouris, K. (1991) 'Disengagement of Greek elite athletes from organized competitive sport', *International Review for the Sociology of Sport* Vol. 24, No. 4: pp. 289–310.

Koukouris, (1994) 'Constructed case studies: Athlete's perspectives on disengaging from organized competitive sport', *Journal of Sport Sociology* Vol. 11, No. 2: pp. 114–139.

Krane, Greenleaf and Snow (1997) 'Reaching for gold and the price of glory: A motivational case study of an elite gymnast', *The Sport Psychologist* No. 11: pp. 53–71.

Massimo, J. (1987) 'Leaving home to train: A critical decision', *International Gymnast* Vol. 9, No. 7: pp. 50–51.

Panagiotopoulos, D. (1993) 'The institutional problem of sport federation in Greece: Structure, administration, legal entity, operation', *Sport Science, theory and Practice* Vol. 8, No. 3, pp. 77–84 [in Greek].

Panhellenic Association of Coaches in Gymnastics (1997) 'Advice to new coaches by the Administrative Council', *Gymnastics* Vol. 4: pp. 6–7.

Patsantaras, N. (1994) '*Der Trainer als sportberuf. Entwicklung und Ausdifferenzierung einer profession*'. Schorndorf.

Patsantaras, N. (1996) 'Changing values and training action in sports performance-championship', in Y. Stamiris (ed) *Sociology of sport*. Athens: K .and G. Zerbini O. E. [in Greek]

Puig, N. and Morrell, S. (1996) 'Relating the method: Use of the itinerary concept in the analysis of sport biographies', *International Review for the Sociology of Sport* Vol. 31, No. 4: pp. 439–454.

Werthner, D. and Orlick, T. (1986) 'Retirement experiences of successful Olympic athletes', *International Journal of Sport Psychology No.* 17: pp. 337–363.

The 'Hand of God'?

Claudio M. Tamburrini

Department of Philosophy,
University of Gothemburg, Sweden

When Maradona scored his famous — or, depending on the geographical context, infamous — "handball" goal against England at the Mexico Football World Cup in 1986, the whole world of sport — except for the Argentinians — accused him of cheating. Maradona, however, showed no repentance. As a matter of fact, he added even more fuel to the controversy by ascribing his goal to the hand of God. Some interpreted his expression as a sign of lack of contact with reality. Others, as a reference to the recent war between Argentina and England for the possession of the Falkland/Malvinas Islands. Still others saw in the argument on divine agency a wider political statement on the historical economic gap between the Northern and Southern hemispheres, and welcomed his goal as supreme compensatory justice. Whichever interpretation we like, the fact remains that Maradona cheated. Indeed, he flagrantly violated the rules of football.

Most sports-interested people — and the vast majority of sports philosophers — believe cheating to be *wrong*. For them, the "handball" goal embodies a regretful tendency of sports at present, with athletes resorting to whatever means they might deem necessary to achieve victory. These pessimistic voices underline that cheating, doping scandals, unsporting conduct and even violence have become common ingredients of current sport practices. And they concur on where the root of all these evils can be found: *widespread professionalisation and commercialisation of sports are made responsible for all the excesses above.*

In this essay, I will question the objection to elite sports that says that commercialism and professionalism encourage (1) cheating, and (2) unsporting behaviour, to the point of spoiling the game. Regarding the former, I will try to show that not all cases of cheating can properly be labelled as wrongful. Particularly regarding the hand of God, I intend to show that Maradona as a matter of fact acted *rightly* when he scored his goal, from a universalistic moral point of view.

Unsporting conduct is often stigmatised by sport critics almost as strongly as cheating. I believe this to be unreasonable. Though at the limit of what is permitted by the rules, this sort of strategic behaviour is part of an extended normative framework — a sort of sport practitioners´ ethos — within which sport rules are interpreted and applied, and should therefore not be considered as reprehensible. As a matter of fact, I will argue that some violations of the code of good sportspersonship should even be encouraged, as they enhance the quality of the game.

I will first proceed to characterise cheating, in order to distinguish it from unsporting behaviour. Following that, I will try to determine when cheating and unsporting behaviour (in short, "foul play") are blameable and, therefore, deserve to be discouraged, as part of my intent to delimit the idea of game-enriching strategic behaviour. Finally, my defence of certain forms of cheating and unsporting behaviour in sports will be presented in more detail.

What is cheating?

Cheating is usually characterised as the intentional violation of the rules of the game, in order to gain an unfair advantage over competitors. In the next sections, I will argue that intentionality is neither a necessary nor a sufficient condition for cheating, and that the advantage obtained by the cheater needs not be unfair either.

Intentionality

Let us begin by discussing the place of intentionality in the evaluation of sporting conduct. Is it the intention *to break the rules* that is relevant here? Suppose Maradona, after touching the ball with his hand, had openly signalised his fault to the referee, before the fault was even noticed. Would we really call his action cheating, simply because the "handball" was intentional? On the contrary, we would rather judge that intentionality was not a sufficient condition for characterising this rule violation as cheating.

By the same token, provided the player who commits a fault tries to get away with it, even *unintentional* rule violations could be said to constitute cheating. Suppose, for instance, that Maradona had no intention of touching the ball with his hand. Nonetheless, we would consider him guilty of concealing the "handball" to the game authorities, particularly to the referee. We would call his action cheating, and rightly so. That means that the intentional violation of a rule is not a necessary condition for cheating either.

It could be argued that such cases might be dealt with simply by postulating intentionality at a previous point of time. As the player now tries to hide her fault, intentionality could be retrospectively ascribed to the (originally unintentional) rule violation. This, however, would be to stretch common language too much. Rather, what these arguments suggest is that it is the intentionality to *deceive*, rather than merely to break the rules, that is morally relevant here.

This, however, is only half the truth. As a matter of fact, not all cases of cheating imply the intentional deception of the game authorities. Consider the so called good fouls. As the term has been defined by Warren Fraleigh (1995: p. 186), a good foul (which also goes under the name of professional foul or rational foul) is a rule violation that occurs when a participant knowingly violates a rule to achieve what would otherwise be difficult to achieve, but violates the rules so as to expect and willingly accept the penalty[1].

A soccer player, for instance, might intentionally and overtly commit an infraction against a rival who is in a position to score, in order to neutralise the danger at the reduced cost of a free-kick. In the good foul, the player does not intend to escape the penalty. There is no deceitful intention in her action. However, Fraleigh — and our intuitions — still tell us that good fouls constitute cheating. How can we support this intuition, in the absence of intentional deception?

In my opinion, good fouls show that the intention relevant for cheating is not so much the intention to deceive (the good fouler commits her fault openly, often in front of the referee), but the intention to obtain a game advantage[2]. What is the nature of this game advantage? Is the advantage obtained by the cheater *unfair*? That will depend on the context in which the game is being played, and on what kind of rule violation we have in mind. Suppose a player indulges in a type of rule-infringing behaviour, B1, and that B1 is, when given the proper occasion, generally performed by game practitioners. Everybody has the opportunity of doing B1, and — more important — everybody actually does it. So, it could be asked, where does the unfairness lie? Rather, the advantage obtained by the cheater has to be characterised as *illicit*, instead of unfair. Thus, "good fouls" are cheating simply because they (are supposed to) yield an advantage to the fouling player through an action which is proscribed in the written code of rules. When illicit behaviour is incorporated in the way game practitioners play the game, when everybody does it, then talk of its being unfair seems unjustified.

Cheating, fair play and sportspersonship

The upshot of the discussion above might then be summarised in the following characterisation of cheating. *Cheating is a violation of the written rules of a game, performed in order to gain an illicit advantage for oneself, or for one's team, over rival players*[3]. The hand of God and Mike Tyson's biting of Evander Holyfield's ear are examples of cheating.

The opposite of cheating is *fair play*. We practise fair play when we abide by the rules of the game. Unlike cheating (which is prohibited by the rules and considered as noxious for the game), fair play is demanded by the rules and expected to enhance its quality. Fair play demands subjection to the letter of current regulations. It implies a ready acceptance of the rules, and a willingness to abide by them. But it need go no further than that.

Another pair of opposites is that constituted by *good* and *bad sportspersonship*. Good sportspersonship is conduct that goes beyond the requirements of fair play, as it demands more than simply abiding by a rule code. Good sportspersonship differs from fair play, not in terms of whether it is good for the game or not (it often is), but rather by not being formalised in the rules of the game. Recall the Maradona situation. He scored a goal with his hand. As he did gain an advantage through his fault, and did it intentionally, he can rightfully be said to have cheated. But what about his teammates, who chose not to tell the referee that Maradona's goal was unfairly scored? By keeping silent, they might be said to accept the advantage granted to them by the cheater's action. Maradona's teammates violated no rule. There is no rule in football stating that players are under an obligation to denounce a cheating team mate. Therefore, they cannot reasonably be charged with cheating. Nonetheless, through their omission, these players violated a rule of good sportspersonship. Good sportspersonship requires that Maradona's teammates address the referee and ask him to annul the "handball" goal. They did not. Thus, they are guilty of unsporting behaviour. Another example of good sportspersonship is, for instance, when a player voluntarily refrains from provoking psychic instability in a rival player, even when that could be done within the limits of the rule framework (for instance, by coughing on purpose at a particular tense moment, or altering the pace of the game by doing up one's shoe-laces when not needed).

Good sportspersonship, then, belongs to the class of *supererogatory acts* in professional sports. Professional players who live up to it deserve to be praised. But, if they fail to do so, it is at least not evident that they should be blamed. The good sportsperson is generous and magnanimous with her rivals. But generosity and magnanimity are not included in the notion of fair play. Nor are they part of any known secularised professional ethics[4]. Though it sometimes might be reasonable to encourage sport practitioners to honour the precepts of good sportspersonship, it is not always reasonable to blame them if they fail to reach its standards.

Bad sportspersonship, in its turn, is considered to affect the quality of the game negatively. Unlike cheating, however, bad sportspersonship, though certainly discouraged, is not a course of action forbidden by the rules of the game. In football, diving and deterrent interventions are considered to be bad sportspersonship. Diving consists in simulating that one has been fouled by a rival in order to get a free kick or a penalty awarded to one's team. An example of a deterrent intervention — also labelled intimidating actions — is the tight marking of a rival player that, though performed within the limits of what is allowed by the rules, is intended to intimidate her from further action.

The English national team provided us with another example of bad sportspersonship in soccer. I will call it the persecution of Schwartz. In the second half of the match against Sweden at Wembley on June 13th 1999, the Swedish midfield Schwartz was given a yellow card by the referee. Some English players began then to play more aggressively against Schwartz every time he got the ball, although without fouling him. Obviously, their intention was to get him to lose his temper, get a second yellow card and thus be sent off the field[5].

English soccer has recently added another case to the bad sportspersonship repertoire. During the match between Sheffield and Arsenal, a Sheffield player intentionally threw the ball out so that medical attention could be provided for a rival injured player. When the game started again, an Arsenal player intended to return the ball to the rivals by kicking it long into Sheffield's half. One of his teammates, however, intercepted the ball and scored a goal. The referee condoned the goal, as no formal rule has been violated. The great majority of the public, however, strongly disapproved of the Arsenal player's action.

The question that occupies us is whether these cases of foul play are reprehensible and should for that reason be discouraged in sports. Are we justified in condemning Maradona´s "handball" goal? Should we really do our best to try to eradicate such cases of behaviour as diving, deterrent interventions, putting off a rival player and the persecution of Schwartz from the world of sports? Does the Arsenal goal differ in any relevant sense from the previous examples of unsporting behaviour?

When is foul play blameable?

Foul play (i.e., cheating or bad sportspersonship) deserves condemnation, and should therefore be discouraged, when at least one of the following conditions is fulfilled:

(a) it introduces unfairness in competition;

(b) it spoils the nature of the game;

(c) it exposes sport practitioners to (an increased risk of) unnecessary physical injury.

Do the examples of foul play listed in the previous section satisfy any of these conditions? Let us discuss them one by one.

Unfair competition

According to a common view on rule-breaking advanced by Gunther Lüschen (1977, quoted in Leaman 1995: p. 193):

> Cheating in sport is the act through which the manifestly or latently agreed upon conditions for winning such a contest are changed in favor of one side. As a result, the principle of equality of chance beyond differences of skill and strategy is violated.

Randolph M. Feezell has similarly formulated this contract idea as a kind of promise-breaking. According to him, "...cheating is a kind of promise-breaking or violation of a contractual relationship, which implies that the cheater has attempted to gain an unfair advantage by breaking a rule" (Feezell, 1995: p. 153). We have then two different ideas here, usually combined in the discussion of rule-breaking in sports. First, there is the notion of a *contract* supposedly agreed to by game participants, and that the cheat breaks. Secondly, in Luschen's and Feezell's definitions of cheating we also find the idea of an *unfair advantage*. The cheat not only fails to honour the previous agreement to respect the rules of the game she has freely and voluntarily engaged in. She also disrupts the equal conditions of competition beyond differences of skill and strategy that existed before the rule violation. While other participants abstain from using proscribed means to attain victory, the argument runs, the cheat resorts to more effective (though illicit) means to win the contest. A sanction is therefore required to *annul* the unfair advantage obtained through rule-breaking, and to *restore* competitive balance between players. I will discuss these two different aspects of the contractarian view of sports in the following two subsections.

Cheating as a contractual breach

What kind of agreement is it that the cheat supposedly breaks? This agreement is obviously not always explicit. Rather, by entering the game, a player is (most often, implicitly) taken to accept submitting herself to the formally sanctioned norms of the sport discipline in which she engages. This acceptance, it is argued, makes respect for the rules mandatory. Thus, by the very action of playing, a sport practitioner puts herself under an obligation to honour the contract she has undertaken, and to abide by its rules. Sigmund Loland (1998: p. 93) has formulated this idea as follows:

> When we voluntarily engage in a rule-governed practice, we enter a
> more or less tacit social contract in which a moral obligation arises:
> keep the formal playing rules of the game! Here, then, we have the
> core justification of the fairness ideal.

Against this contract view of fair play, Oliver Leaman (1995: p. 195) stated
that "(n)on-compliance by some players makes the problem of identifying
precisely what the latent agreement is allegedly about insoluble". Uncertainty
about what the contract actually entails also casts a shadow of doubt on its
validity. The strategy of supporting contractual obligation in sports on the
notion of latent or implicit agreements made by the players is obviously
weakened by the fact that many (even a majority) of them do not act in
accordance with what supposedly has been agreed upon.

Put in this light, our initial question can now be reformulated: Has
Maradona broken the implicit agreement among soccer players, when he
scored his goal against the English national football team? The answer to
this question will depend on whether touching the ball with one's hands runs
counter to the prevailing ethos of football.

Now, according to the traditional understanding of a game ethos, it
certainly does. In Fred D'Agostino's view, "besides the formal, written rules
of a game, there is an unofficial system of conventions which determines how
the official rules of the game will be applied in various concrete circumstances"
(D'Agostino, 1995: p. 47).

On the basis of this notion, D'Agostino distinguishes three different kinds
of sporting behaviour: *permissible* (that is, in accordance with the formal
rules); *impermissible but acceptable* (that is, proscribed though not penalised
conduct); and *unacceptable* behaviour (proscribed and penalised conduct).
There is no question that handling the ball in soccer belong to the third
category. When discovered, this is without exception penalised by referees.

The classical notion of a game ethos is, however, too narrow. It refers
only to the way in which officials interpret sporting behaviour. *It is the ethos
of game authorities, rather than the ethos of game practitioners*. It leaves aside
the conventions, group norms, etc., upon which other participants in the
sporting game base their understanding of the sporting activity in which they
engage. Parallel to D'Agostino's official ethos, there are, for instance, the
ethoses of the public, the media and the players, all different from each other,
which together render a comprehensive understanding of what the game is
about. *D'Agostino's ethos is a set of conventions regulating how rule violations
are to be penalised, rather than how the game is to be understood, much less
how it has to be played.*

In the light of this wider, compound ethos notion, it is pretty obvious
that Maradona's hands-on goal does not run counter to the way soccer is

played today. Particularly among soccer players, handling the ball is not an exceptional fault: when the occasion demands it, they resort to hand touches, and they do so often. It is true that, normally, these rule violations do not take place under the same spectacular and dramatic circumstances under which Maradona scored his goal. But "handballing" is nonetheless relatively common in football games.

This does not mean that handling the ball in soccer should be tolerated by game officials, not even that it should not be criticised. In Maradona's case, for instance, it would be far-fetched to say that the fact that many football players actually commit that kind of infraction turns his fault into a permissible action. But the fact that handling the ball is relatively widespread among soccer practitioners at least weakens the rule formalist objection that hand touches are not part of the normative framework of soccer. If "handballing" is relatively frequent in soccer, then it ought to be seen as part of the reality of the game, as a practice sanctioned by the way in which soccer is played. *If everyone does it — or if everyone would do it, given a suitable occasion — the cheater simply acts as she (reasonably) expects others to act in similar circumstances. No contractual breach can be derived from that.*

Against this realistic approach, it could be objected that, unlike Maradona's goal, hands faults — though indeed common — are often accidental and performed with no intention to deceive the authorities and obtain a game advantage. This move, however, will not do. Even if unintentional at the moment of being performed, the failure to signal one's fault to the referee turns the (originally unintended) action into an intentional strategy to obtain an illicit game advantage. From a contractual point of view, there is no morally relevant difference between trying to get a game advantage through a voluntary infraction, or through concealing an involuntary one. Committing an intentional hands-on fault is on a moral par with doing it unintentionally and failing to acknowledge it.

Finally, it could be objected that my argument unwarrantably takes for granted that the players' ethos should be given priority to the authorities' or the public's. However, *in the present context of fairness*, I believe this is as it should be. Fairness is a relational concept. It requires reciprocity: in the absence of reasons that could justify acting differently, it demands that you treat others as you are treated by them. The public's ethos pays most attention to how the way the play is played affects its quality, particularly its entertainment value. The authorities' ethos is concerned with how to penalise rule violations. The players' ethos, instead, is mainly concerned with how players treat each other, and how they fairly compete with each other within a commonly accepted rule set, rather than with how to preserve the quality (or entertainment value) of the game, or how infractions are to be penalised. Therefore, when fairness is on the focus, among all the complementary ethoses of the game, the players' ethos is the one with most relevance.

Cheating as unfair advantage

According to a wider notion of game ethos, then, handling the ball in soccer is no contractual breach. And, as a matter of fact, it yields no unfair advantage either. Fairness in competitive conditions is not affected if, according to the prevailing ethos (unwritten rules and conventions) of the game, a certain cheating behaviour is accepted and generally performed. Everyone is allowed to proceed according to this (expanded) rule framework. Equal conditions of competition are thereby achieved. There is no unfair advantage in cheating, *provided it is (somehow) considered as part of the game by regular practitioners, and everyone has that option open for herself.*

According to the same line of reasoning, it becomes even more evident that the above mentioned cases of bad sportspersonship constitute no contractual breach or unfair advantage either. They are committed much more frequently than handling faults. But, it could be retorted to this, why should the fact that sport practitioners seldom abide by a regulation have any bearing on whether or not its violation should be accepted, or even tolerated? Think, for instance, of Mike Tyson's biting of Evander Holyfield's ear. Even if that practice were to become generalised (as a matter of fact, it is more common in boxing than one might think), would not such a practitioners' ethos be a perverted one? And, if so, does not this fact speak against giving any consideration whatsoever to the general level of compliance of a rule?

There is, in my opinion, a relevant difference between Maradona's and Tyson's illicit actions. Tyson's bite harmed the physical integrity of his opponent. Thus, it runs counter to one of the basic goals that the rules of the game are designed to achieve: preventing injuries to other players. That is not the case regarding Maradona's goal. Obviously, a hands-on goal still might be said to affect, if not the physical integrity, at least the interests of rival players negatively. But that is exactly what the game is about! Even in cases when the advantage is the result of an action proscribed by the formal rules of the game, that circumstance is tempered by the fact that the action is included in the enlarged ethos adopted by *sport practitioners*.

Thus, with the exception of the Sheffield-Arsenal incident, the examples of bad sportspersonship discussed in this article are not cases of unfair sporting behaviour. As a matter of fact, not even handling the ball in soccer (including the most famous instance, the hand of God) implies unfairness towards rivals, as handling is widely accepted (at least, in the weak sense of being indulged in, in given circumstances) among soccer players. But does this decide the question whether foul play is acceptable? Could we not reject such sporting behaviour on other grounds than unfairness? To see that, let us now discuss condition (b) above.

Spoiling the game

An essentialist interpretation of (b) would establish that rules must be followed because only then can the true nature or essence of the game be preserved. Obviously, this amounts to game Platonism: there are no such entities as games, which remain unchangeable and immune to outer influence or transformation. Rather, condition (b) should be understood as a requirement that games be decided exclusively on grounds of differences in *skills* that are relevant for the actual discipline, and which the competition is expected to measure as objectively as possible. Thus, it could be argued, one reason to have rules in sports, and to discourage rule-breaking, is that without them sport contests would be decided on other grounds — by displaying other abilities — than those considered relevant for the game.

Though appealing, however, this approach does not fully meet the objection from game Platonism. Even skills central to a particular sport discipline evolve. And so does our view of them. At the turn of this century, runners were said to compete in the ability to getting to the finish line as fast as possible without any training or preparation. Today, it is obvious that, in spite of superficial similarities, runners excel in quite another type of abilities, both physical and mental.

Besides, regarding certain examples of bad sportspersonship (for instance, putting off a rival player), it is not evident that the skill a sport practitioner has to display to avoid becoming a victim of that kind of action actually is so irrelevant to sport excellence as the present argument seems to assume. *There is no doubt that psychological make-up (particularly the capacity to resist pressure) also forms part of the skills repertoire tested by the contest.* Björn Borg was admired not only for his tremendous tennis abilities. We also admired him for his coolness of mind in the decisive moments. Other things being equal, this quality makes him superior to other, more temperamental players as, for instance, John McEnroe. At least, that is the way we reason in other professions. Good entrepreneurship is defined not only by the capacity to perform well in business, but also by the possession of a strong character to confront tough, *though licit*, competition. So, putting off a rival player might reasonably be seen as *expanding, rather than distorting,* the skills repertoire required by sporting games. For similar reasons, the English soccer team goes free from the accusation of unsporting behaviour in its encounter with Sweden. They were, so to speak, merely testing Schwartz's psychological excellence.

Perhaps we could, in order to avoid game or skill Platonism, reformulate (b) in terms of the *quality* of the game. On this view, rules — and the sanctions (formal and informal) attached to them — aim at preserving the quality of sport competitions. Cheating, and sometimes even bad sportspersonship, as they are violations of the normative code of a game, lowers its quality and should therefore be discouraged.

The notion of the quality of a sporting game is usually referred to in a rather loose way in the literature on sports, and it has seldom been assessed in a stringent manner[6]. The difficulty of the task suggests such an enterprise probably will not be entirely successful. But this fact can hardly justify the surprisingly few attempts made to characterise the idea of a good game. A tentative characterisation will have to include the following elements:

(i) Flow: a good game cannot be interrupted too often, it needs to have a certain fluidity to allow different game combinations to arise, and the development of game skills to flourish.

(ii) Skill: a good game has to attain a relatively high level in the display of the relevant skills. In a game frequently interrupted by rule violations, in a game with no flow, skills will have difficulty to flourish.

(iii) Challenge: a good game has to be a (roughly) even competition between rivals. An uneven match is not a good match, as it will lack intensity and the outcome will almost be given in advance.

(iv) Excitement: if the outcome is uncertain, and if the skill level is high, then the game will probably turn out as exciting. When the excitement rises above a certain degree, the game might even become dramatic.

(v) Drama: in very disputed and even games, the outcome could be decided only in the final moments of the competition, thus adding drama to the game.

(vi) Joy: when the game has flow, skill level is high and the contest even and exciting, both competitors and the public will experience joy, a sensation of having fun as a consequence of being engaged in a practice of great hedonic quality. Joy, however, is a rare quality in today's professional sports. Athletes need victory too badly to experience any fun in competing: their prestige and economic future are sometimes at stake on the field. And, often, spectators are not dispassionate enough to be able to enjoy a sport contest without suffering the agony of not knowing how their own team or their favourite athlete will do in the competition. In that sense, there is a tension between elements (v) and (vi): the more dramatic a contest is, the less fun the (passionate) spectator will experience.

To return to our previous question, there is no reason to assume a priori that keeping the rules of a game necessarily has a quality-enhancing effect, as characterised in (i) — (vi) above. As a matter of fact, there are several cases in which violations of the rules of a game have led to technical improvements of the discipline[7]. Further, even when no technical adjustments will follow, some cases of rule-breaking are sometimes game-enriching, in the sense of enhancing the challenge and excitement of the competition, without necessarily affecting the skills or the flow of the game negatively. Take, for example, deterrent interventions in football. Tougher play style will probably increase the heat of the game. As long as they stay within the limits of fair play (that is, of what is permitted by the written rule code), we have no reason to regret more aggressive contests. Granted that better skills will be required to elude tougher marking. But that means that players will develop the skill repertoire further.

The same applies to "diving". A goal scored by a simulated penalty no doubt adds to the excitement of the game as it compels the wronged team to play offensively to even the score. The match will then become more disputed and challenging. The flow of the game is not much affected either, as the situations in which it is rational to dive do not occur so often as to yield frequent interruptions in the game. Further, "diving" seems to further, not only the excitement of the game, but also offensive playing skills. "Diving", no doubt, obliges defending players to play in a more cautious manner. Thus, indirectly, it rewards offensive football styles. Dribbling skills will flourish, more goals will be scored, all this adding to the enjoyment of the public.

Spoiling and cheating as free-riding

But perhaps the above discussion of spoiling behaviour renders us another sense in which the above examples of foul play could be seen to be unfair. A condition for not spoiling the game is that, if not all, at least a great majority of players abide by the regulations. Otherwise, the play would become too dull, as a consequence of frequent interruptions, and the different skills and abilities of the players would have no opportunity to unfold and flourish. That means that the reason why cheats do not spoil the game is that others respect the regulations. As Sigmund Loland (1998: p. 99) stated, "[t]he general idea is that it is wrong to benefit from the co-operation of others without doing our fair share". Does not this then turn cheats into free-riders?

I do not think so. Again, with the exception of the Sheffield-Arsenal incident, the kind of foul play we are discussing here (the examples of unsporting behaviour quoted above and such rule violations as handling the ball) are indeed so commonly practised that no player can reasonably be said to profit from other players' obedience to the rules. There is so to speak a fluent rotation in playing dirty among the players. This, in my view, erases any unfair advantage cheaters might get and neutralises the free-rider argument.

Preventing injuries to others

Finally, could it not be argued that, if not all, at least some behaviour (for instance, deterrent interventions and the Sheffield-Arsenal incident) need to be discouraged, perhaps even formally forbidden, on the grounds that those actions increase the risk of physical injury for sport practitioners? I do not think this argument affects deterrent interventions. Obviously, intimidating interventions increase the risk of harm, as they imply playing on-the-limit. That risk, however, does not exceed what can reasonably be demanded from a professional player. Performing a professional activity is always related to the risk of being harmed by the strategies of one's competitors. So is also the case in professional sports.

Things are different regarding the Arsenal goal. If generalised, that action will have the consequence that no team will be prone to throw out the ball in order to provide for the medical attention of an injured rival player. This will increase the risk of injury for soccer players beyond what can be reasonably required from game participants. It is not part of any ethos of the game that, when injured, you will have to manage on your own without any medical attention. In particular, this is totally contrary to the players' ethos. The Arsenal team's action is thus blameworthy. It actually deserves the condemnation it met from soccer fans at the stadium.

What is wrong with cheating?

At the beginning of this essay, I addressed the argument that commercialism and professionalism in elite sports encourage cheating and unsporting behaviour to the point of spoiling sport games. According to this critic, these instances of foul play are wrong or, alternatively, an undesirable element in sport competitions. Such actions, it is said, give an athlete an unfair advantage over others, sometimes lowering the quality of the game or even jeopardising the physical integrity of sport practitioners. Against this, I suggested that at least some instances of cheating and unsporting behaviour do not fit within this description. They might, for example, increase the excitement of the competition, thereby enhancing its hedonic quality for spectators. Further, some of the risks involved in these infractions or actions must be accepted as part of the sport profession.

The realistic approach to sport practices advanced in this essay also answers the criticism that originates in the contract view of fair play. According to this position, by making an agreement to compete, the athlete binds herself with self-imposed rules and conditions. By entering the game, then, she would be accepting, albeit implicitly, the imposition to abide by its rules, even those latent or not overtly formulated. If the athlete then fails to live up to this self-imposed obligation, it is argued by these critics, she might justifiably be accused of cheating, as she obtains an unfair game advantage over other players, an advantage that they have renounced by sticking to the rules.

I have rejected this view. If those actions are open for all practitioners, in the sense of being a part of the enlarged ethos of the players, no contractual breach takes place and no unfair advantage is obtained by the athlete who indulges in them. Obviously, in Maradona's case, the fact that many football players actually commit that kind of rules violations is not sufficient to turn his fault into a permitted action. But at least it neutralises the objection that handling gives an unfair advantage to some players. If everyone does it — or if everyone would do it, given a suitable opportunity — the cheater simply acts as she (reasonably) expects others to act in similar circumstances. No unfair advantage can be derived from that.

From an (indirect) utilitarian point of view, it could even be argued that Maradona's action was right. Indirect utilitarianism states that an action is right when it is performed for optimific motives, even if its direct consequences are not condoned from an act-utilitarian point of view. Derek Parfit (1984: pp. 32–37) has provided an enlightening example of what indirect utilitarianism amounts to. He tells us about Claire, an act-utilitarian girl who has to decide between giving money to a charity organisation (and thereby saving many children from death in a foreign country), or using the money to cure her own child from a serious, though not life-threatening, disease. The disease will cause a handicap to her child, but will not turn the child's life into one that is not worth living. Claire decides to cure her child. In doing so, she fails to save the lives of the children who depended on her aid to survive. From an act-utilitarian point of view, it is evident that Claire acts wrongly. She fails to maximise welfare for all those concerned by her action, and chooses instead to actualise a lesser good. However, according to Parfit, her action, though wrong, is nonetheless blameless, as it is performed for a set of motives (taking care of one's offspring) that, in the long run and indirectly, will make the world a better place to live[8].

By the same token, we could say that Maradona's hands-on goal became a *right, though blameworthy*, action. Blameful right doing stands for an action that, though stemming from a wrong motive, still turns out to be right because of the positive effects that, albeit indirectly, follow from it. Maradona's cheating is to blame, because it stems from the wrong set of motives. Normally, being driven by the motive of getting an advantage over others by circumventing the rule framework tends to produce negative consequences for the game or even for society as a whole. But, some of these actions, although contrary to the formal, written rules of the game, turn out nonetheless to be right, because, in the end, they have a positive impact on the game, either by being innovative for sport techniques, or by enhancing the quality and the excitement of the game, or for all these reasons together.

This is particularly true of the hand of God incident. After it took place, football matches between England and Argentina acquired a special agonistic flavour, that seems to have overshadowed the tragic inheritance of the Falkland/Malvinas war. Thus, his goal had positive effects not only for the game of soccer, but even for the international community at large.

Further, the unfair advantage view also confronts the problem that not all the sanctions actualised by the regulatory rules can properly be described as restoring the previous competitive balance between athletes. Some of them obviously fit under this description. Thus, when a player plays the ball outside the physical limits of the football field, she loses the possession of the ball and the rival team regains it through an out-goal. But take, for instance, a red card for violent fouling. If the game is allowed to continue after the fault is committed, the fouler gets the ball from the fouled player. This is no doubt an illicit game advantage and should therefore be sanctioned. But the game advantage is the same, regardless of the harshness of the fouling. Why then send her out? It the aim is to erase the illicit advantage, why not sanction this one foul, like any other one, with a free kick for the rival team?

Another example is the newly introduced rule of soccer that requires sending out a player who fouls, or simply holds, a rival player in a goal position. Even if the game advantage obtained by the fouler (or, rather, the disadvantage she avoided through her fault) seems to justify a more severe sanction than a free kick, there is nonetheless a lack of proportionality between the type of fault (often, explicit and innocuous), and the sending off of the fouler. Why such harshness?

Similar difficulties arise regarding another rule of soccer sanctioning the suspension from the next match of a player who is booked twice during a tournament. He/she is allowed to finish the match in which the second card is awarded. The team against which the second fault is committed is not benefited by the suspension. Instead, it is the next rival team which is benefited. A highly counter-intuitive situation (from a fairness point of view) arose in the last World Football Cup, in France 1998. The Nigerian national team was not allowed to field some of its best players in the last match of the classificatory group against Paraguay, because they had got a second yellow card in the previous match against Spain. By winning over the weakened Nigerian team, Paraguay qualified for the next round, thereby leaving Spain out of the competition. Not only did Spain not benefit from the yellow cards its performance provoked in the Nigerian team: they were even harmed by it! In that sense, sending out a cautioned player for a period of time during the same match (as, for instance, it is done in ice-hockey) seems a more reasonable way to act. At least, the team benefited by the sanction would be the one against which the fault was committed.

In my opinion, these examples suggest that certain sanctions in soccer (and in other sports as well) are designed to operate as deterrents, rather than as restorative measures for infringements that yield game advantages. In the goal-position example, the severity of the sanction is intended to protect the quality of the game by keeping occurrence of this kind of fouling at a low level. Goals make the game more exciting. So, red cards for fouling a player who is about to score can be justified in terms of (a) above, understood as a quality-preserving condition.

Red cards for violent fouls, instead, seem appropriate for discouraging actions that risk the infliction of physical injury on the players. That means that their justification will have to be formulated in terms of (c) above. However, protecting sport practitioners from injury should not be confused with trying to eliminate reasonable professional risks at all costs. In professional soccer, for instance, dangerous fouls are still prohibited, and so they are in recreational soccer. But while so called intimidating interventions (tough actions on the edge of what is permitted by the rules, intended to instil respect for one's physical strength in rival players) definitely do not belong in the latter, they seem to be, not only acceptable, but even recommendable in the professional field. At least, one positive consequence which might follow from them is the increased excitement of a tough match.

Towards an enlarged sport ethos

The arguments above suggest that in sports, besides the traditional and already established ethos of the game, there is a wider normative framework, directly stemming from the evolving practice of the game, that condones a set of acceptable actions, *(even rule-infringing ones)* that are open for sports practitioners. In this practical, down-to-game normative framework, the sport practitioners' ethos — the particular understanding of the game entertained by players — is the most relevant indication of how the game should be played. This *extended* ethos, I would like to underline, should be clearly distinguished from a perverted one as, for instance, the general acceptance of actions similar to Tyson's bite would amount to. The reason is that, with the exception of the Sheffield-Arsenal incident, the examples of foul play discussed in this chapter are no hinder for achieving the goals of the rule system. They do not spoil the nature of sports. The examples of bad sportspersonship advanced above are not necessarily negative for the quality of the game. Often, they might even be expected to increase its excitement, by furthering the agonistic element of the contest. This is particularly true in professional sports, where so many material gains are at stake.

Bad sportspersonship does not violate the requirement of fairness in competition either. Diving, deterring interventions, persecuting a booked rival player, or the possibility of obtaining a game advantage by disturbing the concentration of one's opponent, are strategies open to everyone who chooses to engage in sport activity. Nor can such conduct be said to deprive individuals from an equal chance to enter the game. At least, not more than in the legitimate sense of putting higher demands on the skills to be mastered by the contestants.

The argument for the idea of an evolving ethos has obvious implications for the issue of fair play and good sportspersonship. Not only the attitudes of sport participants towards the rules of the game will change over time. Also what was previously seen as fair play, and the character qualities associated with it, will be submitted to a transformation, along with changes in values and the concrete situation of the community of sport practitioners. An example of these transformations is the commercial character acquired by sports in recent decades. The prospect of economic rewards and public acknowledgement put athletes under a pressure to increase performance standards. An expected consequence of this process is the relaxation of the system of rules governing sporting activities. Needless to say, the rules and traditions of the practice, as well as current notions of fair play, will have to undergo changes along with such a major transformation. These changes are not necessarily negative for sports. As a matter of fact, many of them can be said to increase competitive tension and the excitement of the game.

The picture of unsporting actions in professional sports that finally emerges is that of a continuum. At one extreme, we have licit and non-blameable actions. At the other extreme, we see those examples of cheating that clearly have a negative effect on the game, as well as on sports practitioners. In between, there is strategic behaviour that can neither be properly labelled as cheating (as it does not violate the written rules of the game), nor rightfully blameworthy (as it does not jeopardise the physical integrity of rival players, is not unfair, and might even increase the excitement of the game).

Finally, within the cheating domain, we find a special type of conduct that, though overtly violating the written normative code, constitutes nonetheless *blameful right doing*. Examples of blameworthy right doing, it should be underlined, are very exceptional. Maradona's "handball" goal, I have argued, is one of them. After its occurrence, encounters between the Argentinian and the English national soccer teams are marked by enhanced competitive character, and the aggressive post-war atmosphere between the teams was definitely eliminated. Therefore, his goal should be placed on a moral par with other actions (such as diving, intimidating interventions, and others), that — though performed from morally suspect motivations — add to the hedonic quality of the sport performance and increase the enjoyment of the public.

If my arguments are correct, it then follows that certain cases of bad sportspersonship and (though in very exceptional cases) cheating should be tolerated or perhaps lauded, rather than discouraged, in professional sports. In my opinion, this is exactly what is happening in elite sports at present. Obviously that encouragement has not been formally sanctioned by rule changes: the rule system is always behind the reality of the practice it purports to regulate. Nonetheless, I believe it is possible to perceive a more condescending attitude towards cheating and bad sportspersonship in at least some professional sports. Is that negative? Traditionally, this laxity has been interpreted as an evident sign of the perversion of sports by commercialism and professionalism. And, indeed, professional elite sports are practised at the intersection of fair play and bad sportspersonship. If the game becomes more exciting, with no increased risks for the physical integrity of the players, I think we should revise that negative judgement. Or, at least, we should think twice before making categorical pronouncements on these matters.[9]

Notes

[1] Immediately after this definition, Fraleigh exemplifies a good foul in basketball as follows: "... a defensive player, moving behind an offensive player with the ball who is dribbling for an easy lay up shot, intentionally holds the player, forcing him to shoot two free throws to make the same number of points". According to him, what makes such faults *good* is that it is in the prudent self-interest of the fouling player to force the opponent to shoot twice from a greater distance to make the same number of points as would have been made by shooting once for a lay up. Incidentally, it should be noticed that, after Fraleigh wrote his article, basketball regulations had undergone changes in this respect. At present, situations as those exemplified in the good foul render three, instead of two, shoots. A similar tendency can be noticed in football. Recent rule changes sanctioning fouls from behind (even innocuous ones, such as holding) to rival players in a goal position with a red card are intended to outweigh the beneficial effects for the fouler and her team of such violations of the rules. Notwithstanding these changes, Fraleigh's argument could be restated by resorting to other examples of good fouls gathered from other sports.

[2] Or, in P. McIntosh's terms, the intention to beat the system by gaining a game advantage even when the violation is sanctioned according to the rules. As he says, "Cheating ...need be no more than breaking the rules with the intention of not being found out...Cheating, however, implies an

intention to beat the system even although the penalty, if the offender is found out, may still be acceptable" (McIntosh, 1979, quoted in Leaman 1995: p. 193.

3 Strictly speaking, the advantage to be gained might also be the fulfilment of one's desire to benefit another competing athlete or team. Suppose, for instance, that a football team that already classified for the final instances of a tournament confronts a match that, if lost, can help the other team to classify. And suppose there is a long tradition of friendship between both teams. If the first team plays to lose, that would be a case of cheating, even if, properly speaking, the advantage they would thereby be getting is not a *game* advantage, but merely a preference satisfaction.

4 For more on the distinction between fair play and a sportspersonlike attitude, see, for instance, Keating (1995), particularly p. 147.

5 A distinction should be drawn here between: (a) provoking a rival player by fouling him (that is, through cheating); (b) provoking by playing at the limit of what is permitted by the rules (that is, through bad sportspersonship); and (c) provoking by displaying outstanding dribbling abilities in front of a cautioned rival player (which is a licit and often game-enriching action). It is (b) that will be discussed in this chapter.

6 See, however, Sigmund Loland´s characterisation of the 'good' game above.

7 Underwater breast swimming, for instance, though not fully allowed after its appearance, amounted to a technical paradigm shift in the discipline. The skyhook (in basketball) and the ´Boklöv jump´ (in ski jumping) are other examples.

8 Parfit´s indirect utilitarianism might be seen as an attempt to reconcile a consequentialist approach with virtue ethics.

9 A version of this paper is also published in C. M. Tamburrini, *The 'hand of God'?* (2000) Sweden: Acta Universitatis Gothoburgensis. The version published in this volume is with the kind permission of Acta Universitatis Gothoburgensis.

References

D'Agostino, F. (1995) 'The ethos of the game', in W. J. Morgan and K. V. Meier (eds), *Philosophic inquiry in sport* (2nd edition). Champaign, IL.: Human Kinetic Publishers, pp. 42–4.

Feezell, R. M. (1995) 'In sportsmanship', in W. J. Morgan and K. V. Meier (eds), *Philosophic inquiry in sport* (2nd edition). Champaign, IL.: Human Kinetic Publishers, pp. 152–60.

Fraleigh, W. (1995) 'Why the good foul is not good', in W. J. Morgan and K. V. Meier (eds), *Philosophic inquiry in sport* (2nd edition). Champaign, IL.: Human Kinetic Publishers, pp. 185–187.

Keating, J. W. (1995) 'Sportsmanship as a moral category', in W. J. Morgan and K. V. Meier (eds), *Philosophic inquiry in sport* (2nd edition). Champaign, IL.: Human Kinetic Publishers, pp. 144–51.

Leaman, O. (1995) 'Cheating and fair play in sport', in W. J. Morgan and K. V. Meier (eds), *Philosophic inquiry in sport* (2nd edition). Champaign, IL.: Human Kinetic Publishers, pp. 193–7.

Loland, S. (1998) 'Fair play: Historical anachronism or topical ideal?', in M. McNamee and S. J. Parry (eds) *Ethics and Sport*. London: E & FN Spon, Routledge, pp. 79–103.

Lüschen, G. (1977) 'Cheating in sport', in D. Landers (ed) *Social Problems in Athletics*. Urbana: University of Illinois Press.

McIntosh, P. (1979) *Fair play: Ethics in sport and education*. London: Heinemann.

Parfit, D. (1984) *Reasons and persons*. Oxford: Clarendon Press.

Leisure Studies Association

LSA Publications

LSA

An extensive list of publications on a wide range of leisure studies topics, produced by the Leisure Studies Association since the late 1970s, is available from LSA Publications.

Some recently published volumes are detailed on the following pages, and full information may be obtained on newer and forthcoming LSA volumes from:

LSA Publications, c/o M. McFee
email: mcfee@solutions-inc.co.uk
The Chelsea School, University of Brighton
Eastbourne BN20 7SP (UK)

Among their other benefits, members of the Leisure Studies Association may purchase LSA Publications at highly preferential rates. Please contact LSA at the above address for information regarding membership of the Association, LSA Conferences, and LSA Newsletters.

ONLINE

Complete information about LSA events and products including contents listings of all LSA Publications:

http://leisure-studies-association.info/LSAWEB

PARTNERSHIPS IN LEISURE: SPORT, TOURISM AND MANAGEMENT

**LSA Publication No. 78. ISBN: 0 906337 89 5 [2002] pp. 245 + iv
eds. Graham Berridge and Graham McFee**

Contents

LEISURE STUDIES: TRENDS IN THEORY AND RESEARCH

**LSA Publication No. 77. ISBN: 0 906337 88 7 [2001] pp. 198 + iv
eds. Stan Parker and Lesley Lawrence**

Contents

SPORT TOURISM: PRINCIPLES AND PRACTICE

**LSA Publication No. 76. ISBN: 0 906337 87 9 [2001] pp. 174 + xii
eds. Sean Gammin and Joseph Kurtzman**

Contents

Contents

VOLUNTEERING IN LEISURE: MARGINAL OR INCLUSIVE?

LSA Publication No. 75. ISBN: 0 906337 86 0 [2001] pp. 158+xi
eds. Margaret Graham and Malcolm Foley

Contents

LEISURE CULTURES, CONSUMPTION AND COMMODIFICATION

**LSA Publication No. 74. ISBN: 0 906337 85 2 [2001] pp. 158+xi
ed. John Horne**

Contents

LEISURE AND SOCIAL INCLUSION: NEW CHALLENGES FOR POLICY AND PROVISION

LSA Publication No. 73. ISBN: 0 906337 84 4 [2001] pp. 204
eds. Gayle McPherson and Malcolm Reid

Contents

JUST LEISURE:
EQUITY, SOCIAL EXCLUSION AND IDENTITY

LSA Publication No 72. ISBN: 0 906337 83 6 [2000] pp. 195+xiv
Edited by Celia Brackenridge, David Howe and Fiona Jordan

Contents

JUST LEISURE: POLICY, ETHICS & PROFESSIONALISM

LSA Publication No 71. ISBN: 0 906337 81 X [2000] pp. 257+xiv
Edited by Celia Brackenridge, David Howe and Fiona Jordan

Contents

WOMEN'S LEISURE EXPERIENCES: AGES, STAGES AND ROLES

LSA Publication No. 70. ISBN 0 906337 80 1 [2001]
Edited by Sharon Clough and Judy White

Contents

GENDER ISSUES IN WORK AND LEISURE

LSA Publication No. 68.ISBN 0 906337 78 X
Edited by Jenny Anderson and Lesley Lawrence [pp. 173]

Contents

MASCULINITIES: LEISURE CULTURES, IDENTITIES AND CONSUMPTION

LSA Publication No. 69. ISBN: 0 906337 77 1 [2000] pp. 163

Edited by John Horne and Scott Fleming

Contents

SPORT, LEISURE IDENTITIES AND GENDERED SPACES

LSA Publication No. 67. ISBN: 0 906337 79 8 [1999] pp. 196
Edited by Sheila Scraton and Becky Watson

Contents

HER OUTDOORS: RISK, CHALLENGE AND ADVENTURE IN GENDERED OPEN SPACES

LSA Publication No. 66 [1999] ISBN: 0 906337 76 3; pp. 131
Edited by Barbara Humberstone

Contents

POLICY AND PUBLICS

LSA Publication No. 65. ISBN: 0 906337 75 5 [1999] pp. 167

Edited by Peter Bramham and Wilf Murphy

Contents

CONSUMPTION AND PARTICIPATION: LEISURE, CULTURE AND COMMERCE

LSA Publication No. 64. ISBN: 0 906337 74 7 [2000]
Edited by Garry Whannel

Contents

GENDER, SPACE AND IDENTITY: LEISURE, CULTURE AND COMMERCE

LSA Publication No. 63. ISBN: 0 906337 73 9 [1998] pp. 191
Edited by Cara Aitchison and Fiona Jordan

Contents

THE PRODUCTION AND CONSUMPTION OF SPORT CULTURES: LEISURE, CULTURE AND COMMERCE

LSA Publication No. 62. ISBN: 0 906337 72 0 [1998] pp. 178
Edited by Udo Merkel, Gill Lines, Ian McDonald

Contents

TOURISM AND VISITOR ATTRACTIONS: LEISURE, CULTURE AND COMMERCE

LSA Publication No 61. ISBN: 0 906337 71 2 [1998] pp. 211
Edited by Neil Ravenscroft, Deborah Philips and Marion Bennett

Contents

LEISURE PLANNING IN TRANSITORY SOCIETIES

LSA Publication No. 58. ISBN: 0 906337 70 4
Edited by Mike Collins; pp 218

Contents

LEISURE, TIME AND SPACE: MEANINGS AND VALUES IN PEOPLE'S LIVES

LSA Publication No. 57. ISBN: 0 906337 68 2 [1998] pp. 198 + IV
Edited by Sheila Scraton

Contents

LEISURE, TOURISM AND ENVIRONMENT (I) SUSTAINABILITY AND ENVIRONMENTAL POLICIES

LSA Publication No. 50 Part I; ISBN 0 906337 64 X
Edited by Malcolm Foley, David McGillivray and Gayle McPherson (1999);

Contents

LEISURE, TOURISM AND ENVIRONMENT (II) PARTICIPATION, PERCEPTIONS AND PREFERENCES

LSA Publication No. 50 (Part II) ISBN: 0 906337 69 0; pp. 177+xii
Edited by Malcolm Foley, Matt Frew and Gayle McPherson

Contents

LEISURE: MODERNITY, POSTMODERNITY AND LIFESTYLES

LSA Publications No. 48 (LEISURE IN DIFFERENT WORLDS Volume I)
Edited by Ian Henry (1994); ISBN: 0 906337 ˙52 6, pp. 375+

Contents